Who is Present in Absence?

Who is Present in Absence?

A Pentecostal Theological Praxis
of Suffering and Healing

PAMELA F. ENGELBERT

Foreword by MARTIN W. MITTELSTADT

◆PICKWICK *Publications* • Eugene, Oregon

WHO IS PRESENT IN ABSENCE?
A Pentecostal Theological Praxis of Suffering and Healing

Copyright © 2019 Pamela F. Engelbert. All rights reserved. Except for brief quotations in critical publications or reviews, no part of this book may be reproduced in any manner without prior written permission from the publisher. Write: Permissions, Wipf and Stock Publishers, 199 W. 8th Ave., Suite 3, Eugene, OR 97401.

Pickwick Publications
An Imprint of Wipf and Stock Publishers
199 W. 8th Ave., Suite 3
Eugene, OR 97401

www.wipfandstock.com

PAPERBACK ISBN: 978-1-5326-3353-9
HARDCOVER ISBN: 978-1-5326-3355-3
EBOOK ISBN: 978-1-5326-3354-6

Cataloging-in-Publication data:

Names: Engelbert, Pamela F. | Mittelstadt, Martin W. (foreword)

Title: Who is present in absence? : a Pentecostal theological praxis of suffering and healing / by Pamela F. Engelbert; foreword by Martin W. Mittelstadt.

Description: Eugene, OR : Pickwick Publications, 2019 | Includes bibliographical references.

Identifiers: ISBN 978-1-5326-3353-9 (paperback) | ISBN 978-1-5326-3355-3 (hardcover) | ISBN 978-1-5326-3354-6 (ebook)

Subjects: LCSH: Suffering—Religious aspects—Pentecostal churches. | Spiritual healing—Pentecostal churches. | Healing—Religious aspects—Pentecostal churches—History.

Classification: LCC BT732 E62 2019 (print) | LCC BT732 (ebook)

Manufactured in the U.S.A.

Scripture and/or notes quoted by permission. All scripture quotations, unless otherwise indicated, are taken from the NET Bible® copyright ©1996–2016 by Biblical Studies Press, LLC. All rights reserved.

To
My Dad

(1929–2017)

While I wrote this project,
you implicitly, although unknowingly, taught me about
being present as you cognitively and physically declined.

Contents

List of Illustrations | ix
Foreword by Martin W. Mittelstadt | xi
Preface | xv
Acknowledgments | xvii
Abbreviations | xix

1 What's It All About? The Introduction | 1

2 What's Your Story? Unmet Expectations in Suffering | 26

3 Where Are You From? Pentecostal Historical Roots | 58

4 Where's God in Suffering? Absence in Presence and Presence in Absence | 86

5 Where Are Others in Suffering? Suffering As an Opportunity for Relationality | 117

6 How to Be Present in Apparent Absence: Empathy | 147

7 Where to Go from Here: The Conclusion | 172

Appendix A: Interview Protocol | 177
Appendix B: Informed Consent Form | 181
Appendix C: Coding Process | 184

Bibliography | 187

List of Illustrations

Figure 1. Four elements of a theological praxis of suffering and healing | 173

Foreword

God whispers to us in our pleasures, speaks in our conscience,
but shouts in our pains: it is his megaphone to rouse a deaf world.

—C. S. Lewis, *The Problem of Pain*

PAM AND I ARE lifelong Pentecostals. We are committed to our tradition, but it has not always been easy.

A long-term commitment to Pentecostal worldviews and practices often poses unique challenges. In the early 1990s, I was meandering through my late twenties, and I was trying desperately to own the tradition of my youth. I enjoyed the exuberance of Pentecostal worship and prominence of experience. I valued the radical edginess of Pentecostal pragmatism, but I began to trip repeatedly over triumphalist theologies that proved inconsistent with my lived experience. Though I certainly did not find my way into young adulthood by way of Pentecostal preachers crazed by 'Word Faith' extremism, I began to sense an inward uneasiness concerning the unwavering rhetoric on the meaning of a life "blessed by God." As I reflected upon my Canadian Prairie upbringing among moderate "name it and claim it" preachers and friends, I lacked theological clarity, and began to question the Pentecostal God of my youth.

I finished seminary and decided it was time to test my Pentecostal worldview, and determine if I would embrace my tribe. I completed my PhD dissertation, a three-year journey on the relationship between the Holy Spirit and suffering in Luke-Acts. I am happy to say that I survived, and I am now at home in my tradition. When people heard that I wrote on suffering, they would pepper me with standard questions such as "why are some not healed?," "why do some people find no relief from pain?," "why does adversity follow her everywhere?," or "what did he do to warrant this predicament?" At this point, I typically dodged the questions, and explained that I wrote on a different kind of "suffering," namely, persecution or opposition because of witness to the gospel. Having said this, I could not avoid consideration of such questions as a pastor, theologian, and believer among family and friends.

In a rather serendipitous manner, I fast forward to the winter of 2014, and my first interaction with Pam Engelbert, then a PhD student at Luther Seminary. She had seen my work, and was embarking on a dissertation of her own. She set out to explore Pentecostals and—you guessed it —our tumultuous theology of suffering. We exchanged a few emails, and soon engaged in several lengthy phone calls. Though I explained to her that I am no expert in Pentecostals and suffering, I sensed a kindred spirit, and I became enthralled with her project. She would search for sufferers willing to share their stories about struggle, grief, and pain in a tradition that identifies strongly with miraculous intervention.

Pam and I continued our conversations, and she eventually invited me to serve as an outside reader for her dissertation, the Pentecostal among readers (and peers) from her diverse community at Luther Seminary. And I am so glad she did. Through ongoing discussion and eventually her research, Pam taught me about myself, and my Pentecostal "family."

I heartily commend Pam's work not only because of her personal impact on my life, but also for the enduring value of her work. I believe Pam writes for readers willing to think deeply about struggle and hardship. What will you discover?

First, Pam traces not only the stories of her interviewees, but she also weaves her story into the project. She writes to locate herself in our tradition. Though it has not always been easy, she also finds her way home, and embraces a more robust Pentecostal worldview. She writes as a mature Pentecostal woman, and demonstrates commitment to her tradition, but she seeks not primarily to argue and defend faith, but to *story* faith. In so doing, Pam provides a model for Pentecostals. In fact, Pam provides a refreshing voice for readers of any tradition. She discovers that answers to or coping with life's most difficult circumstances are seldom ascertained by way of apologetic indoctrination (i.e., theological justification). Instead, she *simply* listens to her interviewees, shares mutual empathy, and finds that God is indeed present even in apparent absence. Pam witnesses God at work.

Foreword

Second, Pentecostals crave miraculous encounter with God. Anyone remotely familiar with Pentecostalism knows the value we place upon extraordinary faith, healing, and utterances. Though Pam recognizes this, she and her interviewees testify, rather paradoxically, to the miracle of God's abiding presence in the course of suffering. Pam recounts stories of people who cannot survive, much less thrive, a superficial faith. She traces stories that should enliven Pentecostal faith. She reveals that the Pentecostal God works miraculously in the midst of pain and grief, and if not by way of a megaphone, surely through God's persistent whisper and abiding presence. In the end, this should not surprise Pentecostals. Testimony serves as a rich Pentecostal practice, a spiritual discipline shared in a gathering of God's people. Authentic testimony, like any compelling story, requires thick plot. Testimonies are not accounts of "glory to glory," but Christian story. The best testimonies witness to falling and rising, success and failure, triumph and tragedy. And the thoughtful listener will note that testimonies do not deliver the final word. Testimonies remind fellow travelers of the need for endurance; they call upon us to embrace vulnerability, fidelity, and trust in God. If Pentecostals sincerely appreciate God's miraculous activity, we should find no better example than stories of God's presence in apparent absence. If Pam and her interviewees do not fulfill the stereotypical testimonies of sensational and spectacular intervention, they declare that God's presence in hardship and the ensuing endurance of faithful sufferers proves no less miraculous.

Finally, Pam writes for caregivers. How should we minister to the sufferer? Pam suggests what amounts to a beautiful yet demanding response. What if we would facilitate God's gracious action through the mundane and unspectacular ministry offered by our presence, space, listening, and service? What if our listening and empathy might offer the charismatic corollary to extraordinary utterance? What if our service would provide much needed comfort instead of futile attempts to explain a way out? You will not find in these stories a formula to address people in pain or easy fix-it guide for ministry. Pam calls for Pentecostals to engage in thoughtful and caring ministry to those in dire pain and struggle.

Today, as I write these words, I anticipate my annual Christmas conversation with Wes, a lifelong friend. Wes grew up Catholic, danced among the Mennonites, and finally landed with Pentecostals. He became Pentecostal, specifically, for reasons cited by so many Pentecostals, not least, our persistent emphasis upon the miraculous. He is ordained with

FOREWORD

the Pentecostal Assemblies of Canada, and maintains a small private counseling practice. Wes is now into his third year with stage four prostate cancer. He remains optimistic for healing, yet he is ready to die. He has witnessed—first hand—many incredible miracles throughout his life, many of them while he has been in personal pain and hardship. Wes regularly attests to God's hand upon family and friends. During every conversation, I listen to Wes. Wes encourages me. We laugh and cry. We testify to God's miraculous provision, to strength manifest in weakness. Every time I hear Wes and Dayna's number on my mobile, I brace for news of Wes's passing. But every time I hear Wes's voice, I feel immediate joy. We share deeply. We marvel at God's grace. We struggle with questions, and we experience God's presence. We inquire "God, where are you?," yet we experience Pentecost together.

Pam brings us face to face with her story and the stories of eight Pentecostals. She inspires personal endurance, community resolve, and further research. She testifies to thick plot, stories of difficulty and challenge, stories beautiful, painful, and ongoing.

Martin W. Mittelstadt
Advent 2017

Preface

As a Pentecostal, the prompting for the topic of suffering for this project occurred after my god had died. My American culture stated, "If you pull yourself up by your own bootstraps, you can be and do anything that you can dream." My American Christianity said, "If you are obedient to God, you will be blessed." My Pentecostal beliefs asserted, "If you are faithful to God, God will be faithful to you and deliver you from suffering." However, for several years these formulaic platitudes had failed me, resulting in questions as to who God was and what I had done wrong for the suffering to not be ameliorated. My pain was intensified when I experienced other Pentecostals as being unable or unwilling to sit with me in my adversity, implying their own belief system fell short.

We Pentecostals are known for our desire for an encounter with God. From the focus on healing to speaking in tongues and from Pentecostal church services to one's personal life, Pentecostals passionately seek, hope, and/or expect to experience God. Our church services are geared toward encountering God, be it through the gifts of the Spirit during worship or at the altar during the closing of the service. We advocate for the telling of stories—testimonies—that support this passionate yearning. Our preaching stresses a response in which we experience God, which is then validated by transformation of the person. While the championing of a victorious Christian life nurtures this longing, it is to the neglect of a formation of a sound theology of suffering. Yet it is this very longing for the presence of God that may teach us how to respond to others who are suffering. As Pentecostals, we speak of experiences with God that do not necessarily change our arduous situations, but these experiences provide a sense of love, peace, and strength. It is also these encounters with God's presence that we learn to cherish. Such encounters with God may also transpire as we participate in God's ministry of presence by being present to others who are hurting.

Preface

This project then is fully Pentecostal. It uses a Pentecostal hermeneutic by lifting up people's stories and the story of the Gospel of John; it centers on Jesus and the Holy Spirit; it underscores pragmatics by focusing on a theological praxis that is also a missional act; and most importantly, it concentrates on an encounter with God.

I have encountered God while in the writing of these pages and have been transformed. It is my prayer for you, as the reader of this work, that you, too, will experience God through the words that follow, even on the paths where God appears to be absent.

In it together,
Pamela F. Engelbert
November 22, 2017

Acknowledgments

I WANT TO EXTEND special gratitude to the following who have revealed God to me and generated healing through their acts of ministry in the power and the presence of the Spirit: to Luther Seminary's administration, faculty, and staff who participated in Christ's ministry in my life by providing this gift to pursue a PhD; to my eight research participants who became vulnerable with a stranger—I continue to grow from your stories; to my ecumenical committee, Martin Mittelstadt, Carla Dahl, and Jessicah Krey Duckworth: Marty, I appreciate your open and teachable spirit that has granted me the permission to say, "As a scholar, I continue to learn"; Carla, through your grace to me, you have invited me to remain curious and to embrace who I am; and Jessicah, I am learning from you to extend hospitality toward those who are different from me for this is where beauty is found—thank you for being my Barnabas; to Rev. Dr. John Gowins, you saw my gifts before I did, and through your steadfast presence I am learning to trust myself, to honor my will, and to learn of my worth, all of which generates transformation; finally, to my husband and my best friend, Lincoln, who has been my greatest encourager through your presence: your willingness to move to Minnesota so I could pursue a PhD; your willingness to be a dialogue partner and help me flesh out my raw ideas; and your contribution by reading each chapter more than once and informing me, "You need to bring your reader along"—I have learned so much from you through your presence and patience. I offer a special thanks to Wipf and Stock for making this publication a reality.

The Lord be with each of you.

To God, the Father, the Son, and the Spirit, be all glory and honor and praise. Thank you for this gift of pursuing a PhD. I have encountered you and have been transformed through this process. You have taught me in

ACKNOWLEDGMENTS

this journey that you are present even in your apparent absence. Thank you for your grace and mercy to me.

Abbreviations

AG   Assemblies of God
NET   New English Translation
NVC   Nonviolent Communication
OFNR   Observation, Feeling, Need, Request
PAOC   Pentecostal Assemblies of Canada
RCT   Relational-Cultural Therapy

1

What's It All About?
The Introduction

IF I HAD PREVIOUSLY given any thought to my beliefs on suffering, I would have affirmed that suffering exists in the world. If I had been asked if I held to the belief that God blessed those who obeyed and punished those who did not, I would have agreed but added some qualifications. I now admit to having held a *just world* belief system.[1] For example, I previously was convinced that ministers were at fault when they departed from a church within a year, or when turmoil disrupted my own life, I frequently asked God, "What did I do wrong?" It was not until I walked on a path of extended suffering that I began to wrestle with this belief system.

The above beliefs or actions are significant when one considers that who I am plays an important role in the words typed on these pages. That is, the aforementioned examples are not merely beliefs or actions that are separate from who I am. Hence, the fact that I am the youngest of three children who were raised on a farm in South Dakota and that I am a woman, a Caucasian, an American, a wife, and a Pentecostal minister cannot be separated from what I bring to the table and from what I offer specifically in the form of this project. Thus, I begin by telling *my* story. My story, as seen on the next few pages, contains an account of three interrelated experiences

---

1. Melvin J. Lerner formulated the *just world theory*, which believes that individuals receive what they deserve and deserve what they receive. Lerner, *The Belief in a Just World: A Fundamental Delusion*.

Who is Present in Absence?

of ministry that have had a hand in shaping who I have become.[2] At the same time, I see the Spirit moving in and through these experiences, leading to this project.

The first place of ministry involved a small group of hurting Pentecostals in which I witnessed healing through authentic relationships in the power of the Spirit. As a deeply wounded congregation, it was the center of gossip in this rural area due to the moral failure of one of its previous ministers; thus, it was incumbent upon subsequent ministers to walk uprightly in the community in order that the Spirit may restore the church's reputation. Interestingly, my husband was the one who initially practiced authenticity; therefore, integrity was maintained among the people in that he shared with the congregation about his struggles, resisting artificiality. Correspondingly, it was his openness that produced a change in my identity as a minister.

The Spirit challenged me to trust others through my own openness and vulnerability, which was contrary to my understanding that a minister was to appear victorious. As we shared our home, our stories, and our struggles, I saw healing and transformation come within us as well as within the congregation. As one congregant exclaimed, "I have never seen two people change so much!" I discovered how our transparency deepened and expanded relationality for it fostered transparency within the members of this Pentecostal congregation. As we prayed for one another, the body learned to share each other's burdens without even involving the minister. As one person insisted, "Pastor, you taught us to do this." My eyes were opened as I saw the importance of being the body of Christ, not only for this congregation's sake but also for the sake of the surrounding community.

I recall a particular occasion when this Pentecostal body embraced a family's grief and suffering, which thereby fostered healing. A Hispanic family within the congregation had learned from their physician that their father, Thomas, had only three weeks to live. As the daughters sat in the second pew singing with the congregation, we were well aware of the news they had received on the previous day. It felt inappropriate to us, and even cruel, to sing songs of celebration while hearts in our midst were filled with deep sorrow. As the congregants greeted each other, my husband asked two of the daughters if it was appropriate for the congregation to visit their parents' home, sing a few songs, and pray with the family. After phoning

---

2. While the events recorded here are genuine experiences, some of the names and locations have been changed to protect those involved.

their mother for permission, it was announced that we were going to *be* the church. That morning this Pentecostal congregation of approximately forty people embodied what it was to be the presence of Christ to this family in their suffering. It informed them, "You are not alone." It also allowed members of the congregation to participate in the Spirit's ministry to Thomas and his family prior to Thomas's death three weeks later.[3]

Such instances were not limited to our church but went beyond the boundaries of the lives of its members. My husband and I had developed strong relational bonds with two other, non-Pentecostal pastoral couples. This friendship formed the basis for these respective congregations to join together in evening worship services on the fifth Sunday of those months that had five Sundays. Healing ensued in the lives of those who had been wounded by the past words and actions of various congregants, and deeper Christian bonds were formed across denominational lines. In short, this first ministry experience communicated to me the significance of the body of Christ, the importance of transparent relationships for the leader, and the healing that comes through relationships through the power of the Spirit. It was this understanding that I carried with me as I departed from this healing space.

This understanding of healing through relationships was reinforced at the second and third places of ministry, not through its copious presence, but through its conspicuous absence. In both places we expected a network of caring relationships, but we regrettably heard pious platitudes or were ignored when we revealed our troubles to those in ministerial or lay leadership. When a local believer stated, "I am praying that you will leave," those who were present neglected to reach out to us. When a different Christ-follower labeled my husband "demon-possessed," a leader informed my husband that it was "an opportunity to grow." Fortunately another leader responded with empathy in this instance when he saw the pain in my husband's face. Following a further instance of rejection, one couple in leadership responded to us by saying, "I can see you are hurting," and they then walked away, leaving us alone to deal with the aftermath. We heard from several that we were to set an example as ministers by living above our problems, which was similar to my own earlier perception of a minister while at our first place of ministry. Certain people overtly opposed the vulnerability we showed through our authenticity. One person asserted,

---

3. With names that end in *s*, I have chosen in this project to use apostrophe *s* (e.g., Jesus's) unless it is a citation.

"Pastor, we pay you to carry our burdens, not for us to carry yours." Unfortunately, at one place of ministry we were forced to depart after fifty-one weeks even though the district leadership plainly expressed our innocence; thus, I had essentially become one of those ministers about whom I had perceived as a failure: a pastor with a short tenure at a place of ministry.

Without the presence of supportive relationships, I entered into a crisis of faith. The frequency with which we were ignored in the midst of pain would have been laughable if it had not hurt so much. As we walked away from these two experiences of ministry, we had come to believe three things: our contribution to ministry was irrelevant; we ourselves were insignificant; and our work was inconsequential. In short, we did not matter. I eventually realized that our first place of ministry had been a lesson in the Spirit's use of relationships to bring healing, and this lesson had been reinforced at the next two places of ministry, albeit by the lack thereof. In essence, while I sought support through relationality, its absence provided a bitter lesson in its importance.

Regrettably, our suffering continued as did our isolation. First, we experienced a job opportunity gone awry, which was followed by a theft and an aborted offer on our house that was for sale, which cost us additional expenses. As weeks turned into months we faced health issues and were unable to find a place of ministry. Our pain deepened when members of the body of Christ ignored us or offered callous comments such as, "at least you don't have it as bad as . . ." I was told at one point that it was my choice to remain in or leave behind my pain. My crisis of faith came to a peak as I wondered, "We had obeyed God. We had followed where God had directed. Why had not God intervened? Why had not God protected? What had I done wrong?" The apparent absence of the body of Christ on this path of suffering only intensified my belief that God had abandoned me. Fortunately, a counselor, who specialized in working with ministers, journeyed with us following our second place of ministry. He participated in the ministry of Christ through his being present to us during this extended period of difficulties that disrupted our theological moorings and spawned our crisis of faith.

WHAT IS THE PROBLEM?

Unfortunately, the story of my own grappling with suffering, of the absence of an expected divine intervention, and the lack of support from others is not a rarity within Pentecostalism. Instead, there is evidence of an underlying need for a more nuanced Pentecostal theology of suffering, which the following pages seek to address.[4]

The need for a more resilient theology of suffering has not gone unnoticed by Pentecostal scholars.[5] Keith Warrington recognizes that Pentecostalism has traditionally disregarded the subject of suffering; thus, he encourages a Pentecostal exploration of a theology of suffering complementary to its theology of healing.[6] Veli-Matti Kärkkäinen comments that one of the ongoing difficult tasks in developing a Pentecostal missiology is the ability to hold in tension both victory and suffering.[7] The concern for a more robust Pentecostal theology of suffering is not limited to the West but is also acknowledged globally.[8] Reuben Louis Gabriel calls for an Asian

---

4. This project includes sections of four papers presented at four meetings of the Society for Pentecostal Studies in the years 2014, 2015, 2016, and 2017, respectively.

5. Allan Anderson, in writing on healing, perceives the majority of current Pentecostals affirms that God does not relieve suffering on every occasion. Anderson, "Pentecostal Approaches to Faith and Healing," 523–34.

6. Warrington, *Pentecostal Theology*, 303, 324; see also Warrington, "Suffering," 201–4. While acknowledging that Pentecostal scholars have mostly neglected the subject of suffering, Warrington in this article notes that recently there have been contributions to a Pentecostal theology of suffering.

7. Kärkkäinen, "The Pentecostal Understanding of Mission," 41–43.

8. While my project's participants are specifically Western Pentecostals, it is significant that the topic of a theology of suffering among Pentecostals has not only been acknowledged but also addressed globally. J. Kwabena Asamoah-Gyadu analyzes various topics within African Pentecostalism, including the topic of suffering. In one chapter he reflects on Martin Luther's theology of the cross and the African prosperity gospel. While he uses a personal example of his preaching of a funeral, this is more for the purpose of illustration than it is for the formulation of a theology of suffering; see Asamoah-Gyadu, *Contemporary Pentecostal Christianity*. In another project, Asamoah-Gyadu combines research and theology and includes a section in which he reconsiders prosperity, healing, and deliverance within the Ghanaian context; see Asamoah-Gyadu, *African Charismatics*. Sang-Ehil Han draws from various models of the atonement to move toward a Wesleyan-Pentecostal theology and spirituality; this is followed by a description of the Korean concept of *han* to portray the anguish and depth of human suffering and by an outline of a holistic theory of atonement that emerges from this concept; see Han, "Weaving the Courage of God and Human Suffering," 171–90. Kwang-Jin Jang forms a theology of suffering by placing the historical experiences of Korean Christians in conversation with a biblical Pauline theology and contemporary pneumatologies. Drawing from the testimonies of persecuted Christians from 1910 to 1953, Jang uses Karl Barth, Jürgen Moltmann, Emil Brunner, Wolfhart Pannenberg, and Pentecostal theology as well as Paul's writings in order to address the role of the Spirit in the midst of opposition for the sake of the Gospel; see Jang, "The Role of the Holy Spirit in Christian Suffering with

Who is Present in Absence?

Pentecostal theology that is more embracing of humanity, which means welcoming the pain that humans experience rather than only upholding success and prosperity.[9] Wonsuk Ma, in writing about issues among Asian Pentecostals, voices his concern about the triumphalist theology that neglects human suffering; yet he is encouraged that Pentecostal scholars are addressing this area.[10]

Some Pentecostal scholars have contributed to a Pentecostal theology of suffering by pulling from the discipline of systematic theology and the work of other theologians.[11] For instance, Kärkkäinen, drawing from

---

Reference to Paul's Experience of Suffering and to Korean Church Suffering 1910–1953." Leonard P. Maré underscores the need for Pentecostals to utilize the Psalms of lament in their worship services when he addresses South African Pentecostalism. By sharing the experiences of the psalmists, Maré argues that Pentecostals are embracing both the majesty of God as well as their own human suffering and offers several ways to use the Psalms in worship services; see Maré, "A Pentecostal Perspective on the Use of Psalms of Lament in Worship," 91–109. Written by a Pentecostal from Ghana, Opoku Onyinah focuses on the issue of God healing some while offering sufficient grace to others; see Onyinah, "God's Grace, Healing and Suffering," 117–27. In another article, Onyinah dialogues with the writings and experiences of Dr. Yonggi Cho in his discussion of Cho's theological perspective of suffering, healing, and prosperity. The author then weaves his own biblical understanding of suffering and healing in solidarity with Cho. While this article is a theological dialogue with another Pentecostal's theology and experience, the experiences are similar to a testimonial rather than systematic research; see Onyinah, "Suffering and Dr. Yonggi Cho's Theology of the Cross," 9–46. As a Pentecostal minister, Isaiah Majok Dau includes experience, theology, and Scripture as well as a Christian response in his study of suffering. He specifically highlights the Christian Sudanese understanding of war within the framework of their faith. His research detects three views of suffering: (1) suffering is God's judgment; (2) suffering is the result of the battle between God and Satan; and (3) suffering is used to reveal the people's faith and purify them. In each view, it is believed that God will intervene and deliver the people from suffering. The author perceives that the church experiences God amidst suffering as seen in the tremendous growth of the Sudanese church. He examines Western beliefs about suffering and evil by using such theologians as Augustine, Luther, Calvin, Karl Barth, and Jürgen Moltmann and concludes this section with an African theological understanding of suffering. Dau then turns toward a biblical understanding of suffering and evil and finishes his project with a biblical and theological response to suffering; see Dau, *Suffering and God*.

9. Gabriel, "Response to Wonsuk Ma's 'Toward an Asian Pentecostal Theology,'" 77–85.

10. Ma, "Asian (Classical) Pentecostal Theology in Context," 63–64.

11. Michael Dusing engages the issue of suffering and Pentecostals by contrasting various Christian beliefs about suffering; see Dusing, "Toward a Pentecostal Theology of Physical Suffering." Terry Tramel seeks a balanced connection in the Evangelical and Pentecostal theologies of suffering and healing; see Tramel, *The Beauty of the Balance*, chapter 6. Daniel Castelo argues that when Pentecostals believe they only need to meet

Martin Luther's theology of the cross, challenges Pentecostals to consider life's dark side rather than highlighting only the sentimentality of God's love.[12] Stephen C. Torr in his project seeks to answer the question: "What does it mean to communicate rightly of and to God in the face of seemingly innocent, meaningless suffering when God appears to be absent, in a way that is conducive to Pentecostal/Charismatic theology?" He examines literature of various Pentecostal/Charismatic responses' to evil and suffering, noting that a Pentecostal/Charismatic response includes the prominence of Scripture and the practical aspect for the believer; however, Torr finds these approaches unsatisfactory due in part to their mishandling of Scripture. In an effort to have a scripturally based approach to suffering, he draws from Kenneth Archer, John Christopher Thomas, and Kevin Vanhoozer to form a hermeneutic that embraces the theology and practices of Pentecostalism. Torr suggests a church practice of not only the offering of testimonies but also "countertestimonies," a lament that is aided by the Holy Spirit.[13] Simi-

---

the right criteria to experience a divine intervention, this belief implies human power is greater than God's sovereignty; thus, he advocates for reflecting on patience; see Castelo, "Patience as a Theological Virtue," 232–46. Chris E. Green sees a deficiency in Pentecostals' starting point in forming a theology of suffering and encourages starting with "Jesus' experience of God as Abba and Spirit" rather than beginning with the "believers' experience of Jesus as savior, sanctifier, healer, and Spirit-baptizer"; see Green, "The Crucified God and the Groaning Spirit," 127–42. Jeff McAffee recognizes that humanity is created for relationships and that humans suffer; thus, he offers a Pentecostal theology of co-suffering that underscores the transformation of both the sufferer and the companion to the sufferer; see McAffee, "The Theology of Co-Suffering." Eldin Villafañe acknowledges that Hispanics in America are being marginalized and oppressed; thus, he seeks to form a Pentecostal social ethic through a communal spirituality that challenges the structures of society while at the same time maintaining the individual's fight with sin and the devil; such a communal spirituality focuses on God's reign and the work of the Spirit in the world and how believers participate in that work; see Villafañe, *The Liberating Spirit*. Edward Decker perceives that Pentecostals offer a unique contribution to ministry by focusing on the whole person; see Decker, "Pentecostalism and Suffering," 51–65. By using global case studies along with the writings of Miroslav Volf, Andrew M. McCoy asserts that Pentecostal worship includes expressions of suffering and affirmation of the materiality of salvation; this is seen in their opposing of evil, the acknowledging of sin, and the voicing of one's faith while he/she suffers; see McCoy, "Salvation (Not Yet?) Materialized," 45–59. Samuel Solivan argues for an understanding of orthopathos within Pentecostal theology as a corrective bridge of orthodoxy and orthopraxis; he perceives American Pentecostal theology as being too cognitive and neglecting the suffering of the oppressed within the United States; see Solivan, *The Spirit, Pathos and Liberation*.

12. Kärkkäinen, "Theology of the Cross," 150–63; his article is also a chapter in *Toward a Pneumatological Theology*, 167–78.

13. Torr, *Dramatic Pentecostal/Charismatic Anti-Theodicy*.

lar to my own project, Torr speaks of the apparent absence of God amidst meaningless suffering; however, unlike my project, Torr does not include personal stories as part of his methodology, even though he recognizes a need for research using contemporary experiences, specifically in how Pentecostal communities respond to suffering. In addition to turning to other theologians, Pentecostal scholars also appeal to their own history in order to discuss a theology of suffering.[14] For example, Oliver McMahan observes that suffering surrounded the Azusa Street Revival in the form of poverty but was infrequently discussed, and this trend continues in contemporary Pentecostalism.[15]

While these contributions are valuable in the ongoing development of a Pentecostal theology of suffering, they are different from my own project in that while it embraces systematic theology, I also uphold a strong biblical approach, which is a Pentecostal preference.[16] There are several Pentecostal scholars who have addressed the issue of suffering by using this preferred methodology. Warrington and Martin Mittelstadt are two New Testament scholars of note, who have participated in the formulation of a Pentecostal biblical approach to suffering and/or healing.[17] Warrington has especially

---

14. Michael K. Adams, drawing from Cheryl Bridges Johns and Walter Brueggemann, believes that early Pentecostalism was birthed out of lament and calls Pentecostals to return to the cries of lament; see Adams, "'Hope in the Midst of Hurt.'" Daniel J. Simmons, who discloses his own questions concerning those who are not healed, examines the history of the doctrine of healing in the atonement along with the views of contemporary theologians; see Simmons, "They Shall Recover."

15. McMahan, "Grief Observed," 296–314. John Kie Vining examines an historical approach of the caring for souls in Pentecostalism, noticing a parallel between the Holiness tradition's shift to embrace both crisis and process sanctification and Pentecostalism's move toward healing that includes both instantaneous cure and natural healing; see Vining, "Soul Care in the Pentecostal Tradition," 15–33.

16. Warrington confirms, "Biblical theology holds more attraction to Pentecostals than systematic theology. Fundamentally, there has been a profound desire to be guided by the teachings of the Bible, rather than the formulations of commentators on the Bible." Warrington, *Pentecostal Theology*, 185.

17. Faith McGhee draws from the Epistle to the Hebrews to bring holiness in conversation with suffering; see McGhee, "Holiness and the Path of Suffering," 57–85. Rebecca Skaggs offers a view of suffering, specifically grief, in light of 1 Peter; see Skaggs, "The Problem of Suffering." Skaggs has also completed a commentary on 1 Peter that includes the topic of suffering; see Skaggs, *The Pentecostal Commentary on 1 Peter, 2 Peter, Jude*. Kari L. Brodin contributes to an understanding of suffering when she discusses the link between suffering, experience, and the Spirit in Gal 3:4; see Brodin, "Experience or Suffer?" Scott A. Ellington, underscoring the Psalter, Job, the prophetic tradition, and the New Testament, highlights the importance of lament when there is a collision of our

considered the Pentecostal issue of healing and/or suffering from a New Testament perspective through several books and articles. For instance, he walks through the Gospels, Acts, Pauline writings, and the Epistle of James, answering questions about suffering and healing.[18] Elsewhere, Warrington examines the place of the Spirit in association with suffering in Scripture in the essay "A Spirit Theology of Suffering."[19] Warrington also implies a more robust theology of suffering is paralleled by a more healthy theology of healing when he suggests the need for Pentecostals to develop "a more carefully scrutinized theology of healing," particularly in the face of the absence of an expected physical healing.[20] Mittelstadt argues on more than one occasion that in the tradition of the theology of Luke-Acts, Pentecostals are not only to welcome the victorious motif, but they also are to embrace the difficulties that correspond to being a witness for Jesus Christ.[21]

---

beliefs and our experience; see Ellington, *Risking Truth*. While Ellington does not specifically address Pentecostals in this work, he does elsewhere; see Ellington, "The Costly Loss of Testimony," 48–59. Valerie Rance adds to the conversation of suffering through her discussion on trauma and well-being; see Rance, "Biblical Personalities and Trauma." She also considers this topic more fully in her dissertation; see Rance, "Trauma and Coping Mechanisms Among Assemblies of God World Missionaries: Towards a Biblical Theory of Missionary Well-Being." John Christopher Thomas offers the New Testament's diverse perspective on the causes of illness while forming a biblical theology of the Satan, sickness, and deliverance; see Thomas, *The Devil, Disease and Deliverance*. William Menzies and Robert Menzies approach a Pentecostal theology of suffering by applying Mark 9:2–10 to expand the understanding of God's providential care; see Menzies and Menzies, *Spirit and Power*, chapter 12. Matthew K. Thomson uses the Gospel of John to provide a model of pastoral care in between divine interventions; see Thomson, "Minister between Miracles," 129–39. Donald Gee in a small booklet invites Pentecostals to continue to pray for healing, while noting that in Scripture God does not always heal; see Gee, *Trophimus I Left Sick*. Matthias Wenk identifies the Spirit as being "God's solidarity with life that is suffering and groaning for liberation"; thus, he argues for the church's participation in the *Missio Spiritu* by being in solidarity with those who are suffering; see Wenk, "An Incarnational Pneumatology"; see also Wenk, "*Missio Spiritu*," 26–33.

18. Warrington, "Healing and Suffering in the Bible," 154–64; see also Warrington, *Healing and Suffering*.

19. Warrington, "A Spirit Theology of Suffering," 24–36; for other examples of Warrington's work, see *Jesus the Healer*; "Healing and Kenneth Hagin," 119–38; "The Path to Wholeness," 45–49; "The Role of Jesus," 66–92; "James 5:14–18," 346–67; "Acts and the Healing Narratives," 189–217; "A Response to James Shelton," 185–93; "The Use of the Name (of Jesus)," 16–36.

20. Warrington, *Pentecostal Theology*, 277.

21. Mittelstadt, *The Spirit and Suffering in Luke-Acts*; see also *Reading Luke-Acts in the Pentecostal Tradition*; "Spirit and Suffering in Contemporary Pentecostalism," 144–73.

While the abovementioned approaches to the topic at hand strengthen a Pentecostal theology of suffering, they, too, are different from this project in that I include Pentecostal experiences of suffering, which is a necessary part of Pentecostal theologizing. Some of the previously mentioned scholars explicitly acknowledge that experience is essential for Pentecostals. Kärkkäinen indicates that historically experience is viewed as first and foremost in a Pentecostal theological hermeneutic when he writes, "Experience came first; theology followed."[22] Warrington comments that experience and praxis are significant for Pentecostals: "Their theology is praxis-oriented and experiential, . . . where life experiences are valid elements of one's hermeneutic and theology as much as conceptual theologizing."[23]

There are those scholars who have maintained the importance of experience in their contribution to a Pentecostal theology of suffering and healing by placing experience in conversation with theology.[24] Robert Gallagher positions his wife's cancer diagnosis in dialogue with Acts 12:1–11, the account of the persecution of the church and Peter's miraculous release from prison.[25] Randall Holm, referencing a friend who was not healed, explores Pentecostal philosopher James K. A. Smith's view that God not only deems creation good in its finitude but also embraces finitude and vulnerability in the incarnation; Holm, then, offers several suggestions to consider in light of the Pentecostal desire for healing, such as vulnerability is the path of wholeness.[26] However, these contributions also differ from my project in that I include a theological praxis of theology and healing (chapter 6) because, as Warrington noted above, Pentecostals are a pragmatic people.

In a similar vein, several Pentecostals have focused on the area of Pentecostal theology and those with disabilities. Amos Yong has addressed this issue on several occasions, offering an interdisciplinary approach by placing

---

22. Kärkkäinen, "Pentecostal Hermeneutics in the Making," 79.

23. Warrington, *Pentecostal Theology*, 16.

24. Mark Cartledge, who does not address suffering per se, speaks to the related topic of healing as well as other doctrines by using conversations conducted from Pentecostal focus groups in combination with theology; he notes the members did not hold that God heals all sicknesses; see Cartledge, *Testimony in the Spirit*. Additionally, sociologist Margaret Poloma has extensively researched Pentecostals, generating theories about their practices. For instance, see Poloma, "An Empirical Study of Perceptions of Healing," 61–82.

25. Gallagher, "Hope in the Midst of Trial."

26. Holm, "Healing in Search of Atonement," 50–67.

in dialogue experience, theology, and the sciences.²⁷ Yong does provide experiences of Pentecostals, but varies from my project in that these are anecdotal and his practices are more an applied theology rather than praxis (see below). Shane Clifton places experiences of disability, Pentecostal theology, and Pentecostal healing practices in conversation with each other as he seeks to reconstruct Pentecostal theology and its practice of healing to be one of well-being.²⁸ Similar to my own project, Clifton includes experiences of those who are not healed, but unlike this project, Clifton's method does not highlight a biblical approach.

Some scholars have approached the subject of suffering among Pentecostals from a practical theological perspective.²⁹ Steven Fettke and the late Michael Dusing acknowledge the tendency of Pentecostals to be pragmatic rather than contemplative, hindering the development of a theology of suffering. The authors turn to Pauline passages, such as Paul's description of his own afflictions, to point out that Scriptures contain more than simply promises of healing and ways to manipulate God. Fettke and Dusing then broaden the possible pastoral responses to suffering when they move beyond the offering of prayers for sufferers to a presentation on lament and testimony. This article is also self-reflective by including Fettke's own story

---

27. Yong, *Theology and Down Syndrome*; see also Yong, *The Bible, Disability, and the Church*; Yong, "Many Tongues, Many Senses," 167–88. Similarly, Luke Thompson asserts that Yong offers a theology of disability while honoring a Pentecostal hermeneutic; see Thompson, "Rising above a Crippling Hermeneutic."

28. Clifton, "The Dark Side of Prayer for Healing," 204–25. While Clifton does not state it in this article, he is a quadriplegic due to an accident in 2010; see Clifton, "Theodicy, Disability, and Fragility," 765–84.

29. Stephen Parker addresses counselors and pastors by discussing Pentecostal beliefs that may impede a Pentecostal's pursuit of counseling and by highlighting ways in which a counselor may attend to these beliefs; while using a case study in this paper and underscoring the importance of using the Bible in counseling Pentecostals, he does not utilize a theological foundation to develop a theology of suffering; see Parker, "Working with Pentecostal-Charismatic Beliefs in Therapy." Andrew Thomas's practical theological study explores the ministry of healing by using a case study of a Pentecostal church, Ablewell Christian Fellowship in KwaZulu-Natal, South Africa. As part of the study, Thomas interviews fifteen congregants about their church's ministry of healing. Some interviewees related their own experiences of healing while others spoke of seeing others healed and/or praying for others who were healed. Thomas includes the participants' beliefs "on partial, prolonged healing and non-healing." Thomas, then, brings these experiences and perceptions in dialogue with both biblical and theological literature in order to formulate a more robust theology of healing; see Thomas, "Pathways to Healing." It is to be noted that this work is different from my own in that Thomas's focus is on healing, not suffering, and his study is not completed within North America.

of a lack of healing for his autistic son. However, while locating themselves as those who are acquainted with suffering, this differs from my project in that I draw from others' experiences through qualitative research, using an analytical process so that the experiences define the process.[30]

Grace Milton conducts a practical theological study, exploring the issue of conversion among Pentecostals through an ethnographic, case study approach of an Elim Pentecostal church in the UK. While this study does not exclusively focus on suffering, she references a theology of suffering when discussing "the crisis" in L. R. Rambo's conversion theory. She wonders "how many people find the triumphalism comforting and how many understood upon their conversion that Christianity involved further suffering" when recognizing the predominant victorious theme within Pentecostalism, which has a less than robust theology of suffering.[31] She notes in her research that all but three out of thirty of her interviewees mentioned "difficult situations, crises or moments of doubt following their conversion."[32] Milton encourages an engagement with lament and the experiences of life's turmoil in order to be whole or complete (*shalom*).

John Bosman and J. P. J. Theron in a practical theological study discuss the results of interviews with nine people from two Pentecostal denominations who had chronic illnesses. The authors identify four categories of the participants' experience of non-healing: spiritual, mental, emotional, and social. The spiritual category centered primarily or secondarily on the person's relationship with God. The mental category, about which most participants spoke, focused on questions such as God's part in the illness or the validity of the Scriptures that speak of healing. The emotional category involved a wide range of emotions including anger at God, confusion, depression as well as positive emotions. The social category highlighted both positive and negative experiences, but the authors note the experiences were predominately negative. Bosman and Theron conclude that by taking into account the experiences of the participants, Pentecostals would benefit

---

30. Fettke and Dusing, "A Practical Pentecostal Theodicy? A Proposal," 160–79. Fettke additionally discusses Pentecostalism and disability. He draws from his own experience as a father of an autistic son and invites his readers to reconsider the meaning of ministry and the *imago Dei* as not only involving the perfect and successful of the church but real people with the Spirit of God in them; see Fettke, "The Spirit of God Hovered," 170–82; this article also appeared in Fettke, *God's Empowered People*.

31. Milton, *Shalom, the Spirit and Pentecostal Conversion*, 97.

32. Ibid., 185.

What's It All About?

from healing being founded in pneumatology rather than in the atonement. Such a move means that healing is not assured but remains a possibility.[33]

This leads to the intention of this interdisciplinary project, which reflects on the Pentecostal experiences of suffering by using the narrative of Scripture, Pentecostal theology, culture, and psychology and then concludes with a theological praxis of suffering and healing. Pentecostals believe God intervenes during periods of suffering, but many neglect to develop a more nuanced theology of suffering and healing that addresses those points in time when God does not alleviate the suffering. This project, therefore, underscores the experiences of Pentecostals when they believe for a divine intervention in the midst of suffering that does not transpire. As such, this project honors both Pentecostals' experiences of suffering and their longing for an experience with God.

Prior to moving forward, it is important to state what I mean by three terms that are essential for this study. *Suffering* is an experience that is perceived as being painful physically, psychologically, socially, and/or spiritually that creates an incongruity between what is and what is believed should be. Unless stated otherwise, *healing* references God restoring or reconciling all of creation to become what God has designed. Because this study focuses on human beings, I particularly highlight the healing of the whole person, which includes not only the physical body but also the emotional, spiritual, and relational aspects as well. Thus, while healing may not occur in the physical body (a cure) for a person, I believe in the continuing work of the Spirit to generate ongoing healing in other ways, transforming the person to be more complete in order to be the human being that God planned from before the beginning of time.[34] In keeping with Ray Anderson (see

---

33. Bosman and Theron, "Some Are Not Healed," 1–16; this article is based on Bosman's dissertation; see Bosman, "Some Are Not Healed: The Theory-Praxis Tension." While not a theological study, Chrystal Jaye researched perceptions of suffering and affliction and views of healing in an anthropological ethnographic study of Pentecostals, Christian Scientists, and medical professionals in New Zealand. I focus here on Jaye's results that pertain to the subject at hand. Suffering, in the Pentecostal group, in the end was believed to be from God in that humans disobeyed God, creating separation from God. Jaye noted that the Pentecostals were hesitant to connect personal sin to personal suffering, but they admitted a person's lifestyle could generate one's own affliction. They tended to believe that God could use a person's suffering for a larger purpose. She also noted that Pentecostals focused more on the internal elements of health, such as spiritual and emotional, and they utilized biomedicine in conjunction with prayer, believing that God intervenes through the use of biomedicine. However, mental illness was viewed as a result of demonization; see Jaye, "Embodied Integrity."

34. For clarification on the concept of "cure," see Yong, *Renewing Christian Theology*,

below) I interchange the usage of such words as *reconcile* and *restore* with healing. That is to say, reconciliation and restoration do not simply mean healing a relationship with God, but they carry a holistic understanding of reconciling or restoring the person to God's intentions. Through Christ believers continue to experience ongoing reconciliation (healing) while they are also completely reconciled to God in Christ. I define *intervene* at this point in the project as God's resolving a person's difficulty, and/or delivering a person from the difficulties, so that the suffering ceases (e.g., healing the sick, protecting the loved one from death, or providing a job when unemployed). This is different from redemption in which God eventually may redeem a situation by working it towards a person's good (Joel 2:25; Rom 8:28). These three terms are foundational for understanding the question in which this project is grounded: When God does not intervene in the midst of suffering, how do Classical Pentecostals understand and/or interpret their experiences and relationships both with God and with others? An effective means to accomplish this task, which includes experience, Scripture, and praxis is through the discipline of practical theology.

WHAT PRACTICAL THEOLOGY STRESSES

Pentecostalism and practical theology share a common interest: the human-divine encounter. This qualifies practical theology as relevant when contributing to Pentecostal theology. I begin this particular section by clarifying what I mean by *Pentecostalism* and *practical theology*.

What Is Pentecostalism and What Is Practical Theology?

Scholars have portrayed the defining of *Pentecostalism* as being an arduous task due to the varieties of Pentecostalisms worldwide.[35] To explain what I have in mind by *Pentecostalism*, I submit four semi-broad definitions that are followed by three commonly used classifications of Pentecostals. Robert Mapes Anderson describes his definition of *Pentecostalism*:

---

loc. 3897–4450.

35. Kärkkäinen explains the usage of "Pentecostalisms"; see Kärkkäinen, *Pneumatology*, 89. The following serve as examples of the challenge of globally defining Pentecostalism: Anderson, "Varieties, Taxonomies, and Definitions," 13–29; Ma et al., "Introduction: Pentecostalism and World Mission," 2–4; Kay, *Pentecostalism*, 5–11; Robeck and Yong, "Global Pentecostalism," 1–10.

> My working definition has been that Pentecostalism is a movement that emerged on the world scene in 1906 during a Los Angles revival in which speaking in tongues was regarded as a sign of Baptism in the Spirit for the individual, a sign of a Second Pentecost for the Church, and a sign of the imminent Second Coming of Christ. I have designated as "Pentecostal" all groups, by whatever name they may use, whose origins can be traced to that revival.[36]

Allan Anderson, referencing R. M. Anderson, describes Pentecostalism as being "concerned primarily with the *experience* of the working of the Holy Spirit and the *practice* of spiritual gifts" (italics in original).[37] Anderson then offers a broad definition that recognizes the global variation of expressions, which share family traits.[38] He writes, "[Pentecostalism] refers to churches with a family resemblance that emphasize the working of the Holy Spirit."[39] Likewise, a study by the Pew Forum states of Pentecostals: "Even more than other Christians, pentecostals and other renewalists believe that God, acting through the Holy Spirit, continues to play a direct, active role in everyday life."[40] As the reader may note, these descriptions focus not only on the Spirit of God but also on the person's experience with God.

Three separate renewal movements are frequently used in narrowing the above descriptions in that these movements mark the origins and thereby the characterizations of Pentecostals worldwide.[41] Classical Pentecostals emerged out of revival movements during the early twentieth century, such as the Azusa Street Revival, and emphasize the baptism of the Holy Spirit with the initial physical evidence of speaking in tongues. These Pentecostals include denominations such as the Assemblies of God (AG), Church of God (Clev, TN), and Pentecostal Assemblies of Canada (PAOC). Charismatics arose from renewal movements in the mid-twentieth century within historic mainline denominations, such as Episcopal, Roman Catholicism, and

---

36. Anderson, *Vision of the Disinherited*, 4.

37. Anderson, "Varieties, Taxonomies, and Definitions," 17; A. Anderson is drawing from Anderson, *Vision of the Disinherited*, 4.

38. Anderson, "Varieties, Taxonomies, and Definitions," 15.

39. Ibid.

40. Lugo et al., *Spirit and Power*, 3.

41. I am following here the examples of other scholars. For instance, Menzies and Menzies, *Spirit and Power*, loc. 353–538; Yong, *Renewing Christian Theology*, loc. 450–75; Anderson, "Varieties, Taxonomies, and Definitions," 17–20. Anderson forms four groups: Classical; Older, Independent and Spirit Churches; Older Church Charismatics; and Neo-Pentecostal and neo-Charismatic Churches.

Lutheran. While choosing to remain in their respective church traditions, Charismatics stress the gifts of the Spirit and "life in the Spirit" rather than focusing only on the Spirit baptism's initial physical evidence of tongues.[42] Neocharismatics, who are also called Third-Wavers, are described by *The New International Dictionary of Pentecostal and Charismatic Movements* as "a catch-all category that comprises 18,810 independent, indigenous, postdenominational denominations and groups that cannot be classified as either pentecostal or charismatic but share a common emphasis on the Holy Spirit, spiritual gifts, pentecostal-like experiences, . . . signs and wonders, and power encounters."[43] Examples of Neocharismatics include John Wimber's Vineyard Fellowship, China's Assembly Hall Churches and the True Jesus Church, and Kenya's the Legion of Mary.[44] There are two things to mention for the reading of the upcoming chapters. First, I use the term "Pentecostal" (capital "P") in this project to include all three classifications unless otherwise noted (e.g., a citation of another author). Second, the reader is invited to pay attention to the Classical Pentecostal in North America since my research involves the experiences of Pentecostals in the United States and Canada who are part of the AG or PAOC.

In defining *practical theology*, I acknowledge there are a variety of sentiments as to what it entails. Thus, my definition is to clarify what I mean by *practical theology*. My starting point is the two words "practical" and "theology." The word "theology" may conjure up images of reciting particular tenants of faith such as, "We believe in the one triune God" and/or "We believe in Jesus Christ, the only Son of God." When *practical* is placed in front of *theology*, some mistakenly equate this to *applied theology*. Applied theology places precedence on the development of the doctrines of God, which is followed by the relating of those same doctrines to life.[45] This means that the formation of theology comes first and is ensued by the development of application.

Contra to beginning with theological constructs, practical theology usually starts with experience. Bonnie Miller-McLemore confirms,

42. Burgess and van der Maas, "Introduction," xix.
43. Ibid., xx.
44. Ibid., xx–xxi.
45. Cartledge perceives that Pentecostal practical theology is currently "underdeveloped" because it "has been limited to an Evangelical paradigm of 'applied' theology, and tended to view such theology as an extension of the sermon." Cartledge defines applied theology as "the application of biblical precepts to pastoral practice in a fairly linear fashion." Cartledge, "Pentecostal and Charismatic Theology," 370.

What's It All About?

"Practical theology is seldom a systematic enterprise, aimed at the ordering of beliefs about God, the church, or classic texts. More often it is an open-ended, contingent, unfinished grasp or analysis of faith in action."[46] John Swinton and Harriet Mowat also highlight the beginning point of practical theology when they write, "[T]he common theme that holds Practical Theology together as a discipline is its perspective on, and beginning-point in, human experience and its desire to reflect theologically on that experience."[47] For example, Don Browning perceives that when a Christian community is faced with a crisis, the community reflects on their practices and eventually rethinks the "norms" that they used to develop those practices, such as Scripture, tradition, or theological documents, and this in turn shapes the community's practices. He describes this movement as "practice-theory-practice."[48] Because of this emphasis on experience, practical theology is a fitting method for developing a Pentecostal theology of suffering.

While the aforementioned "practice-theory-practice" is a good starting point for understanding practical theology, it does not completely satisfy who I am as a Pentecostal. Focusing on "practice-theory-practice" for me runs the risk of centering on human action while avoiding divine action. Andrew Root critiques Browning in saying, "[H]ermeneutics is done by human agents that seek to interpret human actions through the best of human thought and action (tradition) for the sake of better human practice."[49] In other words, if I only reflect theologically on human practices

---

46. Miller-McLemore, "Introduction," 14.

47. Swinton and Mowat, *Practical Theology and Qualitative Research*, loc. 65–66.

48. Browning, *A Fundamental Practical Theology*, 6–7. While "practice-theory-practice" is discussed throughout his book, specific examples of his usage of this phrase are on pages 7 and 9. Rather than Browning's movements of three, it may be helpful for me to offer another perspective for those not familiar with the meaning of practical theology. Richard Osmer perceives that practical theology includes four tasks that function like a spiral in which one returns to the tasks again and again. These tasks include: *descriptive-empirical*, which asks, "What is going on?"; *interpretative*, which inquires, "Why is this going on?"; *normative*, which seeks to discover, "What should be going on?"; and *pragmatic*, which answers the question, "How might we respond?" Osmer, *Practical Theology*. In essence, one deeply describes the experience (descriptive), reflects on that experience by using science and culture (interpretative) as well as theology and Scripture (normative), and offers a new action in light of this reflection (pragmatic). I have chosen to use Browning's framework as an example because it is from this model that Ray Anderson formulates his own model of Christopraxis, which I use in this project.

49. Root, *Christopraxis*, loc. 1315–6. Root's whole project addresses the field of practical theology and its absence of speaking about divine action and lived experiences in

or actions, I may neglect God's action, which can result in the equating of human practices within the Christian community with God's activity. As a Pentecostal, the "concrete and lived" encounter between the human and the divine is critical, which leads to my use of the practical theological interpretative method of Ray Anderson called *Christopraxis*.[50]

WHAT IS CHRISTOPRAXIS?

I begin this section with some introductory remarks concerning Christopraxis prior to moving toward a more detailed explanation. Unlike the previously mentioned *applied theology*, Anderson adheres to the understanding that church doctrine flows from ministry/experience.[51] As Anderson states, "What makes theology practical is not the fitting of orthopedic devices to theoretical concepts in order to make them walk. Rather, theology occurs as a divine partner joins us on our walk, stimulating our reflection and inspiring us to recognize the living Word, as happened to the two walking on the road to Emmaus on the first Easter (Lk 24)."[52] Thus, similar to other practical theologians, Anderson begins with experience; however, unlike Browning, Anderson's Christopraxis centers on the reflection of the experience/actions of Jesus while asking, in light of both what Scripture says and what the Spirit is doing, "How then should we live?" and "What should we do?"[53] Anderson recognizes that Jesus is the one who continues to minister today, and it is upon their experiences with Jesus, which believers are to reflect. This leads to Anderson's definition of Christopraxis as being "the continuing ministry of Christ through the power and presence

---

which humans encounter God today. For a more in-depth exploration on the discussion of Browning, see chapters 2 and 4.

50. In using the phrase "concrete and lived," I am drawing from Root's *Christopraxis*.

51. Anderson, *The Shape of Practical Theology*, 61–62. See also his discussion on modernism and postmodernism in the same volume, 18–21.

52. Ibid., 12.

53. Ibid., 52. Root comments about the use of Scripture in Christopraxis, "Anderson's Christopraxis approach allowed him to herald that the norm of practical theology is not *the Bible* but the *ministering of the living Christ*. It is the Bible that is needed to discern the action of the living Christ that the Spirit calls us to join in the world. The Bible, then, for Anderson remains a central norm, not as a destination, as it appears in the other approaches to which to conform, but as a tool to move into practical theological engagement" (italics in original). See Root, "Evangelical Practical Theology," loc. 2400–2403.

of the Holy Spirit."[54] Elsewhere Anderson clarifies, "Christopraxis means the real presence of Christ as the one who has been raised from the dead and the one who is coming again, but also as the *eschatos* who is even now present in the world."[55] Hence, Christopraxis is appropriate for developing a Pentecostal theological praxis of suffering and healing because it focuses on experiences with the person of Jesus in light of Scripture.[56]

Keeping in mind that practical theology begins with experience/action, Anderson bases Christopraxis on the understanding that what humanity knows of God is a result of God's own action in our world. It is God's action that produces theology. God took the first step to reveal Godself to the world and to reconcile the world to God through acts of ministry.[57] This, then, is ministry: to reveal God and to reconcile humanity to God.[58] "All ministry is God's ministry," says Anderson, because God first ministers to humanity and continues to minister through Jesus Christ, and it is this "ongoing ministry of Jesus Christ" that "gives both content and direction to the church and its ministry."[59] This makes ministry not simply a human endeavor, but it is a divine one in which humans participate. When we respond in obedience to God's ministry, writes Anderson, it "becomes our ministry, which in turn, serves" to reveal God.[60]

Anderson offers an effectual example of how humanity participates in God's acts of ministry through the story of Moses. Anderson points out that Moses experienced God's ministry of redemption prior to writing a

---

54. Anderson, *The Shape of Practical Theology*, 29.

55. Anderson, "Christopraxis," 28.

56. From my perspective, Christopraxis was developed in part with Pentecostals in mind. Anderson explains in his writing about his purpose of the book *Ministry on the Fireline: A Practical Theology for an Empowered Church*, "[T]his book is an attempt to heal the breach between pentecostal and mainline church theology by providing the contours of a mission theology that is centered in the Pentecost event as a continuing praxis of the Holy Spirit in the encounter between Christ and the world for the sake of liberation and reconciliation." Anderson, *Ministry on the Fireline*, 10.

57. Anderson writes, "[M]inistry precedes and produces theology . . . [M]inistry is determined and set forth by God's own ministry of revelation and reconciliation in the world, beginning with Israel and culminating in Jesus Christ and the church"; see Anderson, *The Shape of Practical Theology*, 62. Anderson states, "All of God's actions in history are what we mean by God's ministry"; see Anderson, *The Soul of Ministry*, 3.

58. Root points out that practical theology for Anderson is ministry. Root, *Christopraxis*, loc. 2095–273.

59. Anderson, *The Shape of Practical Theology*, 62.

60. Anderson, *The Soul of Ministry*, 3.

theology about God as Creator and Redeemer as seen in the Pentateuch.[61] Moses, an elderly man who is an ineloquent speaker, encounters God in a bush that is burning but not consumed. It is here that God reveals to Moses, "I am that I am" and calls Moses to go to Egypt and to tell Pharaoh, "Let my people go."

Anderson accentuates the impossibility of this situation. Moses has been in the desert for forty years after his failed attempt to free the Israelites forced him to flee for his life. The Israelites, having been slaves for four hundred years, did not accept him as a leader. For Anderson, this is nothingness (*ex nihilo*), an impossible situation.[62] However, when Moses acts by obeying God and joins God's own action, "the Word of God creates the response out of nothing."[63] Thus, not only does God reveal Godself, but God also provides the response, the redemption or healing of God's people (reconciliation). Root points out that when Moses encounters God's being and obediently goes to Egypt, Moses joins God's own acts of ministry, which are simultaneously revealing God; thus, through Moses's action, Moses is participating in God's very being.[64] Root explains, "We take the divine being's form not in the way of ontological essence (this is not possible) but through action, by ourselves becoming ministers, joining God's being (ontology) not through shared essence but through concrete shared action of ministering (Matthew 25 seems to point in this very direction)."[65]

Christopraxis particularly centers on God's ministerial act in Jesus who reveals God to humanity and reconciles humanity to God. John 3 reminds us that God's love for the world initiates God's act of the sending of the Son into the world. Thus, the Son, who is the being of God, is simultaneously the action of God. This means revelation and reconciliation occur in the very person (body) of Jesus. That is to say, Jesus, as the human-divine

---

61. Ibid., 3–4.

62. Ibid., 35–42. Anderson explains that *ex nihilo* is Latin for "out of nothing." He reminds his readers that Genesis proclaims that "the earth was a 'formless void,'" but when God spoke, "creation emerged out of this formless void—this nothingness." For Anderson, this is similar to the words spoken to Pharaoh in Exodus, "Let my people go!" Thus, Anderson argues, "It is by the power of the Word of God that the people were redeemed from bondage, and it is by the power of that same Word that all things were created out of nothing." Hence, for Anderson, nothingness or the void (which he calls *ex nihilo*) is essential "for the Word to bring forth God's creation." Ibid., 37–38.

63. Ibid., 37.

64. Root, *Christopraxis*, loc. 2130–81.

65. Ibid., loc. 2137–39.

What's It All About?

one, reveals God to humanity and responds completely and wholly to God in his very person (body).

John's Gospel informs the audience in the first chapter that Jesus, the Word of God, enters the world that he created by becoming flesh and blood to reveal God to humanity and to reconcile the world to God through his very being. In this event of Jesus coming to humanity and walking among us, God is present with us, being revealed as a God of grace and truth (John 1:14). At the same time, humanity is reconciled to God (healed) as Jesus obediently responds to God in a complete and holy way.[66] Thus, Anderson accentuates this one event, which is God's act of sending the Son, and it contains both revelation (the Word of God) and reconciliation (the response), making them "reciprocal movements of a single event."[67] Thus, God acts through God's being.

While I have stressed God's ministry in the sending of the Son, Christopraxis emphasizes that this ministry is ongoing in the world through the Spirit. Anderson illustrates Christopraxis through a scriptural example from Acts 10, the story of Peter and Cornelius.[68] This incident occurs after Peter and the other disciples already have encountered Jesus in their powerlessness, being empowered by the Spirit at Pentecost (Acts 2).[69] Peter in Acts 10 has an experience with God through a vision of unclean animals being lowered from heaven, which is followed by a command to Peter to eat them. After Peter refuses, the voice declares, "What God has made clean, you must not consider ritually unclean!" When Cornelius's men arrive, the Spirit instructs Peter to accompany them. Upon choosing to obey the Spirit and go to Cornelius's household, Peter preaches and the Spirit falls upon the Gentiles, and Peter responds by baptizing Cornelius's household. As Anderson points out, this is praxis, which is "truth in action" that includes a telos.[70] Peter unites with God's ministry to Cornelius's household, entering

---

66. Anderson describes reconciliation as "that movement by which humans are conformed to the Word of God and through which humans are constituted as possessing health and holiness." Anderson, *The Shape of Practical Theology*, 65.

67. Ibid.

68. See Anderson, *The Soul of Ministry*, 28–31; Anderson, *The Shape of Practical Theology*, 81–82.

69. Anderson perceives nothingness at Pentecost in that the disciples "were powerless until the Spirit came upon them at Pentecost." Anderson, *The Soul of Ministry*, 112.

70. Anderson, *The Shape of Practical Theology*, 48–49; see also Anderson, *The Soul of Ministry*, 29–30.

into the Gentiles' nothingness of powerlessness.[71] Anderson perceives that when Peter witnesses the Spirit baptizing the Gentiles, he concretely joins God's ministry to the Gentiles by baptizing them in water, revealing God's truth that God has no partiality between Jews and Gentiles.[72]

In the above example, Christopraxis is operating in two forms. First, in the same way Peter encountered the divine, Christopraxis is based on people continuing to experience Jesus Christ today. Jesus comes to people and ministers to them, bringing healing and wholeness. When believers reflect on their encounters, they obediently respond to God, ministering to the other in his nothingness through the power of the Spirit, by which God is revealed.[73] Thus, the second way in which Jesus is experienced is in ministry, person-to-person. Root clarifies, "The experience of the living Jesus in communities of persons is for ministry itself; the Christ who encounters us is Christ at work, ministering to our person by sharing in our lived experience. This experience is praxis, not only because it is action (not pure mysticism) but because it is action with a telos, for the sake of ministry (relationally sharing in the life of other)."[74]

Such ministry is not the same as imitation but is participation. When believers participate in Christ's ministry, this is not *imitatio Christi* or simply practices, forcing believers to fall back on their own strength. Instead, participating in Christ's ministry occurs through the power of the Spirit.[75] Root writes, "The ministry of Jesus is not a past happening . . . but is *the ongoing possibility of God's encounter*" (italics in original).[76] This means that in the same way we encounter God through the act of ministry in Jesus, Jesus is now encountered through acts of ministry as we participate in his ministry. Root explains, "To participate in Christopraxis is to take on the

---

71. Anderson's assertion that the church experienced nothingness (powerlessness) until the Spirit came upon them at Pentecost and empowered them (Acts 2) is being applied here in reference to the Gentiles. Anderson, *The Soul of Ministry*, 112.

72. Ibid., 29–31.

73. I have chosen throughout this project to alternate my usage of gender when employing the third person indefinite pronouns to avoid the cumbersome language of he/she, him/her, or his/her.

74. Root, *Christopraxis*, loc. 2082–84.

75. As Root points out, if we are only imitating Christ, our acts of ministry fall short as we seek to build ourselves up. Ibid., loc. 1532–60.

76. Ibid., loc. 2072.

form of and join Jesus' own action, which is to join the praxis of ministry itself."[77]

When we join with the other person in her nothingness, in her place of impossibility, we are joining with God in God's ministry to that person. It is here in this act of ministry in her nothingness that God continues to reveal Godself and to reconcile her to Godself. Root comments, "So we can know God (epistemology) only through the priority of encountering God's being (ontology) as it is revealed in the act of God's coming ministry to humanity."[78] This is Christopraxis. It is where, to quote Anderson, the "truths of God are discovered through the encounter with Christ in the world by means of ministry."[79]

WHAT TO EXPECT

In keeping with a project in practical theology that employs Christopraxis, the upcoming chapters focus on participants' experiences of suffering (nothingness); reflect on experience/action with the divine by using Scripture, theology, culture, and psychology; and closes with how we are to respond. Each chapter also includes experiences of the participants in adherence with the foundations of both practical theology and Pentecostalism.

Chapter 2 centers on the experiences of extended suffering of Pentecostals out of recognition that experience is important in the development of Pentecostal theology. I recount the experiences of extended suffering of eight Classical Pentecostals who believed for a divine intervention but did not obtain one. I include in these accounts: the participants' beliefs about God and/or suffering prior to their stressor events; a description of unmet hopes and/or expectations; and a portrayal of their losses and grief. This chapter, then, emphasizes what Root refers to as nothingness, relating it to the apparent absence of God, and discusses the apparent absence of Jesus in the Gospel of John. That is to say, this chapter centers on apparent absence over and above presence.

Chapter 3 investigates the historical roots of Pentecostalism in order to show that the participants' believing for a divine intervention is part and parcel of Pentecostalism. This chapter's objective in studying the history of Pentecostalism's theology of encounter is to confirm how an experience

77. Ibid., loc. 2093–94.
78. Ibid., loc. 2101–2.
79. Anderson, *The Soul of Ministry*, 29.

with God is the ethos of Pentecostalism. This is accomplished by underscoring six aspects of historical Pentecostalism as it relates to divine encounter, which are also represented in the lives of the participants: (1) restorational revivalism supplies a doctrine of divine encounter; (2) worship provides a space for divine encounter; (3) altar presents a place for divine encounter; (4) prayer makes a request for divine encounter; (5) transformation gives the verifiable evidence of divine encounter; and (6) testimony offers a report of divine encounter, which is the theologizing of it. This chapter then stresses God's presence.

Having examined in chapter 2 the experiences of suffering of eight Pentecostals, chapter 4 continues reflecting on the research participants' stories in conjunction with theology and Scripture. This chapter relates the participants' experiences with God in the midst of suffering, the encountering of God in their nothingness. It depicts how the participants interpreted and/or understood the apparent absence of God, which is the meaning they drew from their suffering. The formation of meaning involves three aspects: (1) being transformed; (2) making sense; and (3) embracing uncertainty, ambiguity, and mystery. I reflect on the participants' experiences and interpretations with the aid of James K. A. Smith's discussion on Pentecostalism's *non-interventionist supernaturalism,* which sees Pentecostalism embracing the ongoing work of the Spirit in the world as well as the intense, unique instances of divine intervention: thus, I emphasize not only the apparent absence in presence but also presence in apparent absence. I then consider the Gospel of John's theme of Jesus's presence and provide several aspects of his presence that is evidenced in this Gospel and in the lives the participants.

Chapter 5 conveys how the body of Christ responded to the research participants in their suffering. I accent Christopraxis's emphasis on experiencing God as we join God's own act of ministry to others in their nothingness through relationality. In essence, I stress experiencing presence in the midst of apparent absence through person-to-person ministry. I recount the participants' experiences of others' unhelpfulness through the lens of individualism, which is portrayed as part of culture's influence on Western Pentecostalism. This is followed by relating the participants' experiences of the helpful responses of others, which are placed in dialogue with John Bowlby's attachment theory and Brené Brown's discussion of vulnerability. I conclude this chapter with the command from John 13 to minister to one another through love, supporting my assertion throughout this chapter that suffering is an opportunity for relationality.

Chapter 6 focuses on the participants' answer to the question: "How would I now respond to someone who is suffering?" In other words, this chapter answers Christopraxis's questions: "How then should we live?" and "What should we do?" It is here that I clearly spell out a theological praxis of suffering and healing through the expression of empathy by drawing from Marshall Rosenberg's Nonviolent Communication. Inherent in empathy is a relationality that embraces suffering, which aides in healing. I continue the theme from the Fourth Gospel of the disciples' loving each other by asserting Jesus is God's embodied expression of empathy; thus, we participate in Christ's ministry of empathy by loving each other through the expression of empathy when others are suffering. That is to say, I offer a theological praxis of experiencing presence in the midst of apparent absence. This expression of love, however, is not only an end in itself, but it also is a testimony to the world that we are followers of Christ. I conclude with chapter 7 by offering future ways in which this project may be advanced.

Additionally, I offer the following delimitations in order to clarify what the reader is not to expect in the upcoming chapters. This project does not offer an in-depth theological or philosophical treatise on the reasons for suffering in light of the Christian belief in an omniscient, omnipotent God. Instead, it strives to embrace mystery and ambiguity by holding in tension both the reality of suffering in the world and the existence of a God who is all powerful/all knowing. As a qualitative study, this project is unable to generalize its findings beyond the experiences of the participants of this research; thus, it embraces this limitation while seeking to contribute to the conversation of a Pentecostal theological praxis of suffering and healing. It is my hope, in keeping with Christopraxis, that this project of practical theology joins God's ministry by ministering to its readers, revealing God and bringing healing (reconciliation).

2

What's Your Story?
Unmet Expectations in Suffering

I'm starting to question God, and I'm like, "Okay, God, why? You parted the Red Sea. You did this. You did that. I mean, God just have mercy. Just have mercy." So then I'm starting to blame God for some of these different . . . positions just heading south, and I'm like, "God, we did what was right here, and we were out. We did what was right here, you know. Why is all this happening?" And now, Jason mentally and physically he can't do anything. "God, where are you? What are you doing?" And I got very angry. Very angry.

—Christy, a participant

I RELAYED IN THE previous chapter my own experience of a crisis of faith and how this path of suffering became a call to contribute to a Pentecostal theological praxis of suffering and healing. The reader is now invited to join me on a journey of discovering how other Pentecostals interpreted their experiences with God and with others when God did not intervene as they had hoped. I introduce in the next few pages eight Classical Pentecostals and relate the stories of their experiences of suffering and unmet expectations. For Pentecostals, the stories of our experiences are a vital foundation for the forming of our theology as seen in the sharing of testimonies in

What's Your Story?

a Pentecostal community and with the emphasizing of biblical narratives, such as Luke-Acts.[1] Thus, in this chapter I invite the reader to enter into the nothingness of these participants by listening to their stories of extended suffering. After presenting the stories, I explore the narrative of Jesus as pictured in the Gospel of John, in which I underscore the apparent absence of Jesus. However, prior to turning to the stories themselves, it is essential to clarify my understanding of nothingness as it relates to the participants' experiences of suffering.

WHAT IS NOTHINGNESS?

As previously stated, Anderson's paradigm of Christopraxis accentuates nothingness. That is, creating out of nothingness is at the very heart of God's ministry. Anderson shows how this is repeatedly demonstrated throughout the Scriptures.[2] For instance, in the story of creation (Gen 1–2) Anderson notes both that "the earth was a 'formless void'" as well as the absence of a partner for Adam.[3] In Genesis (11–22) we read that Abraham and Sarah were unable to have children, and in Exodus (2–4) Moses was not capable of freeing his people from Egyptian slavery. In Acts the Early Church was ill-equipped to proclaim the Gospel of Jesus to the world, and in Romans we are reminded that humanity was incapable of keeping the commands in order to have relationship with God. According to Root, nothingness, then, is one of impossibility and may include "human limitation, finitude, and need."[4] Anderson describes it as the "hopelessness of the situation," which is "marked by powerlessness from the human side."[5]

Nothingness is central to Christopraxis because, as Root explains, we know God's being through God's acts of ministry as God holds in God's

---

1. Warrington writes, "Pentecostals have always emphasized experiential Christianity rather than doctrinal confession. Rather than describe or explain doctrines in the mode of systematic or dogmatic theologians associated with the seminary and scholar, they typically explore them in the biblical narrative and by the testimony of those affected by them"; Warrington, *Pentecostal Theology*, 15–16. See also Archer, *A Pentecostal Hermeneutic*, 94–126; Smith, *Thinking in Tongues*, 48–85.

2. Anderson writes, "There is an *ex nihilo* located at the very core of the paradigm that portrays the ministry of God." Anderson, *The Soul of Ministry*, 37.

3. Ibid., 38.

4. Root, *Christopraxis*, loc. 2342.

5. Anderson, *The Soul of Ministry*, 37.

arms "our experiences of *ex nihilo*" (italics mine).[6] In order for God to act, nothingness has to be present. As Root says, all "human possibility must be removed."[7] This is confirmed when we read that Adam is unable to find his own partner and why Ishmael is not God's chosen, both of which are failed attempts of human action. The same is true when the Hebrew children are not liberated by Moses's act of killing an Egyptian, or when humanity attempts to do good works in order to be righteous before God. Instead, as Anderson stresses, it is "[t]he Word of God [that] creates the response out of nothing."[8] Root captures this thought:

> The Word always speaks of possibility: The Word speaks over the void of nothingness and creates (Gen. 1:1–6). The Word speaks of a dead womb bringing forth the promise (Genesis 21). The Word speaks of an old man leading a people from slavery (Exodus). The Word speaks of a poor nobody virgin bearing the Word itself (Luke 1:30).[9]

In short, it is not human action that is able to change the impossibilities faced in life. The unrelenting depression. The broken marriage. Unemployment. An incurable diagnosis. A head injury. Death. It is only the Word of God.

For Pentecostals, however, nothingness may be not only impossibilities such as those mentioned above, but it may also include the absence of a hoped-for divine intervention. For example, when faced with the human limitation of an incurable disease, the Pentecostal turns to the only one who can cure the infirmity: God. This Pentecostal believes and hopes that God intervenes and physically heals the one that is afflicted. He holds that God continues in this day and age to intervene in human affairs, and he, no doubt, has heard many accounts of said deliverance from suffering. Thus, the Pentecostal is expected to seek God for a divine intervention since it is believed and hoped that a divine intervention will occur when suffering interferes in a person's life.[10]

However, when no divine intervention comes as one has hoped, the Pentecostal believer experiences, what I call, the apparent absence of God.

---

6. Root, *Christopraxis*, loc. 2340–42.

7. Ibid., loc. 2344.

8. Anderson, *The Soul of Ministry*, 35.

9. Root, *Christopraxis*, loc. 2849–51.

10. According to John 9:3 and 11:4, Craig Keener perceives that we are reminded that suffering is an "opportunity for divine intervention." Keener, *The Gospel of John*, 839.

This means I am equating the experience of the lack of an expected divine intervention with God's apparent absence. Don't get me wrong. Pentecostals believe in the omnipresence of God, but there are times in a person's life when God is apparently absent in God's presence. This is particularly noticeable when humans have an expectation or a hope as to the manner in which God will respond to a situation, believing for or hoping in God for a specific outcome.[11] In other words, an experience of God's apparent absence emerges in the unfulfilled prayer request for a divine intervention. While on some occasions God may eventually heal, there are other times when there is an apparent lack of response from God—God remains silent. This is an event of God's apparent absence in that God did not intervene (deliver) as the Pentecostal prayed. Many times there is no explanation as to why God did not eradicate the suffering in a person's life. Instead, only silence prevails. It is here the sufferer comes face to face with her own

---

11. Mittelstadt, in remarking about "Pentecostals in the global North," writes, "Since Pentecostal Christians expect 'the blessing of God,' suffering seems to infringe on this right to happiness, causing an increasing gap between expectations and any potential suffering connected with God and/or godliness"; see Mittelstadt, "Spirit and Suffering," 165. Ma also writes of expectations and extended suffering: "The triumphalist attitude of the modern Pentecostal/Charismatic theology and ethos has left very little room for human suffering . . . [T]he overly simplistic and triumphalist theology of 'kingdom now' (or its variety) has betrayed the true reality of human life where suffering is an integral component. It has also been destructive of the eschatological tension that New Testament believers had been taught to live with for so long. These problems have almost created a sense that Pentecostalism is a cheap version of Christianity . . . This not only distorted the concept of commitment in Christianity but also fostered unscriptural expectations of God's power on our behalf. Although this is not preached explicitly it is conceivable that Christians with long-term illness may likely lose their place in a local Pentecostal church when the message of unconditional healing, which actually only requires faith is implicitly proclaimed from the pulpit. In reality the old fallacy is recycled: if one is not healed, it is either because of hidden sin or lack of faith, since Jesus paid for all healing"; see Ma, "Asian (Classical) Pentecostal Theology in Context," 63–64. Kärkkäinen also comments about expectations: "One of the persisting challenges to a movement such as Pentecostalism is to find a balance between the mentality of 'overcoming' and suffering, between the patience of sticking with the disappointments of life and the expectation of God's 'supernatural' intervention. Pentecostal/charismatic Christianity has (re)introduced to Christian spirituality an ideal of victorious Christian living, an intensive faith expectation, and emphasis on spiritual power to overcome problems in one's life. The attitude of 'overcoming' is characteristic to Pentecostal and charismatic preaching. Often there is a heightened expectation of divine intervention, even in situations that seem impossible"; see Kärkkäinen, "The Pentecostal Understanding of Mission," 41.

vulnerability—her uncertainty, her being at risk, and her own emotional exposure, to use Brené Brown's definition.[12]

Such apparent absence in and of itself becomes nothingness (a human limitation, finitude, or need) for a Pentecostal. Even though the Pentecostal has prayed and fasted, confessed sin, studied and memorized Scripture, and believed God for a miracle, all these human actions may have failed to generate the much-desired divine intervention. This is a human limitation, nothingness. It means that not only is the Pentecostal in his own self incapable of ridding himself of the suffering, but he is also powerless to make God miraculously remove the suffering. Thus, the experience of the apparent absence of God, the lack of a divine intervention, also becomes the place of impossibility. This, then, is the human experience, according to Root, which "is not one of strength and power but of death and impossibility."[13]

The experience of the apparent absence of God, to say again, is the lack of a divine intervention in the midst of suffering, and this is classified as nothingness. There is nothing a human can do to force God to respond. We are powerless to manipulate God to deliver us from our afflictions. As will be shown in the next section, the actions of the participants did not generate a divine intervention in which God removed the suffering. God did not heal the diseases, disability, or mental illness. God did not miraculously generate employment nor did God suddenly mend a marriage that was torn asunder. With the lack of a divine intervention, God appeared to be absent, and none of the participants' actions generated a much-desired miracle on their behalf.

WHO ARE THE PARTICIPANTS?

I previously stated that Pentecostals rely on experience and Scripture to form their theology. Therefore, I begin this contribution to a Pentecostal theological praxis of suffering and healing by recounting the stories of Classical Pentecostals' experiences of extended suffering. While I am relating accounts of real people, the names, locations, and other minor details have been changed in order to maintain confidentiality. Prior to telling the participants' stories of suffering, I describe the procedure of finding the participants, and I delineate the characteristics of suffering that arose from the stories.

12. Brown, *Daring Greatly*, 34.
13. Root, *Christopraxis*, 2799–2800.

What Was the Process of Meeting the Participants?

I chose to conduct semi-structured interviews in order to hear the stories of experiences of suffering of Pentecostals. It was through the help of family and friends and postings on various Facebook pages of Pentecostal groups that these participants learned of this research project and contacted me. That is to say, I did not have a personal relationship with any of these participants at the time of their interviews.

After the participants contacted me via email, I sent them a screening questionnaire to verify that they were within my established parameters for this project. Each of the participants needed to have experienced an extended period of suffering for a minimum of one year. Furthermore, they needed to indicate they had had an expectation or a hope that God would intervene and deliver them from their difficult situation, but no miraculous intervention came forth. Such expectation or hope meant that the person desired or thought that God would or could intervene. Following their submission of the screening questionnaire, I had a telephone conversation with each of them, after which I extended an invitation to participate in an interview.[14]

The interview was semi-structured in that I had formulated eight main questions with several possible sub-questions (see appendix A). It was my desire that the eight chief questions would begin a conversation that would allow the participants to tell their stories. The interview, as Herbert Rubin and Irene Rubin suggest, was structured to rise slowly with emotional intensity that eventually reached a peak that was followed with an attempt to lower the affective level.[15] It inquired about Pentecostals' experiences and relationships with God and others prior to, during, and after the stressor events. The recorded interviews lasted ninety to one hundred and twenty minutes and were conducted face to face in the region in which the participant lived except for one participant that was interviewed via FaceTime. An informed consent form was signed prior to the interview (see appendix B). After I recorded and transcribed each interview, I entered into a process called "coding" in which I analyzed the interviews in order to

---

14. Not all individuals who inquired were accepted into this study. If I determined through the screening questionnaire or through the telephone interview that they neglected to meet the criteria (e.g., not currently attending an AG or PAOC church; not having an expectation of a divine intervention; or perceiving that God did intervene), I did not invite them to participate in an extended interview.

15. Rubin and Rubin, *Qualitative Interviewing*, 107–12.

form concepts, topics, and themes from the data that was formulated into categories (see appendix C).

What Is the Path of Suffering?

As readers consider the stories in the next several pages, I invite them to notice various characteristics that emerged from the data. Prior to making note of these qualities, it may be beneficial to place some handles on the abstract concept of suffering. As I contemplated the data as well as my own suffering, I found it helpful to use the image of journeying on a *path of suffering* when speaking of the experience of extended suffering. I first rejected the phrase "a space of suffering" because *space* is nebulous and difficult to clearly delineate. *Space* lacks the clarity that enables one to grasp it, and this exacerbates the sense of helplessness. I then considered the phrase "place of suffering," which seemed to generate an increased sense of empowerment. Unlike *space,* which is nebulous and without boundaries, *place* offers a definitive locale. If, for example, I ask someone to come to where I am, my place, I state a specific street address. The word "place" provides a quality of concreteness and clear boundaries that may stimulate healing.

Nevertheless, I realized that *place* was too static, causing me to reflect upon the word "path," which speaks of movement. *Path* implies a route that deviates from the normal road, and it also may encompass the trait of an unexpected trajectory. *Path* is different from *detour* in that *detour* expects to return once again to normal. I acknowledge that in the past I have treated suffering as a detour by chastising and blaming myself for not being able to return to the normal road. However, when one finds herself on a path of suffering, she will never again traverse the road of perceived normalcy. It is possible she may eventually journey on a path that is parallel to her prior perception of normalcy; however, suffering has altered the events of her journey thereby transforming her. In essence, she enters a new normal.[16]

In keeping with the Pentecostal tradition of using stories to develop theology, in this chapter I introduce the reader to the eight stories, allowing them to speak for themselves. There are three qualities of the path of suffering that emerge from the stories, and I invite the reader to identify these

---

16. As Alan Wolfelt explains, when writing of a person who has experienced a death of someone close to them: "The unfolding of this journey is not intended to create a return to an 'old normal' but the discovery of a 'new normal.'" Wolfelt, *Understanding Your Grief,* 147.

characteristics, which are embedded in these accounts. First, the so-called normal road appears in the stories of the participants as they describe their lives prior to the stressor events. This road is paved with expectations, hopes, and dreams. It contains beliefs about suffering and how God interacts with the world. For some, there are indications of a belief in a just world such as, "If I obey God, God will protect me." For others, there was an openness to struggling and wrestling with tough concepts and life. Second, the participants' stories include unmet expectations of God, of others, and of their own theology. The expectation for some participants bordered on certainty, and for others it is more closely related to having hope or trust. Third, the participants experienced loss and grief. While many people tend to equate loss and grief only to the death of a person, experiencing other losses and grieving those losses transpires in a variety of ways throughout life. Nancy Hooyman and Betty J. Kramer describe loss as being "produced by an event that is perceived to be negative by the individuals involved and results in long-term changes to their social situations, relationships, and patterns of thought and emotion. Even perceived positive changes, such as a career move, relocation, or retirement, may evoke feelings of loss and grief."[17] Grief is the natural response to losing that to which we were attached.[18] While by no means an exhaustive list, these attachments may include places, persons, jobs, abilities, marriages, health, and even particular ways of thinking or theologies.[19] The grief that ensues in the aftermath of a loss is messy and chaotic with many emotional and physical responses.

One final note is to be made. The stories as presented in this chapter are limited to the path of suffering, emphasizing the experience of the apparent absence of God. That is to say, they do not contain the participants' interpretation of their experiences with God and others in their suffering. There is an absence of a resolution. This is intentional so that in the

---

17. Hooyman and Kramer, *Living through Loss*, loc. 229–31. For more information on the way loss pervades our lives, see the classic text, Viorst, *Necessary Losses*.

18. Hooyman and Kramer write, "Grief is a natural reaction to loss, and loss is a necessary and natural part of existence"; Hooyman and Kramer, *Living through Loss*, loc. 236.

19. Hooyman and Kramer state, "Losses can be physical or symbolic, but they always result in a deprivation of some kind; in essence, we no longer have someone or something that we used to have. Physical loss is something tangible that becomes unavailable . . . Symbolic loss refers to a change in one's psychological experience of social interaction." Ibid., loc. 231–33.

introduction of these stories, the reader is encouraged to enter into others' nothingness, the apparent absence of God.

What Are the Stories?

I interviewed five women and three men who were currently a part of the AG of the United States or the PAOC. In adherence with the AG and PAOC theological position of Spirit baptism, each of the interviewees have been baptized in the Holy Spirit with the initial physical evidence of speaking in tongues. Six out of the eight have been in full-time ministry, and out of those six, five had been credentialed with the AG or the PAOC, and the sixth was married to a minister and equally engaged with her spouse in ministerial leadership. The two individuals who had not held ministerial credentials have participated in ministry as laypersons.

During the next pages the reader will be introduced to the eight participants. I have included actual quotes of the participants in order to enhance the telling and the reader's experience of hearing their stories.[20] It is my intention that in the same way that Pentecostals share testimonies of God's provision to assist in formulating a theology of encountering God, I offer these stories of suffering to aid in constructing a more robust theological praxis of suffering and healing.

Joan

Joan testified that she "had been living in that wonderful bubble that God would protect." While she admitted they had "normal" struggles, she and her husband, Craig, "had this pretty protected life." For instance, when a factory exploded near their home, destroying houses and causing damage to many other homes, their home remained untouched. Such experiences colored her worldview, generating an expectation of divine intervention in her life. This was particularly evident in her understanding of a prophecy

---

20. I have chosen in this project to clean up the quotes by removing immaterial words such as fillers (e.g., uh, um), stammers, or the repeated words when a participant starts and restarts a sentence. This has been done to eliminate distractions from the thrust and power of the message. For instance, I present this quote in chapter 5 thusly: "They were there, I mean, every month we'd go, and I saw their love. I saw their support, and they were just there." This is what the participant actually said: "They . . . they were there, I mean, every ss . . . every month we'd go and I saw their love. I saw their support, *(uh huh, uh huh)* and they were just there" (italicized words are mine).

that was spoken over her and her husband a few years prior to the interview. She and her husband attended a week of prayer and fasting at their church in which others prophesied that their latter years would be greater than their former years. Based upon the many experiences of divine interventions, she interpreted "greater" to be equated to a greater status or position. If her husband was already a leader of an institution, she wondered what could be greater than that? Would they "go out in a blaze of glory?"

When one combines her experiences of divine interventions with a Pentecostal emphasis upon obedience, one may understand how Joan correlated her charmed existence with obedience and any experienced difficulties to being divine discipline. Being raised as a Pentecostal, she admits there is an expectation of healing that is coupled with an understanding that "all things work together for good to them who love God and are called according to his purpose." Joan clarifies, "So if I'm seeing a lot of trouble, maybe there's some things I need to straighten out in my life or maybe there's some things that I've done and you know, God is catching me up on this and, you know, calling me to account." However, since life for Craig and Joan appeared to be relatively free of trouble, in her mind they were being obedient. Since they were obeying God and God loved them, God would continue to protect them.

Yet, difficulties began to brew on the horizon. During this time Craig was having physical issues with his back, but based upon her experiences with God and her interpretation of the prophecies, she believed that "this back pain would just be a bump in the road." In addition to the back pain, she began to notice that Craig was becoming "like a two-year old." Normally, Craig was very organized so that she had to sprint to keep up with his pace; however, while traveling for a speaking engagement, she observed that he was anxious, forgetting details, and his lectures were lacking substance. She witnessed a "discrepancy between what he was able to do and what we were suppose to be doing on this trip." In short, "We're losing it." Yet, she identified this change as being associated with his back pain. She believed that after his back surgery, he would come "back to normal," and they could move "onto greater things."

Unfortunately, rather than his mental faculties improving after his back surgery, she noticed they continued to deteriorate. This was confusing because she perceived that God was orchestrating the minute details of their lives as they made a major move to another state; therefore, it was difficult for her "to believe that there wasn't going to be healing." She also knew they had many people praying for them, and so she was "just believing that this is gonna be a wonderful miracle and then we can get on with what we're suppose to do." She had in part attributed the prayers of others throughout the years as the reason for God's protection.

When Craig's mental capacity continued to progressively decline, their regular physician announced that it was frontal lobe dementia and encouraged them to see a neuropsychologist. Following a battery of tests, the neuropsychologist confirmed the regular physician's diagnosis: Craig had frontal lobe dementia and was given two to five years to live.[21]

At the time of the interview Joan noticed the increasing signs of loss as the man she had known slowly disappeared. He lost the capacity to operate his computer and his cell phone. He also was becoming less talkative, and he was reading less and less. She spoke of the loss of "the ability to be appropriate," such as hugging and/or kissing both acquaintances and strangers in various public settings. He also repeatedly misplaced material items. She aptly stated, "He just lost one more thing." One may wonder when she wrote in her journal, if she was speaking both metaphorically and literally when she stated, "I accept that everyday we will look for a lost item."

Christy

Unlike Joan who had been raised in a Pentecostal family, Christy grew up in a non-Christian home that was described to me as one of suffering. Her father was an alcoholic; she experienced a home life that had a shortage of food and clothes; and her family was labeled "poor white trash." When she became a Christian in a Pentecostal church in her late teens, she was under the impression that all of her suffering would disappear, and her life would be "perfect." She believed, "God would send this knight in shining armor. He would be so solid. We would just have the happiest life forever and all would be joy and all would be bliss." She met Jason, her "knight in shining armor," at college. Jason's gregarious personality plus his academic excellence matched her extrovert and high achieving tendencies. Together they planned to go out and make a difference in the world.

However, life did not go as expected. Jason's family of origin was one of serious dysfunction. After getting married, she began to witness Jason struggling with severe bouts of depression. When she saw him crying and

21. Craig passed away during the writing of this project, approximately one year after the interview with Joan.

asked him what was wrong, he related to her stories of terrible abuse in which he was not treated like a human being. Furthermore, their personal employment history did not unfold as anticipated. While Jason was at his first place of employment, the overseer called Jason into his office one day and said, "I want you out now." They discovered later that this particular man went through a variety of employees, mentally and emotionally harming them and then abandoning them in their misery. Unfortunately, a short-term employment pattern began to take hold. While some of these short-lived jobs were due to Jason's mistakes, in other positions Jason had done what was right but was forced to leave. Christy maintained that while Jason's characteristic of being a self-starter did not always fare well with his overseers, he also was not always the one in the wrong. Repeatedly, they had done what was right, but they continued to experience hardship.

After several years of unpredictability both personally and professionally, Jason became mentally and emotionally exhausted and determined to make it end. He got in his car and headed for the Grand Canyon with the intention of taking his own life. Christy was frantically contacting whomever she could in hopes that someone could assist her in keeping Jason safe. On that occasion one of Jason's long-time friends made a connection with Jason, resulting in his returning home and entering counseling.

Yet the divine intervention of healing for Jason did not materialize. Jason even lamented, "I fast. I pray. I do all these things, Christy," but he was unable "to conquer" what he was feeling. Instead, Jason became progressively worse. He isolated himself in another room in their home for hours and hours; he slept for long periods of time; and he neglected showering for several days at a time. He also became more violent, becoming verbally abusive and hurling things across the room; thus, she began to fear for her safety and that of her children. Consequently, Christy separated herself and her children from Jason by moving to another state, and approximately one and a half months later, Christy received word that Jason had taken his own life.

She acknowledged that although life without Jason was now different, it, too, has been an arduous path of suffering. While she no longer was fearful for her own safety, she was grieving the loss of her husband. Without him, she now began to wonder, "Oh, my goodness, how am I suppose to take care of everybody?" Jason had not worked for two years; therefore, they had used all their resources in order to live. He had in previous years bought cars, repaired them, and resold them; however, most recently he had bought cars but not fixed them. As a result, Christy and Jason had accumulated debt, which meant she was forced "to sell everything." Christy said, "We were just like starting over." This raised new concerns: "What are we gonna drive? Where are we gonna live? How am I gonna feed my kids?"

Jeremy

Upon meeting Jeremy, I was struck by his strong belief that God is significantly directing and participating in the affairs of humanity. For Jeremy, this means that God was involved in his life prior to his becoming a Christ-follower as seen in his giving credit to God for his success at his job. He recalled others telling him: "We don't know how you did that. We don't know how you ever accomplished all that stuff." He knows he worked hard, but he, too, is unsure how it happened, except through God's help.

After his becoming a Christ-follower, Jeremy admits God not only continued to help him professionally but also personally. He confessed that prior to his conversion he drank, smoked heavily, swore considerably, and had a horrible temper, and then, "I mean, well, my life has dramatically changed." In short, Jeremy was a successful businessman with responsibilities that resulted in a six-figured salary, and who had witnessed the Spirit moving in his life, transforming and helping him. For Jeremy, God was protecting and would "protect" him.

However, on a fall day a few years prior to the interview, Jeremy was involved in a car accident that changed his life. He does not recall the details of the accident or the month and a half immediately following it, but he has been told that his vehicle rolled three to four times, and the jaws of life were required to remove him from his truck. He had to be flown to a larger city in order to receive the proper medical care, during which time they had to resuscitate him twice. Some of the resulting damages included a broken jaw and a head injury, both of which continue to have their impact.

After being discharged from the hospital but while he was still rehabilitating, Jeremy continued to make plans for his life. His physician had put him in touch with an individual who was to assist him on his journey of recovery. After having several good phone conversations, Jeremy informed the other person of his future plans, but the person discounted this possibility. Jeremy asserted that he served a loving God for whom nothing was impossible and curtailed the conversations. He now admits that underlying his assertion was an expectation. For Jeremy, God was like a "vending machine." He expected that because he had invested in God, God would give him what he wanted.

This may have appeared to be the case when Jeremy was cleared by his physician to return to work within a few months of being discharged from the hospital. His expectations, unfortunately, remained unmet. On his first day of work, he was able to find his office, but then he could not recall how to sign on to his computer. That same day he was informed that other employees would join him for a conference call to another city, but he was unable to remember how to go about implementing the call. He also realized he was now inept at developing spreadsheets with Microsoft's Excel. As a result of his incompetence, he was let go from his job within a short period of time and placed on long-term disability.

Up to this point, Jeremy's work had determined his purpose and identity, but now his sense of identity and worth were stripped away. Not only was his wife maintaining their financial records since the accident, but now he also was no longer the main wage earner in the home. Jeremy perceived, "I couldn't be the man of the house. I couldn't be the worker, the man that goes out and earns an income." He viewed himself as no longer being "a man the way I define a man." His crisis was not only limited to his own identity, but it also influenced his expectations about God. Jeremy described the impact: "And so, now I'm out of work, and I'm feeling like, 'God, did you leave me? You've been with me through this whole process. Have you left me?'" Consequently, Jeremy entered a deep depression. It became so challenging that one day he decided it was time "to end this nonsense," and he loaded his pistol. Even though he chose not to take his life that day, Jeremy's life has not returned to how it used to be. He continues to have memory issues, and he has difficulty reading aloud when asked to do so in a public setting. He said to me that he still has tough days in which he prays, "I don't get it, God."

Bob

During my face-to-face meeting with Bob, I quickly learned that Bob was not a stranger to suffering. By the time he was three years old, Bob had a need for hearing aids due to complications during his birth. This in itself created its own snags since his family attended a Pentecostal church where people wanted to pray for his ears. "They always wanna see me healed because that's in the Assemblies of God Pentecostal theology is that we get healed." Since he was not healed, he saw himself as "a monkey wrench in people's theology" in that other Pentecostals did not "know what to do with me in terms of my disability." It was a combination of these types of experiences and Pentecostal preaching and teaching that generated his ambivalence about suffering. Since suffering was not normalized in his Pentecostal context, he did not reflect on his own suffering because he had learned "that it [suffering] was something to be avoided."[22] Instead, he resolved within himself to persevere and overcome adversity independent of others. He simply "learned how to push through it."

After completing college and working full-time for a season, he sensed God was directing him to graduate school, the place where he met his wife, Deanna. Little did Bob know that this decision coincidently placed a definitive marker post in his life's journey: from the time he quit his job to go to graduate school until the time of the interview, Bob "was not able to have a full-time job with benefits." While he was completing his Masters degree, he learned that his brother had brain cancer, prompting this young family to move to be closer to his brother after Bob's graduation. Following his brother's death, they found a place of employment that provided housing, but they had to supplement their income with other jobs in order to make ends meet. In spite of this, Bob told me that their experience was positive. They unfortunately discovered after two years that the company's housing contained mold, making his wife and children quite ill. While they attempted to work out the situation, they eventually were forced to leave this position, which broke their hearts. Bob said, "Since then, we haven't had a place to be," something Bob expected God would provide.

During the two years that followed, they had to move every three to six months until they finally were able to be in a house for one year. There were moments when Bob was "feeling almost totally emotional despair," which effected him physically. "I could physically feel the sorrow weighing down on me." He repeatedly applied for jobs that never came to fruition. He thought he would attempt to become certified as a teacher since he had a teaching degree, but that turned out to be "a dead end." Bob described their dire financial straits: "We have no financial support at all. I mean, we have money, but it's barely enough to live. So we have no savings. We have no anything. You know, no safety nets at all. There's nothing there." I

---

22. In speaking of American culture, Hooyman and Kramer comment, "In our culture, pain is seen as something that can and should be avoided, instead of being viewed as an inescapable part of being human." Hooyman and Kramer, *Living through Loss*, loc. 473.

heard a sense of vulnerability when he said, "I'm trying to do my best. So I feel frustrated when we're trying to do what we can and nothing's getting anywhere."

Bob and Deanna believed that God had finally opened a door for them when Deanna was hired full-time as a director of a daycare in another state. Unfortunately, problems arose, chaos unfolded, and they departed from that position after ten months. Bob said it was "a traumatic experience" for both of them, and they left feeling betrayed by someone they had deeply trusted. Prior to Deanna's departure from her job, Bob had been accepted into a one-year program that offered additional paid training. At the time of the interview, he only had a few more weeks until this position ended, and the future was holding uncertainty and generating concern. Would they be placed in the same situation they had experienced previously? Bob voiced his apprehensions: "I've been applying for jobs, but nothing's really opened up yet. So we're not sure what's going on. What's gonna happen. So it's been hard to not, you know, get tensed up about what's gonna lie ahead because we don't wanna be where we were before."

Kyle

Growing up in a non-Pentecostal minister's home, Kyle heard from his father that speaking in tongues was of the devil. However, that changed when his family moved into a community in which the only church was Pentecostal, altering Kyle's course in life. After graduating from high school, Kyle attended a Pentecostal college, met his wife Adel, and together they launched into full-time ministry, resulting in a variety of ministry positions through the years.

As a Pentecostal minister, Kyle was previously reluctant to reflect on suffering, but rather he concealed his hurt. "I was aware of my pain, very much aware of my pain, but I was a Pentecostal pastor. I couldn't let that out, so I controlled it." Even in Bible college, Kyle did not sense an invitation to reflect on the subject of suffering. Instead, he perceived the class on Job to be "very dry, very sterile, very academic," and they never examined "the foundational concept and problem for Job," which he saw as, "why do people suffer." Consequently, Kyle reasoned, "I couldn't wrestle with that because I was already in a huge state of suffering in my inner self."

Kyle's recent path of suffering began several years prior to the time of the interview when their daughter, who was married and a mother of two teenagers, became ill. Her general practitioner believed in the beginning it was an allergy; however, after a frustrating period of no improvement, she was referred to specialists, who argued with each other without being able to arrive at a diagnosis. At one point, Kyle asked a doctor what his daughter's prognosis was, and the doctor replied, "We have not any prognosis. We don't know what we're dealing with." After one and a half years without a definitive diagnosis, their daughter passed away at the age of thirty-five. An autopsy was performed, and six months later Kyle and Adel received the test results: their daughter had had a rare form of leukemia.

When their daughter died, both Kyle and Adel were devastated—the unexpected had occurred. As a Pentecostal minister, Kyle believes what the Scriptures state about God, such as God is his healer. He and his wife had fervently prayed for their daughter's healing, and other Christians anointed her with oil and prayed. "Yet to our eyes to our understanding this side of heaven, she wasn't healed." Kyle also was made aware of a disruption in the order of things. "The natural way is for us to bury our parents and grandparents, but it is not the normal to bury your child." Thus, his daughter's death was not expected on two fronts: in his understanding of God and in the typical cycle of life.

While Kyle and Adel chose to attend counseling to assist in healing from their traumatic loss, the losses continued to mount. Three months after losing their daughter, Adel ceased to attend counseling with the intent of moving on with her life. Although she returned to work, she lost her job due to her poor job performance. Kyle also suffered the loss of his job. He had taken several months off of work, and when he returned, he discovered they had hired someone else to replace him. The unthinkable, then, occurred in Kyle's life: he lost his wife. She left the marriage. Kyle explained the unexpectedness of this event: "I never thought it would happen to me. I mean, we were Pentecostals. We were former pastors. It's not gonna happen to us. It did."[23]

In the turbulence of such pain, Kyle admitted he contemplated taking his own life in the several days following Adel's departure. He cried out to God, "Why God? Why me? Why us?" But rather than hearing an answer to his cries, Kyle's isolation continued to increase. His two remaining children

---

23. Hooyman and Kramer remark, "When faced with a major loss, the world no longer makes sense; there is no comprehensible person-outcome contingency, no guarantee of safety and protection. With our fundamental assumptions shattered, disillusionment and disbelief are pervasive as we struggle with 'I never thought it could happen to me.'" Ibid., loc. 1270–72.

refused to talk to him for approximately one year because they had heard only their mother's reasons for leaving their father after forty-two years. In the depth of his pain, he was unable to discover a good reason to attend church. He could not "find the correspondence between what was happening" in his "life and what preachers were preaching about the goodness of God and all those kind of nice things." Kyle wondered, "Why was I in the middle of what I was in if God was so good? If God is love? If God heals?" To contribute to his suffering, Kyle is currently having physical issues with his back. Having had four surgeries, he learned a few days prior to the interview that the surgeon was reluctant to do a fifth surgery. Others had repeatedly prayed for him, but he still was not healed. Was God judging him for a lack of faith?

Kirsten

Similar to Bob, Kirsten's early life was one of suffering in that she was abused at the hand of another. Thus, she "always understood suffering to happen." She admitted to experiencing frustration about the subject of suffering, so she avoided the development of her own theodicy. Instead, she chose to identify herself as a "survivor." If she saw herself as the one who managed to survive the abuse, she no longer had to reflect on the reasons for both her suffering and for God's failure to save her. Kirsten explained, "And so there's a sense of independence from God because if I succeeded at it, then I don't have to ask why God did it that way."

Even though she was familiar with suffering, she maintained expectations of divine intervention. She recounted an experience during her time in college in which she did not have the finances to return the following semester. Having heard a sermon on God's provision, she went to the airport, expecting God to prompt someone to give her the money prior to her boarding the plane. She went home empty-handed that day, but her eyes had been opened. Yet, this did not put an end to Kirsten's unmet expectations.

To appreciate Kirsten's story, it is necessary to know that prior to her recent path of suffering, Kirsten was "an active person." She had traveled to Europe and Greece as well as all over the United States. Her activities had included diving, spelunking, and the ability to deadlift 160 pounds. In college she had obtained a level of responsibility in the dormitories as she served as a resident assistant and as a resident director assistant. Following graduation, she worked at various Christian institutions, walking to and from work. However, all that changed in the ensuing months.

Two factors engendered what Kirsten referred to as "a crisis of faith." First, Kirsten experienced one the happiest days of her life when she married her husband Dillan. Unfortunately, her whole being responded negatively when she became sexually intimate with Dillan; she unexpectedly re-lived the sexual trauma of the past both physically and emotionally. Within a year, she struggled to walk as she developed pelvic floor problems. Kirsten was in physical pain, and this was compounded when the medical field did not give her the proper treatment for eight years but told her "the pain was mental." In essence, she was informed she was crazy and treated as if she was. Her physical problems continued to multiply as she developed a two-year-long urinary tract infection, fibromyalgia, mini-strokes, heart arrhythmia, and eventually seizures. The emotional impact of such problems were exacerbated since she was Pentecostal. "And so it's like you just have this people not believing you. You know. Then you go to church and as a Pentecostal, you're suppose to have enough faith to be healed, and you have them not believe you."

Second, her job became a place of high stress as conflicts erupted, and she was sexually harassed. When the stress became too bad at her first place of employment, Kirsten said, "[I was] coming home from work everyday crying in the midst of all this mess, so I quit." She then chose to become a receptionist at another Christian institution. She admitted, "I had a tendency to be overzealous about things, so that could get me in trouble." Yet, she enjoyed this new job until she received a new boss. Once again, she was sexually harassed, resulting in her being moved to an alternative department; however, because of the previous sexual harassment, she was "treated badly." She was eventually transferred to yet another department where in due time she began feeling increased pressure. "They watched everything I did all the time because they were really looking for any excuse to have fired me because of the sexual harassment and the legal things I'd seen."

Within a short period of time, Kirsten went from being an active young woman to a young woman with multiple physical issues who needed a cane. It was not a surprise that in the midst of this she confessed, "I'm questioning God, 'Why is this happening to me?'" Kirsten was well aware of what she was "missing out on" due to her physical issues; thus, one can understand her wanting to be "prayed for as much as possible," but at the time of the interview, healing for Kirsten had not yet appeared.

Lindsey

I discovered that Lindsey was raised in Pentecostal minister's home in which she was granted space to wrestle with questions. As a young teen she asked her dad, "Do I believe what I believe just because I'm the pastor's daughter or how do I know this is all real?" Rather than criticizing her for her doubts or saying, "Don't feel that way" or "Of course it's true," he offered her an invitation: "Honey, why don't you go next door to the church and just spend some time telling God everything you told me." For Lindsey, this began "a transformation for me of my relationship with the Lord."

Not only did Lindsey's upbringing allow her to wrestle with issues, but also a previous desert experience was preparation for her to handle subsequent difficulties better. She had experienced an arduous journey of several years of infertility and poverty. Lindsey watched for six and half years as "everybody around me is getting pregnant, and it's like one month after month after month question, question, question." Although she eventually had two children, the wilderness experience had not ended. They underwent such extreme poverty that they were "dumpster diving for cans to turn them in for five cents a piece in order to buy bread." In both cases, she had struggled and had asked, "God, don't you see? Don't you care? Aren't you listening? Aren't you ever gonna answer?" She confessed to me, "It just seemed like it was endless," with the infertility and the poverty. After those difficulties had ended and they had finished walking that path of suffering, she believed, "We can survive anything."[24]

That theory was eventually tested when her sixty-five year old father passed away, and several weeks later her thirty-one year old brother was diagnosed with brain vasculitis. Five years prior to her dad's death, he had developed cancer; however, this path of suffering was not a steady decline. In the beginning her father had been diagnosed with multiple myeloma, but a year and half later the doctors stated, "We misdiagnosed you," to which her parents testified, "He's healed." After another year and half, Lindsey's father was told he had Waldenström's, a type of leukemia. Six months before he passed away, Lindsey's dad had a physical crisis "where he went septic and was in ICU," but "he somehow miraculously made it through that." Her dad

---

24. Hooyman and Kramer write, "Research indicates several ways in which to find meaning through our loss. We need to change our life's scheme or cognitive representation of our life to be consistent with the loss experience . . . [Some examples are:] adapting our self-image in a positive way that incorporates the loss [such as saying] . . . after this, I can handle anything." Ibid., loc. 1293–7.

believed, "If I was raised from such an experience, God has total healing for me." Several months later after conducting his mother-in-law's funeral, he was unable to fight off a cold and died. Lindsey described the journey this way: "So that was a bit of a roller coaster. You know. You have it. You don't have it. You have it. You almost die from it. You come through that, then you die." Her grief was compounded in that the days prior to her grandma's death, they had moved to be near her parents; thus, she grieved not only two deaths but also the transition—the loss of life at her previous location. She journaled at the time: "I'd like to get on with life here, but it's just so hard."

When her brother developed his illness, he had not been serving God but came back to God "at the early part of his sickness." Due to the nature of his illness, her brother was placed in a facility, and his body deteriorated over time. "In the course of six years from thirty-one to thirty-seven, he became like an old man and not able to care for himself at all." She watched as he went from being able to have a conversation to "staring into space or maybe giving you one word." Such a gradual decline meant Lindsey mourned for him by degrees. "We lost him long before we lost him." When he died, Lindsey accordingly sensed "relief and a release" as well as gratitude in that "thank God he's not suffering anymore."

Two family members. Two extended illnesses. One a minister. One restored prodigal. Yet healing did not come to either. Nevertheless, Lindsey's parents had prayed for others and had seen them healed, and Lindsey's mom had been healed of diverticulitis. Lindsey also confessed that she has prayed for people with serious illnesses, and they experienced miracles. Thus, Lindsey had a measure of expectation for healing. Speaking of God, Lindsey asserted, "So, I knew he could. I hoped he would, but I had no assurity that he would." Yet, the reader may wonder, "Why not her dad? Why not her brother?" How did Lindsey interpret this lack of a divine intervention?

Danielle

Having been raised in a Catholic home prior to becoming a Pentecostal, Danielle embraced both beliefs that God is good and that suffering happens in this life. When suffering did come a person's way, she was taught, "You just go on with your life. Pull the straps up on your boots, and that's it." When her husband Reagan was diagnosed with leukemia at age forty, the prognosis was grim as Danielle and her husband were told "to get a will together." Seeking medical treatment at a well-established, cutting-edge clinic, Reagan received two rounds of chemotherapy, and his siblings were tested to find the best possible match for a bone marrow transplant. For Danielle, "miracle[s]" occurred when one "brother was a perfect match, as perfect as you could be without being a twin" and when Reagan did not get the "big side effect" from the transplant, "graft versus host disease." Even when they had spent all their savings, monies were provided so that they were able to survive and "keep on living." Danielle testified, "You know, you think it's only God that could do all that, put it all together." For Danielle, God had provided both healing and finances. Her miracle had come.

Several years later when it was discovered the leukemic cells had returned, Danielle and Reagan immediately revisited the same clinic for treatment. Once again, Reagan received chemotherapy, which was followed by receiving his brother's "T-cells," the ones that fight cancer. When Reagan made a complete recovery, Danielle once again perceived, "God is in control." Even though the cancer returned again and again over the next several years, Danielle attested, "He never has medication that he's on when we come home. We just have to get [over] that bump. [We] never lose faith in the Lord."

The fourth time the leukemia came back, however, Danielle noted it had only been a year since the last episode. Hence, the doctors determined that Reagan needed another bone marrow transplant. Unfortunately, after they prepared Reagan for the transplant, he developed a fungus that stopped him from having the procedure. He now was to have a thoracotomy on each lung. Despite this disappointing news, Danielle confirmed she was still trusting and believing that Reagan would be healed. "He was all this other time. Why wouldn't he be this time?" Even with the absence of a bone marrow transplant, he was able to receive medicine for six hours a day that aided in his healing and facilitated his return to work. Yet, his blood counts eventually became not what they needed to be, bringing about the necessity for blood transfusions. The blood transfusions were helpful for a while, but after developing a fever, he died within several weeks.

Danielle relayed to me that she continued to believe for her husband's healing even just days before his death. Although Reagan had experienced "kidney failure," which placed him on dialysis: "I'm still believing he's gonna get well. I'm not doubting." One morning while a nurse was giving Reagan medication, Danielle inquired as to its purpose, and she heard the nurse say, "It's to keep his heart going." Danielle learned her husband would die within four hours without that medication. Because she did not want to "keep him alive on medicine," the decision was made to place Reagan, who was unresponsive, on hospice. Danielle described with tenderness the moment Reagan died. While she lay on the bed hugging her husband, she noticed a wall hanging of Jesus with his arms outstretched. "I said, 'Reagan, Jesus is waiting for you. He's got his arms extended. Go home and be with him.' So it was shortly after that that he did, you know, he did go home with Jesus. So it was beautiful. His death was painful, but yet in the sense it was beautiful."

Danielle related to me her immediate reaction as she admitted, "I believe right after that I became anesthetized." She described herself as "strong" as she "really didn't cry." Such a demeanor was maintained over the next couple of months as Danielle became very busy, traveling here and there. However, when she went back to work two months after Reagan's death, it all changed. As the other employees came up to her, she began to cry to the point that she became unable to work, so she excused herself to the break room. She said of her experience of sitting in the break room: "I'm just like kind of out of it, and I'm seeing lights in heaven." For Danielle, "reality or something" was being awakened in her. She said, "I think this is when I grieved. I started my grief."

WHERE IS JESUS?

The participants in the above stories experienced an occasion when God did not protect them from suffering. When extended suffering entered the participant's life, God did not eradicate it, being apparently absent at a time when the Christ-follower believed for God to intervene. When God does not remove the suffering even though the participants may have prayed, it complicates the nothingness since the lack of God's response indicates their powerlessness to cause God to respond as they had hoped. Unfortunately, the participants remained in the midst of their own impossibilities, their nothingness, experiencing unmet expectations. I now turn to the biblical narrative to aid in developing a theology of apparent absence in the midst of presence.

In keeping with Pentecostalism's focus on narrative, I draw from the Gospel of John's theme of unmet expectations and the absence of Jesus. Besides the apparent attractions to John that exist for a Pentecostal, such as a story that focuses on Jesus, the Gospel also emphasizes the Spirit; therefore, John not only points towards christology but pneumatology as well, both of which have prominence in Pentecostalism.[25] It additionally underscores relationality: individual relational encounters with Jesus; the trinitarian relationships; our relationship with Jesus Christ; and the relationships among Christ-followers. Its chief significance for this project, however, is its support of Christopraxis, such as we know God through God's action of sending Jesus, and more importantly, its accent on Jesus's presence and its sub-theme of his absence. After a brief discussion on the purpose of John, I begin an exploration of Jesus's absence and the people's unmet expectations found in this Gospel. This is accomplished by surveying three wide-ranging facets of Jesus's absence in John in order to portray its prominence in this Gospel and by concluding with a discussion on how this applies to Pentecostals today.

What Is the Purpose of the Fourth Gospel?

The Fourth Gospel's purpose is found near the conclusion when John writes in 20:31, "But these are recorded so that you may believe that Jesus is the Christ, the Son of God, and that by believing you may have life in his name." As some New Testament scholars note, some manuscripts of the Greek text use *pisteusēte* (the aorist subjective case), which is translated "you may believe," while other manuscripts have *pisteuēte* (the present subjunctive) which is translated "you may continue to believe." Thus, it may be argued, as some do, that the former is a call to believe, an evangelistic approach, and the latter is the call to persist, a pastoral approach.[26] However, as Craig Keener, Marianne Meye Thompson, and others assert, this is not simply a matter of preference concerning Greek manuscripts, and neither

---

25. Kärkkäinen writes, "Against the assumptions of uninformed outside observers, pneumatology does not necessarily represent the centre of Pentecostal spirituality. Jesus Christ, rather, is the centre, and the Holy Spirit in relation to Christ. At the heart of Pentecostal spirituality lies the idea of the 'Full Gospel,' the template of Jesus Christ in his fivefold role as Saviour, Sanctifier, Baptizer with the Spirit, Healer, and Soon-Coming King. Consequently, the key to discerning and defining Pentecostal identity lies in Christ-cantered charismatic spirituality with a passionate desire to 'meet' with Jesus Christ as he is being perceived as the Bearer of the 'Full Gospel.' This is a particular form of 'Spirit-Christology.'" Kärkkäinen, "The Pentecostal Understanding of Mission," 34.

26. Keener, *The Gospel of John*, 1215–16; Morris, *The Gospel of John*, 755–56; Harris, "John," paragraph 75055–57; Thompson, *John*, 429–30.

Who is Present in Absence?

is one to base the purpose of the Gospel on the verb tense alone.[27] Instead, support may be made for both positions. John underscores the invitation for individuals to have an encounter with Jesus through many of its characters who also have had personal encounters (e.g., Nathanael in John 1; the Samaritan woman and centurion in John 4; the blind man in John 9). At the same time, it encourages believers to endure when considering its emphasis on the persecution of Christ-followers (7:7; 15:18–20; 17:14) and the references made of being thrown out of the synagogue (9:22; 12:42; 16:2). Keener suggests that the way for those to hear the gospel who are not Christ-followers is for the believer to share its message; thus, Keener comments that "[f]rom the perspective of marketing strategies," the Fourth Gospel addresses believers. But he also perceives that it portrays that "many people become initial believers, but their initial faith proves insufficient without perseverance"; therefore, he concludes that the author desires "not simply initial faith but persevering faith."[28] While I believe there is evidence in John for both approaches, this project's focus is on Christ-followers' experiences with God in the midst of suffering, thereby centering on believers who continue to believe. As indicated in Jesus's words to Thomas in 20:29 as well as John's address to the readers in verses 30 and 31, John seeks to speak to those who believe but have not seen, and this encompasses today's believers, including those who have experienced unmet expectations and the apparent absence of God.[29]

Where Are Examples of Absence and Unmet Expectations in John?

Having briefly explored the purpose of John's Gospel, I now introduce the concept of the absence of Jesus, and this is followed by exploring three categories of Jesus's absence, noting when they periodically are accompanied

---

27. Keener, *The Gospel of John*, 1215–16; Thompson, *John*, 429–30; Harris, "John," paragraph 75055-57.

28. Keener, *The Gospel of John*, 1216.

29. Jesus says to Thomas in 20:29, "'Have you believed because you have seen me? Blessed are the people who have not seen and yet have believed,'" and John writes to the readers in 30–31, "Now Jesus performed many other miraculous signs in the presence of the disciples, which are not recorded in this book. But these are recorded so that you may believe that Jesus is the Christ, the Son of God, and that by believing you may have life in his name." Thompson comments on verses 30 and 31, "But the Gospel has been written for those who did not see Jesus' signs, who were not privy to his resurrection appearances"; see Thompson, *John*, 429.

by unmet expectations. The Fourth Gospel's theme of Jesus's absence is in stark contrast to its emphasis on Jesus's presence (to be discussed more fully in chapter 4 of this project). For instance, John presents Jesus as the one who surpasses rituals and the Temple. Thompson sees that John portrays Jesus as the one now present to purify his followers "through his word and his death" rather than John stressing "matters affecting of ritual purity," such as touching a leper, a corpse, or those deemed unclean.[30] Jesus also identifies himself as God's Temple when he cleanses the Temple (2:13–22). Concerning this pericope Thompson writes, "Jesus is then both the Messiah, the guardian of the temple where the glory of God and the name of God dwell (2:13–17), and himself the locus of that indwelling glory."[31] For my purposes in this chapter, however, I highlight John's focus on Jesus's coming to earth, having been sent by God the Father and who is now present with humanity but also appears paradoxically absent. That is, Jesus is apparently absent while present on earth.

The idea for studying the absence of Jesus in John comes from Robert Sloan, who maintains that Jesus's absence is adjacent to discussions of Jesus's identity and people's belief/unbelief.[32] Wendy North also underscores Jesus's absence, asserting it to be essential in addressing the Johannine community's feeble faith in the face of persecution and the delay in Jesus's return.[33] While being influenced by both of these scholars, I introduce a classification of Jesus's absence in the Fourth Gospel in which I divide the instances into three broad categories that also overlap with each other. Due to limited space, I offer only one story in each category to illustrate my argument.

First, Jesus is not where he is expected. This particularly emerges in the people's expectation that Jesus will be in Jerusalem at the celebration of the Feast of the Tabernacles (7:1–13). The chapter begins with Jesus's brothers asserting that Jesus should openly attend the Feast, which, Thompson observes, is an apparent expectation that Jesus will join his brothers in going to Jerusalem.[34] After all, if a man wanted to make a name for himself, the Feast of the Tabernacles was an opportunity to acquire quite a following!

30. Ibid., 7.
31. Ibid., 73.
32. Sloan, "The Absence of Jesus," 207–28.
33. North, "'Lord, If You Had Been,'" 39–52.
34. Thompson, *John*, 166.

Who is Present in Absence?

This is placed alongside the religious leaders wondering, "Where is he?" (7:11).[35]

In the second category Jesus's absence appears in his revealing that now that he has come, which raises hopes of some of the people, he is going away. This is powerfully portrayed in Jesus's speaking of his soon departure adjacent to the expectations or beliefs about the Messiah in 7:14—8:59. Jesus discusses his leaving more than once in this section (7:33–34; 8:14, 21), which provokes questions and assumptions as to where he is going (7:35–36; 8:22). Additionally dispersed throughout these two chapters are statements and questions about Jesus's identity: he has a demon (7:20); he is the Christ (7:26–27, 31, 41); he is a Prophet (7:40); he is a Samaritan and possessed by a demon (8:48, 52); and he is asked, "Who are you?" (8:25) and "Who do you claim to be?" (8:53). Moreover, the people substantially indicate in this pericope their own beliefs or expectations about the Messiah. Since they know from where Jesus comes, they assert, "Whenever the Christ comes, no one will know where he comes from" (7:27). At the same time, they acknowledge that Jesus is from Galilee, but the Messiah is from Bethlehem (7:41–42; 52), contradicting themselves. They also believe the Messiah will perform as many miracles as Jesus (7:31).[36]

The people's expectations and hopes in relation to Jesus being the Messiah in John is not a surprise because, as Thompson remarks, such expectations and the questions pertaining to Jesus being the Messiah occur more often in John than in the other Gospels.[37] One of the most distinctive examples of the people's unmet hopes for Jesus being the Messiah (but that is not connected to absence) is 12:12–16, the Triumphal Entry into Jerusalem. Keener remarks that the combination of shouting "Hosanna!" with the waving of the palm branches "suggests that the crowds hoped for him as a king or national deliverer." Such a "royal expectation" also occurs in 6:15, notes Keener, but in that incident Jesus withdraws, which is unlike chapter

---

35. Other incidents include: Jesus is not where he is to be expected in 11:54–57 when the people are looking for him at the Passover and in 20:1–18 when Mary, Peter, and the beloved disciple do not find Jesus's body at the tomb. Additional incidents of Jesus not being where he is expected are also observed in conjunction to his miracles, which is the third category (6:22–26; 11:1–45).

36. Jesus also speaks of his soon departure with his disciples in 13:31—14:31; 16:5–28 and with his Father in 17:1–19.

37. Thompson, "John, Gospel Of," 378. For example, see 1:41; 4:25–29; 7:25–31; 12:34–50.

12 in that he "does not retreat."[38] As Thompson writes, no one expects that this king, rather than "vanquishing the Romans to accomplish his royal vocation, . . . will die on a Roman cross."[39]

The third category of Jesus's absence in John's Gospel is connected to Jesus's miracles. There are seven miracles recorded in the Fourth Gospel (eight if one includes Jesus's resurrection), and the sub-theme of absence emerges in all but one (2:1–11).[40] In essence, Jesus is apparently absent at a time when Jesus appears powerfully present, during his miracles. In this section I focus on the account of the death of Lazarus (11:1–45) because it is connected so vitally to unmet expectations. While the story speaks of the mighty miracle of raising Lazarus from the dead, I underscore four elements that are relevant for this chapter's emphasis: absence, expectation, love, and grief.

John 11 begins with the notice to the reader that those whom Jesus loves are not immune to suffering (11:1–3). Lazarus is sick, and Jesus loves him. Yet, rather than immediately journeying to Bethany, Jesus chooses to linger "in the place where he was for two more days" (11:6). In other words, Jesus remains absent rather than directly intervening on the behalf of a loved one. This is an unmet expectation as seen in the statements of both Martha and Mary (11:21, 32), compounding their grief. In essence, Jesus had the power to heal their brother if only he would have just shown up! While such a comment speaks of the desire and the need for Jesus's presence, it is in contrast to John's story of Jesus's healing of the official's son without being present (4:46–54), demonstrating Jesus is capable of healing Lazarus from afar. Thus, in light of the healing of the official's son, Jesus

---

38. Keener, *The Gospel of John*, 869.

39. Thompson, *John*, 265.

40. The other incidents of absence adjacent to miracles are: healing of the official's son (4:46–54); healing of the lame man (5:1–15); feeding of the 5,000 and Jesus's walking on water (6:1–58); and healing of the man born blind (9:1–39). Concerning the healing of the official's son (4:46–54), Sloan notes the father insists that Jesus is to be present to heal his son (4:47, 49) but Jesus's asserts his absence (4:50), which is opposite of the healing of the centurion's son in Matthew and Luke; Sloan sees this connected to the subject of unbelief/belief; see Sloan, "The Absence of Jesus," 208–9. In the story of Jesus's walking on water, Jesus is absent from the disciples when the storm arose, which is followed by the crowd looking for Jesus. In the healing of the man born blind, absence is adjacent to a false expectation that a man from God does not heal on the Sabbath (9:16). This belief/expectation hinders the religious leaders from believing that the man is who he says he is, a man born blind (9:18). In 12:36 Jesus hides from the people after the Father speaks from heaven (v. 28) and immediately prior to John mentioning Jesus's miracles and the people's unbelief (v. 37).

is completely absent from Mary and Martha in two dimensions: (1) he is physically absent, and (2) he does not heal from a distance.

To preclude any presumption that Jesus's actions may express a lack of care on his part, the author speaks three times of Jesus's love for the sisters and Lazarus (11:3, 5, 36). This love corresponds with four allusions to Jesus's absence (11:6, 21, 32, 37). Keener notes that this "love for the family" points to John's stress on God's love for humanity, serving as encouragement to the original hearers of this Gospel as well as contemporary Christ-followers who certainly undergo "untimely deaths and suffering that on the level of human understanding" appear "to conflict with the assurance of God's love."[41] As Thompson also asserts, such a delay in his being present, or I would add his choosing not to heal from a distance, signifies that the divine-human one may not be forced to respond.[42] This, as I have argued above, amplifies the suffering family's nothingness, their impossible situation.

This narrative additionally calls attention to grief/bereavement in the aftermath of a lack of a divine intervention even though there is hope in the resurrection. Martha obviously believes in the resurrection (11:24), but still she grieves. Jesus, too, grieves (11:33, 35, 38) full well knowing that he is about to raise Lazarus from the dead. Thompson maintains that Jesus sheds tears when those whom he loves mourn and when they die. His weeping then becomes "the penultimate expression of Jesus' love for Lazarus" (11:36); thus, Thompson concludes, "That Jesus will soon raise Lazarus to life, and so manifest God's glory, does not mute the genuine sorrow that he experiences and expresses."[43] Keener also sees Jesus's tears as an expression of his care: "It reveals his character, which leads to his suffering on others' behalf . . . By weeping, Jesus shows his solidarity with the

---

41. Keener, *The Gospel of John*, 839.

42. Thompson writes, "Jesus' delay and his reference to God's glory (v. 4) again emphasize that his actions are not coerced: Jesus acts in his own time and in order to bring glory to God." Thompson, *John*, 241.

43. Ibid., 248. This is contrary to Morris and George Beasley-Murray (see notations below). Scholars discuss the meaning of Jesus's weeping and the use of the words *enebrimēsato* (11:38), which may be translated "greatly disturbed," and *etaraxen* (11:33), which may be translated "troubled." Some believe these words carrying an understanding of anger, indicating Jesus is angry at sin, Satan, and death; see Harris, "John," paragraph 73786–89. Some believe Jesus is indignant over the unbelief concerning who he is and his ability; see Beasley-Murray, *John*, 192–94; Keener, *The Gospel of John*, 846; Morris, *The Gospel of John*, 493–95.

mourners (11:35)."⁴⁴ In essence, for those who experience the absence of a divine intervention, this passage portrays the divine-human one embracing their loss and grief, the apparent absence of divine deliverance.⁴⁵

What Does This Mean?

I have argued in the preceding paragraphs that the Fourth Gospel at times emphasizes Jesus's absence alongside Jesus's presence. Furthermore, I have attempted to show how people's unmet expectations also periodically arise in this Gospel. This may be seen specifically in the story of Lazarus's death but also more generally in the people's expectations of the Christ.

Similar to the stories of the research participants who held beliefs and expectations, the people in John's Gospel hold beliefs and expectations about Jesus and the way in which he is to act. John expresses the people's desire to make Jesus king on more than one occasion (6:15; 12:12–16) with a desire for Jesus to deliver them from the oppression of the Romans. It is only when Jesus's time has come (2:4; 7:30; 8:20; 12:23, 27; 13:1; 17:1) that he permits them to honor him as king, but this king does not act as expected for he goes to a cross. When John relates the story of Jesus's healing the official's son (4:46–54), Jesus resists two requests of the official to travel to the official's home to heal the son, choosing to heal while being absent from the boy. When Martha and Mary entreat Jesus to come to heal their brother, he refuses to journey immediately to Bethany but deliberately waits (11:1–6). In essence, Jesus remains sovereign in each instance. He may not be forced to do the people's bidding. This is an additional theme in this Gospel in that Jesus is in control of his destiny as seen when Jesus is speaking about his life, "No one takes it away from me, but I lay it down of my own free will" (10:18).⁴⁶ Such a theme sheds light on sufferers' powerlessness and vulner-

---

44. Keener, *The Gospel of John*, 846.

45. Thompson comments, "Jesus does not promise that he will prevent death, but that he has the power to raise the dead to life." Thompson, *John*, 245.

46. Joel Green writes, "When turning from the Synoptic versions to the Johannine account of Jesus' suffering and death, one is immediately struck with the majesty of Jesus in John. He has long known his betrayer (6:70) and actually sets in motion the act of betrayal (13:27). In the arrest scene it is neither Judas nor the arresting party that is in charge, but Jesus himself, revealing himself as the 'I Am' (*egō eimi*) and negotiating the release of his disciples (18:1–11) . . . Requiring no assistance, he bears his own cross (19:17). He cares for his mother from the cross (19:25–27) and, before the soldiers can perform the *coup de grâce*, breaking his legs to speed his death, he dies of his own accord

ability: the impossibility, or human limitation, of making Jesus the King intervene and deliver them from their extended suffering.

Yet, such a lack of a divine intervention is not equated to a lack of love on God's part, as underscored in John 11. Jesus embodies God, who is love (1 John 4:8), which means Jesus embodies love. Therefore, since Jesus is the embodiment of divine love, when he appears absent and does not act as desired, the love of God remains. In other words, Jesus's being is love in action (3:16) even in his apparent absence. Neither does a lack of a divine intervention mean humans are not to grieve; to the contrary, Jesus who is divine and human weeps in experiencing the lack of a divine intervention. Thus, not only does Jesus identify fully with humanity's experience of loss and grief through his humanity, but through his divinity he also is alongside the human who grieves even as the one who is the resurrection and the life (11:25).[47]

I have lifted up the absence of Jesus in John because it portrays the human encounter of experiencing Jesus as apparently absent in the unmet hopes or expectations of people. As Pentecostals, we are not to miss the strong parallelisms from John concerning the people's experiences with Jesus and their unmet expectations of Jesus. John underscores the people's unmet hopes and expectations of where Jesus will be and what he will do as the Messiah and/or Healer in addition to the encounters people have with Jesus's presence. In short, people experience Jesus's absence as well as Jesus's presence in John. Such are the human experiences with Jesus both then and now.

CONCLUSION

In this chapter I have ventured into the nothingness of the apparent absence of God in the midst of presence. I have peered into the participants' impossibilities, their lack of a divine intervention, and their unmet expectations. I have painted the human limitations to cause God to respond as people desire, amplifying their nothingness. I have portrayed eight Pentecostals'

(19:20–33). In this manner John demonstrates the truth of Jesus' words, 'No one takes my life from me, but I lay it down of my own volition' (10:18)" (italics in original). Green, "Death of Jesus," 162.

47. Keener writes, "Assurance that Jesus did care, that God did have long-range purposes in the suffering, even that Jesus joined in weeping with the bereaved as well as ultimately held power over life and death, would mean much to believers facing that universal human predicament of death." Keener, *The Gospel of John*, 839.

experiences of the apparent absence of God through the lens of Scripture, specifically the Gospel of John. I have referenced ways that John accents the absence of Jesus even while the divine-human one is present on this earth. I have pointed out the periodic attempts to force Jesus to act in accordance with the people's hopes or beliefs, demonstrating Jesus's sovereignty. It has been argued that the Gospel of John puts forward Jesus's absence in addition to the encounters people have with Jesus's presence. Thus, the encounter of Jesus's absence and presence is a human experience among Christ-followers in both stories from Scripture and from today. In chapter 4 I highlight the presence of God, particularly presence in suffering, but in the next chapter I argue that the hope and expectation for a divine intervention, the presence of God, is the ethos, or the DNA, of Pentecostalism, making the absence of a divine intervention a glaring disparity.

3

Where Are You From?
Pentecostal Historical Roots

[The minister is] *up there and just getting everybody excited and* [said], *"If you've never been baptized and you don't know the power of the Holy Spirit, come on down."* . . . *And so I just ran . . . I just run to the altar because I was like, "I need that. I need that." And I just felt the presence of the Holy Spirit so powerful and so strong and before I even got all the way to the altar, no one touched me or anything, I started speaking in tongues. And I just went down on my knees and I was just whoosh. I will just never forget that day because it was a day like no other when I sensed such power and such peace.*

—Christy, a participant

It was with a divine encounter in 1906 that Pentecostalism began in North America.[1] I stressed in the last chapter the unmet hopes and expectations of a divine encounter to eradicate suffering. As will be emphasized in this chapter, an expected encounter with God is a central theme

---

1. I am drawing from Nancy Hardesty who states, "Pentecostalism began with a healing." Hardesty, *Faith Cure*, 101.

in Pentecostalism.² Such a belief in encounter does not emerge from a vacuum; it unfolds from the tradition's origins that were inaugurated with an experience with God, as stated above. This dynamic is observed in the research participants' hopes and expectations of a divine encounter that are in line with their Pentecostal tradition and heritage. As will be discussed, Pentecostal heritage has shaped the hopes and expectations of contemporary Pentecostals. While it is true that Pentecostals' personal divine encounters fashion their continuing expectations, it is also the case that their tradition shapes their expectations thereby molding their experiences. As Peter Neumann argues, experiences (such as those of the research participants that are discussed in this chapter) have a "mediated quality," which means they are shaped by and understood within one's Pentecostal tradition.³ The purpose in this chapter, then, is to demonstrate how Pentecostalism historically emphasizes divine encounter, which in turn influences one's own expectation of an encounter with the very presence of God.

While there are many well-researched projects that have detailed Pentecostalism's history around the world, this chapter is not another of

---

2. Warrington views an encounter with God as central to Pentecostalism; see Warrington, *Pentecostal Theology*, 20–27. Smith perceives that Pentecostals have "a position of radical openness to God, and in particular, openness to God doing something *differently* or *new*," which for him is "at the heart of being pentecostal, and so at the root of a pentecostal worldview" (italics in original); see Smith, *Thinking in Tongues*, 33–34. Examples of other Pentecostal theologians who stress the importance of divine encounter for Pentecostals include: Kärkkäinen, "Pneumatologies," 223–44; Cartledge, *Encountering the Spirit*.

3. Neumann, *Pentecostal Experience*, 6. Neumann writes in his Preface that because of his educational pursuits, he began to appreciate how "theological understanding and doctrine" as well as experiences with the divine were "shaped and mediated by the traditions and (sub) cultures in which we find ourselves." As he reflected on Pentecostalism, he began to see, "[T]he very Pentecostal theological and spiritual tradition in which I had been raised actually served to shape the ways that those within that tradition were experiencing the Spirit. I had grown up assuming that experience of the Spirit was more or less direct or immediate, but now it was becoming clear that other theological and cultural factors were influencing my experience of God. Further, it appeared that these factors were operating more or less unacknowledged, but nevertheless authoritatively, within my own Pentecostal tradition and the shaping of its theology and doctrine. I began to wonder whether a more nuanced view of experience of God—one that more explicitly acknowledged the mediated nature of experience—might produce some theological fruitful results for Pentecostalism itself, in particular its ability to grow in its self-understanding and interaction with the broader ecumenical Christian community." Ibid., loc. 52–79.

those accounts.[4] This chapter seeks to support the claim that the search for a divine encounter is part of the roots of Pentecostalism, its very ethos. I begin by providing a brief summary of the Pentecostal roots in North America, focusing on the Azusa Street Revival, specifically the factors that led to the revival and its beginnings, and then offer six aspects of divine encounter that surface in the history of Pentecostalism and in the stories of the research participants.[5]

SUMMARY OF PENTECOSTAL ROOTS

Although North American Pentecostalism may be said to have erupted during the Azusa Street Revival, it did not emerge out of a vacuum as some Pentecostals may like to believe.[6] As Donald Dayton has demonstrated through his now classic text, there was the presence of several streams of theology that paved the way for Pentecostalism. One stream was Wesleyan-Methodism whose influence is particularly seen in the belief of the experience of the second blessing of entire sanctification, subsequent to the experience of salvation.[7] Dayton writes of John Wesley's belief: "[W]ithin the *process* of sanctification there was a 'moment' of entire sanctification" (italics in original).[8] However, as David Courey notes, it was Wesley's understudy, John Fletcher, who stressed "an instantaneous experience of perfect love based on a post-conversion reception of the Spirit."[9] Not only is there a definitive experience with God in Methodism that is subsequent to salvation but as Courey comments, Methodism also was promoted through

---

4. For example, see Anderson, *To the Ends of the Earth*; Synan, *The Holiness-Pentecostal Tradition*; Hollenweger, *Pentecostalism*; Hollenweger, *The Pentecostals*.

5. While recognizing there were pockets around the United States where people experienced Spirit baptism with the evidence of speaking in tongues, I chose the Azusa Street Revival because of its significant and far-reaching impact on a variety of contemporary Pentecostal groups. It is to be noted that the work of Cecil Robeck Jr. is the main source for this chapter's focus on the Azusa Street Revival.

6. David Courey states that through some publications such as *The Apostolic Faith Restored* (1916) and *Suddenly . . . from Heaven* (1961), "the notion was perpetuated that the Pentecostal revival was simply an act of God, entirely discontinuous from historical or social factors, to restore primitive Christianity." Courey, *What Has Wittenberg*, 26–27. It is to be noted that Courey's work also addresses Pentecostal triumphalism by constructing a Pentecostal theology that includes Martin Luther's theology of the cross.

7. For a fuller explanation, see Dayton, *Theological Roots*, 45–51.

8. Ibid., 48.

9. Courey, *What Has Wittenberg*, 40.

a revivalism that included "[e]motionalism, physical manifestations, and supremely, altar calls."[10] This leads to another person of influence, the revivalist Charles Finney.

Charles G. Finney is described by Kimberly Ervin Alexander as the man "most responsible for the shape of evangelical America in the years preceding the Civil War."[11] Finney practiced extemporaneous preaching, which was charged with emotion, and also utilized what was known as the "anxious bench."[12] According to Mark Noll, the "anxious bench" was the place near the pulpit where individuals came to receive prayer "or to be admonished about the condition of their souls." Noll mentions Finney held that God directed persons in Scripture to repent, and thereby God also provided a way for persons to do so immediately. This understanding, however, was different from previous revivals that tended "to leave the timing of the conversions to God" rather than to the individual's own agency.[13] Noll writes of this ritual: "The anxious bench led to the modern evangelistic practice of coming to the front at the end of a religious service to indicate a desire for salvation."[14] Therefore, as I will attempt to show, Finney's emphasis on revival, emotional preaching, and the altar have a bearing on the Azusa Street Revival and Pentecostalism's expectation for divine encounter.

A third influence on the birth of Pentecostalism is the rise of the Holiness revival, particularly through the influence of the prominent figure, Phoebe Palmer.[15] Alexander remarks that after Palmer received the

10. Ibid., 50–51. Courey is drawing from Murray's *Revival and Revivalism*.

11. Alexander, *Pentecostal Healing*, 11.

12. Ibid.

13. Noll, *A History of Christianity*, 176. Steve Latham articulates "six levels in the understanding of revival": (1) a Christ-follower being spiritually invigorated; (2) special planned meetings particularly among Pentecostals to strengthen the spiritual walk of Christ-followers and draw non-followers to Christ; (3) a spontaneous time of a spiritual wakening in a congregation, which invigorates Christ-followers and brings non-followers to Christ; (4) a spiritual revitalization in an area with extensive new converts—for example, "the Welsh, Hebridean, East African and Indonesian revivals, and possibly Pensacola in the 1990s"; (5) "societal or cultural 'awakenings,' e.g., the transatlantic First and Second Awakenings"; and (6) "the possible reversal of secularism and 'revival' of Christianity as such"; see Latham, "'God Came from Teman,'" 171–72.

14. Noll, *A History of Christianity*, 176.

15. Dayton writes, "Phoebe Palmer and her sister Sarah Lankford came into the experience of sanctification. Phoebe, for whom this experience provided the assurance that others found in conversion, was to become the major figure of the Holiness Revival—first as primary leader of the 'Tuesday Meeting for the Promotion of Holiness' that met in the Palmer home for almost sixty years . . . and . . . as an itinerant evangelist who

experience of entire sanctification, she began regular Tuesday meetings in her home. Palmer eventually developed what was called "altar theology," which comprised three steps to obtain total sanctification: (1) consecrating oneself completely; (2) having faith; and (3) giving a testimony. The name "altar theology," Alexander notes, is due to its "emphasis on instantaneous experiences which take place at the altar."[16] Courey additionally observes "revivalistic meetings were also a part of her ministry," believing "God blessed her meetings simply because she employed God's methods."[17] He stresses that the Holiness movement in time adopted "more demonstrative manifestations" that evolved into "an institutionalized form of the camp meetings" with "spiritual vitality, experiential focus and agitated expectation," which "looked and sounded like Azusa Pentecostalism."[18] Thus, not only was there the presence of revivalism but also an emphasis on immediacy, faith, and testimony.

The final influence that I mention is the nineteenth-century healing movement, of which Alexander writes, was fathered in America by Charles Cullis.[19] Alexander defines the Divine Healing Movement as that movement in Christianity that "maintains a belief that physical disease or illness can be cured or healed by God's supernatural intervention, when the prayer of faith is prayed; this healing is available as part of salvation."[20] After Cullis had the experience of entire sanctification, according to Alexander, he began to reflect on James 5:14 and 15, which spoke of praying for the sick. Cullis, a physician, started praying for his patients at the same time he offered them medicinal care, and individuals began to be cured. Alexander cites one of the more dramatic examples of healing, a woman named Lucy Drake who had been in bed for months due to a brain tumor. After Cullis prayed for her, she got out of bed and was completely cured in three months. It was Cullis who persuaded further members of the Holiness movement that not only was salvation provided in the atonement but so also was healing.[21] In essence, the healing movement stressed an expecta-

---

traveled widely both on the North American continent and in the Old World." Dayton, *Theological Roots*, 65–66.

16. Alexander, *Pentecostal Healing*, 12.
17. Courey, *What Has Wittenberg*, 51.
18. Ibid.
19. Alexander, *Pentecostal Healing*, 16.
20. Ibid., 9.
21. Ibid., 16–17. In Ronald Kydd's six models of healing, he calls this "the soteriological

tion for a divine intervention, specifically a cure. In summary, then, each of the abovementioned streams, Wesley's Methodism, Finney's revivalism, Palmer and the Holiness movement, and Cullis and the healing movement, contributed to the emergence of the Azusa Revival, the roots of Pentecostalism in North America to which I now turn.

The Azusa Street Revival: The North American Birth of Pentecostalism

As Cecil Robeck Jr. records, at the beginning of January of 1906, William Seymour, an African-American Holiness preacher, sat outside Charles Parham's classes at Parham's Bible school in Houston and listened to the Caucasian Holiness preacher as he instructed his students that speaking in tongues was the initial, physical evidence of the baptism of the Holy Spirit.[22] There are two items of note in this record. First, such teaching by Parham was not typical for Holiness preachers of that era. Robeck explains that terms such as "Pentecostal" and "Spirit-filled" were used in the Holiness tradition to describe a second work of grace following salvation in which a believer was sanctified. It was not until later that these terms were used to describe those who believed in a Spirit baptism accompanied by speaking in tongues.[23] That is, *Pentecostals* at that time were those who expected an additional encounter with the Spirit after salvation—one of sanctification. Second, Robeck writes that Seymour was not permitted to sit in the classroom with the other Caucasian students due to the Jim Crow laws in Texas that forced segregation between Blacks and Whites in schools.[24] Yet, unknown at the time, this son of former slaves would in several weeks be the pastor the Spirit would use to lead the highly influential Azusa Street Revival. It was at that revival that a specific encounter with God, the baptism of the Spirit with the evidence of speaking in tongues, was stressed and became the distinguishing mark of Classical Pentecostalism.

When Seymour was listening to Parham's instruction, it was not Parham's first time teaching on Spirit baptism at a ministry training school. Approximately five years earlier, as noted by Anderson, Parham had left

model"; see Kydd, *Healing through the Centuries*, chapter 14.

22. Robeck, *The Azusa Street Mission*, 4. For more information on Parham, see Goff, *Fields White unto Harvest*.

23. Robeck, *The Azusa Street Mission*, 31–33.

24. Ibid., 47.

instructions with his students at his Bible school in Kansas to study the Acts of the Apostles in order to determine the evidence for Spirit baptism. After instructing them to fast, pray, and study, he departed for several days. Upon his return, the students informed their teacher that they concluded that speaking in tongues was the evidence of the baptism of the Holy Spirit. Desiring all that God had for them, they set aside December 31, 1900, as a time of seeking this divine encounter with the verifiable evidence of speaking in tongues. They were still praying on January 1 at 11:00 P.M. when student Agnes Ozman requested that Parham pray for her to receive this baptism, and thereby she became the first among several students to speak in tongues. By 1905, it was reported that several thousand had received the baptism of the Spirit with the evidence of speaking in tongues through Parham's ministry.[25] Anderson comments that it was Parham who "formulated the 'evidential tongues' doctrine that became the hallmark" of Classical Pentecostalism in the United States and Canada.[26]

Robeck writes that Seymour, who had yet to be baptized in the Spirit with the evidence of speaking in tongues, had been attending Parham's school in Houston for only a month when he received an invitation to pastor a Holiness church in Los Angeles. The pastor, Julia Hutchins, felt called to be a missionary to Liberia and was seeking an individual to oversee her congregation.[27] However, as Robeck points out, Hutchins adhered to the Holiness Association's belief that when one received Pentecost, one was sanctified but did not speak in other tongues; thus, she held that Spirit baptism generated "purity." Those within the Holiness churches had declared that the doctrine that promoted three "works of grace," which were salvation, sanctification, and Spirit baptism, was "heresy."[28] Yet, asserts Robeck, "Seymour did not teach that the baptism in the Spirit was a work of grace. He taught that it was merely an empowering *encounter* with the Holy Spirit that was evidenced by speaking in tongues" (italics mine).[29] Thus, after hearing Seymour proclaim to her congregation that tongues was the initial evidence of Spirit baptism, an experience he had yet to encounter, Hutchins locked the church doors.[30]

25. Anderson, *An Introduction to Pentecostalism*, 34.
26. Ibid.
27. Robeck, *The Azusa Street Mission*, 50.
28. Ibid., 62–63.
29. Ibid., 63.
30. Ibid., 62–63.

Robeck writes that after being shut out of the church, Seymour, who was staying at the home of Mr. and Mrs. Edward Lee, was invited to teach and conduct prayer meetings in their home. Within a short while, the prayer meetings outgrew the Lee's residence and had to be moved to a house on Bonnie Brae Street. As the people in the prayer meetings began to embrace Seymour's teaching on Spirit baptism, they sought God more fervently for such an encounter. In April, the attendees decided to not only pray but to also initiate a ten-day fast as they earnestly sought the baptism of the Spirit with the evidence of speaking in tongues. On day three of the fast, Mr. Lee was not feeling well and requested prayer so that he would be able to attend the prayer meeting that evening. Seymour and another individual not only prayed for Mr. Lee's healing, but they also prayed for Mr. Lee to receive the Spirit baptism, resulting in Mr. Lee falling on the floor and speaking in tongues. When they attended the prayer meeting that evening and Seymour shared about Mr. Lee's experience, someone else began to speak in tongues. As the group continued to pray, others experienced an encounter with the Spirit as evidenced by speaking in tongues. And three days later on April 12, 1906, Seymour also received the baptism of the Spirit with the evidence of speaking in tongues.[31]

As news spread of the revival, Robeck reports it became evident that the house on Bonnie Brae Street was too small to accommodate the ongoing rise of people attending. This was particularly indicated when the house's porch collapsed under the weight of the attendees. In response to this unfortunate incident, the group rented a former church at 312 Azusa Street and planned to open its doors on April 15, Easter Sunday, which was only two months after Seymour had arrived in Los Angeles. By June 10, the newspaper reported that several hundred people, a mixture of Blacks and Whites, were attending the revival services.[32] According to Robeck, the Azusa Street Revival continued until early 1909.[33] Many people testified to experiencing salvation, sanctification, Spirit baptism, and/or healing. Some were called into full-time ministry or experienced miracles. The Azusa Street Revival became the birthplace of several Pentecostal denominations, whose adherents have traveled the world stressing the Good News of salvation through Jesus Christ. While it ended over a hundred years ago,

---

31. Ibid., 64–69.
32. Ibid., 69–81.
33. Ibid., 313.

the divine encounters experienced at 312 Azusa Street continue to have a paradigmatic effect on Pentecostals today.[34]

SIX ASPECTS OF PENTECOSTALISM'S DIVINE ENCOUNTER: THEN AND NOW

Having briefly outlined four streams that influenced Pentecostal origins and having summarized the beginnings of the Azusa Street Revival, I turn to six aspects of the Pentecostal belief in divine encounter that appear in Pentecostalism's historical roots as well as in contemporary Pentecostalism. I became cognizant of these aspects while researching Pentecostal history, particularly in reading Robeck's work. I then saw how these same aspects were directly or indirectly a part of the stories of the research participants, demonstrating Neumann's assertion that the Pentecostal tradition "mediates" Pentecostal contemporary hopes and expectations of divine encounter. In this section I provide each aspect with examples of its prominence within the Azusa Street Revival, offer a brief explanation of each aspect's significance, and present the experiences of the participants for current substantiation. These six aspects of divine encounter in Pentecostal history and contemporary Pentecostalism are:

(1) restorational revivalism supplies a doctrine of divine encounter;

(2) worship provides a space for divine encounter;

(3) altar offers a place for divine encounter;

(4) prayer makes a request for divine encounter;

(5) transformation gives the verifiable evidence of divine encounter; and

(6) testimony presents the report of divine encounter.

---

34. I recognize there are diverse views concerning the origins of Pentecostalism so that questions arise as to whether or not Azusa is the origins of North American Pentecostalism; for example, see Espinosa, *William J. Seymour and the Origins of Global Pentecostalism*. Michael Wilkinson has coined the term "Azusa-*ization*" and argues that even if the Azusa Street Revival is not the origins of Pentecostalism, the influence of Azusa continues to be seen in that the Azusa Street Revival is a paradigm that Pentecostals embrace; see Wilkinson, "Pentecostalism in Canada," 3–12; Wilkinson, *The Spirit Said Go*.

Restorational Revivalism: A Doctrine of Divine Encounter

I begin by noting that a restorational understanding is underscored in the Azusa Street Revival's publication, *The Apostolic Faith*. The second edition's headline declares, "The Pentecostal Baptism Restored: The Promised Latter Rain Now Being Poured Out on God's Humble People."[35] The paper's third issue proclaims:

> The Pacific Apostolic Faith Movement stands for the restoration of the faith once delivered unto the saints—the old time religion, camp meeting, revivals, missions, street and prison work and Christian unity everywhere. We are not fighting men or churches, but seeking to displace dead forms and creeds or wild fanaticisms with living, practical Christianity.[36]

Robeck observes that these statements were printed time and time again.[37] This observation is significant for Robeck in that for him "both the Azusa Street Mission and the larger Pentecostal movement" understood "themselves as restoring an ineffective or a compromised church to its former state."[38] Such a perception was also evident in the years just prior to the Azusa Revival, remarks Robeck, when forerunners such as Parham and Frank Sandford held to "the restoration of the gifts" of the Spirit (1 Cor 12–14) as well as in the experience of speaking in tongues, which was viewed as a gift "to speak languages of the world without prior study."[39]

At this point, it may be helpful to define *restoration* to shed light on the phrase "restorational revival movement." Pentecostalism has been described as a restorationist movement.[40] Courey states that restorationism is "an effort to recapture the vitality of New Testament Christianity, by returning to apostolic ways."[41] Robeck writes:

> Restorationists believe that at some time in the history of the church—usually, it is said, around the time when the church emerged from "persecuted sect" status to become the Roman

---

35. "The Pentecostal Baptism Restored," 1.
36. "The Apostolic Faith: 312 Azusa Street," 2.
37. Robeck, *The Azusa Street Mission*, 9.
38. Ibid., 121.
39. Ibid., 41–42.
40. For example, see Wacker, "Searching for Eden," 139–66; Althouse, *Spirit of the Last Days*.
41. Courey, *What Has Wittenberg*, 10.

> Empire's state religion—genuine Christianity was lost . . . Restorationists have generally taught that now, at last, God has begun his final intervention on the human stage to bring about the full restoration of the church.[42]

Robeck goes on to note that each restorationist group declared the manner in which God would restore the church, and for the "holiness and Apostolic Faith groups," this would transpire through "the outpouring of the Holy Spirit."[43] Courey asserts that Pentecostals were different from other restorationists, however, in that "[t]hey experienced an ontological immediacy with the New Testament church that others may have claimed, but proved theirs with the crowning experience of the supernatural gifts of the Spirit, and the restoration of Pentecost itself."[44] That is, for Pentecostal restorationists, God, Godself, had intervened.

Early Pentecostals were also revivalists in that the ways of the New Testament church were restored through a revival. For them, this occurred not of human agency but by divine action. Early Pentecostals perceived the church's human traditions and creeds as lifeless products of tradition (see above). Edith Blumhofer comments, "History—with its accumulation of tradition—was irrelevant. The church was called to be ahistorical, or at least to exist untainted by historical currents."[45] Pentecostals eschewed the creeds and relied solely on Scripture, which was seen as divinely inspired.[46] For Pentecostals, then, Scripture not only described God's acts but was also the result of divine agency while historical creeds were of human agency. Blumhofer writes of the fervently held position of early Pentecostals that God had deserted "organized religion."[47] It was God who would, in Blumhofer's words, "sovereignly restore the faith in the end times."[48] For Pentecostals, this restoration occurred through revival; thus, they became restorational revivalists.[49]

42. Robeck, *The Azusa Street Mission*, 121.

43. Ibid.

44. Courey, *What Has Wittenberg*, 83. *Ontological* for Courey refers to more than "an existential sense of union, but an essential unity of being with the apostolic church"; see 82n35.

45. Blumhofer, *Restoring the Faith*, 13.

46. As Blumhofer remarks, "As restorationists, early Pentecostals intentionally ignored historical tradition, opting rather for biblical terminology and precedent." Ibid., 4.

47. Ibid., 14.

48. Ibid., 15.

49. I am borrowing this from Kenneth Archer who uses the term, "restorational

Ironically, a restorational revivalism that resists creeds and church tradition yet holds to the belief that God revives the church becomes in itself a doctrine. It believes in a divine encounter that renews God's people so that the church is restored to the New Testament church, a time in which the church thrived spiritually. Pentecostals tacitly believe, "If we can simply return to an earlier spiritual state when we experienced an impassioned spirituality, we will experience a divine encounter." Thus, Pentecostals tend to be gazing backward to a previous time rather than perceiving how the Spirit is moving at this location and time and seeking how to best participate in the Spirit's work now. In this way, their revival experiences have become doctrine. William Kay implies this theologizing of a divine-human encounter when he indicates that Pentecostalism as a whole "is revivalistic." Kay writes, "Patterns of revival behaviour became part of Pentecostal worship . . . In effect, Pentecostalism normalized revival behaviour and could claim to be a 'revival movement.'"[50] This normalization for me is the formulation of a doctrine of divine encounter, which leads to practices, such as intentionally creating room in services that invite God to move and revive the church to be what it once was.

This thread of restorationism within revivalism continues in current Pentecostalism and is evidenced in some of the interviews of the research participants. When Jeremy was asked how he defined a Pentecostal, he pointed towards the restoration of the New Testament church when he said a Pentecostal was "an Acts Christian, 'cuz you'll hear speaking in tongues; you'll have prophecy or being led by the Spirit . . . What you read in Acts, we see at the church." Kyle spoke of his sister hearing the Spirit speak to her to go to the front to receive the Spirit's baptism at a "Holy Ghost revival type crusade" in which an evangelist was the speaker. Kirsten told of revival services at a Pentecostal school that she attended at which prior to the service the students were "praying and praising out loud." She stated, "[T]he sound of praise was so piercingly beautiful . . . It was the most beautiful, pure thing my ears have ever heard." Joan implied revivalistic meetings when she spoke of an evangelist visiting their church. She said the evangelist talked about the baptism of the Spirit when he said, "You know, it's just a matter of breathing in the Holy Spirit and just opening yourself up to the Holy Spirit." She then received "the baptism of the Holy Spirit very unemotionally and very calmly, sitting in a chair." Such experiences of divine encounters as

---

revivalism"; Archer, *A Pentecostal Hermeneutic*, 12.

50. Kay, *Pentecostalism*, 59.

described by the research participants are encounters shaped or mediated by the Pentecostal tradition's doctrinal heritage and beliefs in restorational revivalism.

Worship: A Space for Divine Encounter

The second aspect is worship, which is the space created in a Pentecostal service for God to move in their midst.[51] Robeck comments that originally worship was the response to experiencing God at the Azusa Street Revival.[52] As Robeck relayed, an encounter with God transformed lives in a single moment, generating assorted responses. Some danced while others jumped. Some stood still with arms raised high, but others shouted or sang "with all the gusto they could muster." Still "others were so full of awe" that "they fell to the floor."[53]

The meetings in the beginning of the revival, Robeck remarks, had no songbooks, hymnals, musical instruments, or what I would call *organized* worship leading. Instead, one person led out in a song as the Spirit moved on her, and the attendees joined her, singing a cappella and harmonizing their voices. When she was done, another person, being moved by the Spirit, started a different song. These songs were from the repertoire of the revival attendees' previous church experiences of "African American and Wesleyan holiness groups."[54] That is to say, their very singing was an experience of the Spirit in that their singing of the songs were believed to be prompted by the divine. Such worship experiences also included periods of singing in the Spirit in which the attendees sang together in tongues. Robeck informs his readers that those in attendance "believed that this music was inspired

---

51. There are three ways that Pentecostals define *worship*: (1) the whole service; (2) the singing of songs in the service; and (3) the act of honoring and glorifying God. The way I use *worship* unless stated otherwise is as a noun that speaks of the singing of songs. Daniel Albrecht comments that in his ethnographic study of three Pentecostal/Charismatic churches, he seldom heard "the whole Sunday liturgy referred to as a worship service." Instead, it usually signified the first twenty-five minutes or so of the service. Albrecht, *Rites in the Spirit*, 155. Albrecht's study examines the "Pentecostal experience and the rites and rituals that express, shape, nurture, transform and authenticate the spirituality of Pentecostals." Ibid., 7.

52. Robeck, *The Azusa Street Mission*, 131.

53. Ibid.

54. Ibid., 144–45.

completely by the Holy Spirit."[55] Worship was such a part of experiencing God that Robeck states that Frank Bartleman, an attendee who recorded much of the events, "vehemently condemned any worship singing ordered by the intervention of some leader who would direct the 'song service.'"[56] Robeck writes:

> Bartleman was convinced that some of the leaders of the revival were actually quenching the Spirit because they moved from hymns in the corporate memory or "singing in tongues," to singing from published hymnals and pre-selected songs led by designated song leaders. From his perspective, these practices were nothing more than human attempts to control people who would prefer to embrace the spontaneity of the Spirit.[57]

While the Azusa Revival's worship was a response to their encountering the divine, contemporary Pentecostal churches utilize worship to cultivate a divine-human encounter. It is no secret that the entire contemporary Pentecostal service is centered on the divine-human encounter.[58] Smith writes, "[P]entecostal worship makes room for the unexpected. Indeed, we might say that, for pentecostals, the unexpected is expected."[59] Daniel Albrecht in speaking of the all-encompassing milieu of Pentecostal churches ("the ritual field") asserts, "It is both a conscious and intuitive effort to construct a sphere in which together a congregation most likely will *encounter* their God" (italics in original).[60] Albrecht notes that if various human efforts of the worship service foster divine encounter, these efforts are perceived in a "positive" manner; however, if any effort hinders the people's encounter with God, it is suspect.[61] These perceptions will be clearly seen in the research participants' comments concerning their experiences in contemporary Pentecostal services. This points not only to the divine element in an encounter but also to the human element.

55. Ibid., 149–50.
56. Ibid., 148.
57. Ibid., 149.
58. Smith sees Pentecostalism's "radical openness to God" as translating "into a dynamic ecclesiology *in practice*—where worship is shaped by a persistent openness to surprise and an expectation of the miraculous" (italics in original); see Smith, *Thinking in Tongues*, 39. Other examples include: Ingalls, "Introduction," 6–7; Albrecht, *Rites in the Spirit*, 141–42; Land, *Pentecostal Spirituality*, 70–71.
59. Smith, *Thinking in Tongues*, 33.
60. Albrecht, *Rites in the Spirit*, 149.
61. Ibid., 142.

While the construction of the entire service focuses on a divine-human encounter, the song service itself is that space in the service specifically created for the people to meet with God.[62] Warrington, when writing of Pentecostal worship, states, "Pentecostals expect to experience an intimate relationship with God in which he is felt and they are moved emotionally."[63] As such, many contemporary Pentecostal song services are crafted in such a way as to assist in generating a space for an encounter with God. Frequently, as the music begins, people stand to their feet in order to participate fully in worship.[64] The worship usually begins with songs that are celebratory in nature. These songs, which tend to have an upbeat tempo, underscore praising God not only with one's voice but also with handclapping and at times with dancing. Eventually, the worship moves towards slower, more contemplative songs that are sung with many Pentecostals raising their hands. Albrecht remarks, "The tone and the words of the [more meditative] songs help to move the worshipers into a more 'intimate communion.'"[65] Albrecht reports that many of his study's participants spoke of sensing "the proximity of the Holy Spirit and the reality of close communion with the divine heightened during the singing, listening and participating in the music and the other sounds of worship."[66] If a congregant exercises one of the vocal gifts of the Spirit (1 Cor 12), it often occurs during the segment of more meditative worship. Whether the gift is expressed as a prophecy or a message in tongues with an interpretation of tongues, the congregation becomes still as they intently listen to a Christ-follower who they believe is being used of the Spirit. In essence, they believe they are encountering God in that moment.

In considering the above discussion and the way in which Pentecostal tradition mediates contemporary Pentecostalism, it is not a surprise that worship was stressed when I inquired of the research participants' current church experiences. Both Joan and Danielle expressed how wonderful the worship was in the church they currently attended. Joan revealed

62. Albrecht notes, "The music of the Pentecostal song service . . . seeks to help usher the congregation into the presence of God." Ibid., 143.

63. Warrington, *Pentecostal Theology*, 219.

64. Albrecht comments, "With the chords of the first song many spontaneously stand. It is reminiscent of the contemporary rock concert, where fans endeavor to become more actively involved in the music by standing and engaging themselves kinesthetically in the music." Albrecht, *Rites in the Spirit*, 157.

65. Ibid., 159.

66. Ibid., 143.

how worship in her church became a space for divine encounter: "A service would have lots of worship with beautiful music and praise to God. It's very free and open worship. Many times there will be a message in tongues and an interpretation or a prophecy." Danielle talked of a "great worship time" in which the congregation is brought "into the worship of Jesus" by the leader. Jeremy, whose responsibility was to select photographs for the background of the words to the songs, spoke in amazement of the most recent church service when the congregation spent "five minutes of non-stop praise and worship" to one song with one photograph as background.

Some participants acknowledged personal preferences in how churches conducted worship, exhibiting how the human element encourages or inhibits the divine-human encounter. Lindsey mentioned her partiality for a worship style that included current, contemporary worship songs. Bob expressed disappointment in his worship experience, such as when the leader centered on the congregants' involvement rather than focusing on God. Kyle voiced irritation of being unfamiliar with the songs, which interfered with his ability to enter into worship. He asserted, "When people aren't singing and really involved in what's going on, worship does not ensue as naturally as if everybody was involved in the music and really reveling in the presence of the Lord." Accordingly, Kyle believed the gifts of the Spirit were "somewhat restricted . . . based" in part on "the way the pastor [led] the service." That is to say, worship for the participants was vital for creating a space for divine encounter, and the way in which it was conducted either fostered or hindered this encounter.

Altar: A Place for Divine Encounter

The third aspect is the altar, which is a place for divine encounter.[67] At the Azusa Street Revival, the altar was a significant place at which people encountered God. The first edition of *The Apostolic Faith* states, "People are seeking at the altar three times a day and it is hard to close at night on account of seekers and those who are under the power of God."[68] *The Apostolic Faith* also included an account of a mother and daughter:

---

67. I am not the only one to hold this view. For instance, the title of Daniel Tomberlin's book is telling: *Pentecostal Sacraments: Encountering God at the Altar*. Albrecht also comments of the research participants in his study that they "look to the altar space as a meeting place with the divine"; see Albrecht, *Rites in the Spirit*, 132.

68. "The Old Time Pentecost," 1.

> A young lady who came into the meeting unsaved, went to the altar during the sermon, under deep conviction, and was saved in about five minutes. Before that evening was over, she was sanctified and baptized with the Holy Ghost and had the gift of the Chinese tongue and was singing in Chinese in the Spirit. Her mother followed her to the altar and has also been saved, sanctified, baptized with the Holy Ghost and healed of asthma and heart trouble, which the doctors said was incurable.[69]

As the reader may observe, the two women experienced salvation, sanctification, Spirit baptism, and one was also healed *at the altar*. Divine encounters at the altar like these were not just an occasional happenstance, but, as Robeck notes, *The Apostolic Faith* reported such occurrences again and again.[70] The attendees were so drawn that *The Apostolic Faith* portrayed the opening of the altars as being a time that people streamed to the altar without any pleading.[71] There was this expectation that at the altar one would meet with God. Robeck summarizes the altar's importance at Azusa in that while attendees enjoyed all the aspects of the service (i.e., worship, testimonies, sermon), "if they wanted to encounter God, they were told that they needed to spend time seeking him either at the altar or in the upper room."[72]

There is a certain significance in Pentecostalism's emphasis on going to the altar to encounter God. Such an approach is an act of humility before both God and the other persons in attendance. It is a physical demonstration with one's whole being that communicates, "I want to meet with God." It bodily indicates to the divine, "I need you"; thus, the person is calling out to God through this action, displaying an expectation or a hope of encountering the divine. In many ways, the altar is seen as a pre-designated meeting place with God, which is indicated in variations of the old-time phrase, "Come to the front to be under the spout where the glory comes out!"

The idea of *altar* has changed slightly over the years in Pentecostalism. I recall as a child two benches at the front of the church where people knelt and prayed at the close of a service; however, many Pentecostal churches today reference the space between the front row and the platform as *the*

---

69. "No Bottom," 3.
70. Robeck, *The Azusa Street Mission*, 167.
71. "Bible Pentecost: Gracious Pentecostal Showers Continue to Fall," 1.
72. Robeck, *The Azusa Street Mission*, 168.

front, or *the altar*.[73] During a service and/or at the close of today's services, a pastor often invites congregants to the front for prayer. The pastor and/or other designated *altar workers* often meet individuals in this place in order to join together to seek a divine encounter.[74] Albrecht describes this ministry, "Here they will meet together in order to stand, kneel or bow before their God."[75]

Daniel Tomberlin states this place is for the benefit of humanity, not for God. Humans are "creatures of time and space," so it is necessary to have a specified place that is viewed as holy.[76] Tomberlin notes the altar in Scripture is "a place of sacrifice" where a nation or individuals brought "offerings" to present "to God."[77] Albrecht confirms that this understanding continues today when he writes, "The altar space functions symbolically as . . . a sacred space, a place for meeting God, a place for humans to make self-offerings in prayers, actions and ministry rites."[78]

The altar is also painted as a place of victory, or instantaneous deliverance. If it is a meeting place with God, such an encounter points to change (see below). The minister may proclaim, "If you have a sin over which you need victory, come down to the altar and find freedom from sin. If you have a problem, come and lay your burden on the altar, and God will give you victory today!" The altar then becomes the place of an expectation of instantaneous transformation because one is experiencing the divine in that place.

Several of the research participants referenced the altar or going to the front of the church building where they sought and/or encountered God. Joan spoke of the altar at a previous church as being important as a place for encounters with God, including the receiving of divine direction.

---

73. Albrecht writes, "The altar space, frequently called 'the front' is in each of our three churches the area between the platform and the first row of chairs or pew. The altar space is a meeting place. Where the established ritual leaders and congregants meet, there the congregation symbolically meets their God." Albrecht, *Rites in the Spirit*, 131.

74. Albrecht remarks, "Leaders come from their leadership space on the platform as congregants come from their primary space in the pews, and together they meet at the altars." Ibid., 132–33.

75. Ibid., 133.

76. Tomberlin, *Pentecostal Sacraments*, loc. 359–60. Albrecht agrees and likens this place to a "temporary 'container' of sorts for the sacred, for the human to engage in the sacred"; see Albrecht, *Rites in the Spirit*, 133.

77. Tomberlin, *Pentecostal Sacraments*, loc. 371–72.

78. Albrecht, *Rites in the Spirit*, 133.

She additionally indicated how the altar at her current church was a place for divine encounter: "They always have a time of anointing where during the worship time people could come forward and be anointed with oil and be prayed over by the prayer team." Kyle told of an instance of going to the front for prayer to receive the baptism of the Spirit. Danielle talked of her pastor extending an invitation to pray with people at the close of the service and also saying, "This altar is for anyone. It's not that you're having trouble, and for people to think, 'What's wrong? What's going on in their life so that they need to come up front?'" Despite one's expectations, Kirsten reported a divine encounter may not occur at the altar as one desires when she said, "I had a lot of different experiences where I didn't get healed at altar services."[79]

Prayer: A Request for Divine Encounter

The fourth aspect is prayer, which I see as a request for divine encounter. The emphasis on prayer is evident when one researches early Pentecostalism, specifically the Azusa Street Revival. Robeck writes that when one investigates the accounts of the revival, one will "conclude that prayer was probably the centerpiece of the revival."[80] Correspondingly, Warrington notes that God is believed to be responding to prayer when a revival occurs.[81] Additionally, Robeck describes Seymour as "a man of prayer," which is demonstrated by his extensive praying for the arrival of a revival and his continued praying after its inception.[82] Robeck states of Seymour that he "provided the norm for the whole revival when he reportedly sat with his head tucked into the makeshift pulpit, praying, while other things went

---

79. Kirsten illustrated how the human element may also be a factor in hindering a divine-human encounter at the altar. She related an experience in which the minister at the altar continued to speak into a microphone while ministering to her, causing her embarrassment. When he informed her that unforgiveness was the reason she was not healed, it caused her to forgive everyone that came to mind. The minister then had her parade around the sanctuary without her cane, claiming she was healed. In reality, she was not completely dependent on the cane, so to walk without using it was not evidence of her healing. As will be discussed (chapter 5), this incident illustrates an unhelpful response to suffering that occurred at the altar. According to Christopraxis, it did not reveal God and generate reconciliation with God.

80. Robeck, *The Azusa Street Mission*, 139.

81. Warrington, *Pentecostal Theology*, 214.

82. Robeck, *The Azusa Street Mission*, 139.

on about him."[83] Robeck summarizes, "Prayer . . . seemed to bathe all the events of the revival."[84]

Early Pentecostals believed that when one made a request in prayer, God answered. This is seen in *The Apostolic Faith* encouraging Christ-followers to be baptized in the Holy Spirit: "Pray for the power of the Holy Ghost, and God will give you a new language."[85] Besides praying for the baptism of the Spirit, Robeck notes, "Prayer for healing also became a staple of the mission."[86] For example, *The Apostolic Faith* declared, "A man who was deaf and said he had not been able to hear for half his life was prayed for. God instantly gave him his hearing, when he was anointed and prayed for."[87] If the prayer request was not answered, *The Apostolic Faith* offered the suggestion: "If you do not get the answer right away, perhaps there is something on your part that needs to be gotten out of the way."[88]

Since the significance of prayer as ministry is discussed in chapter 5, my comments here focus on divine encounter. Warrington states of the Pentecostal understanding of prayer: "Prayer is primarily an encounter with God" in that it is a dialogue.[89] Warrington continues, "Fundamentally, it is intended to be a God-conscious moment when the transcendent God opens a window into the world of the believer and announces his presence."[90] Prayer for us as Pentecostals is not only expected to occur in churches with other Christ-followers, but we also emphasize regular, personal times of prayer, believing God hears us whenever we pray. Warrington writes, "Pentecostals assume that God listens when they pray and are consequently expectant of his intervention into their lives and in response to their prayers."[91] William Menzies acknowledges that there are

83. Ibid.
84. Ibid.
85. "Two Works of Grace and the Gift of the Holy Ghost," 3.
86. Robeck, *The Azusa Street Mission*, 142.
87. Evans, "Fire Falling at Oakland," 4.
88. "To Our Correspondents," 4.
89. Warrington, *Pentecostal Theology*, 214.
90. Ibid., 214–15.

91. Ibid., 216. Candy Gunther Brown conducted research among Pentecostals and discovered that Pentecostals who desired healing "took the position that failure to continue praying for one's needs until physical symptoms were 'completely' resolved diminished the likelihood of ever experiencing complete healing"; see *Testing Prayer*, 187. Brown surveyed Pentecostals who attended the healing conferences of Iris Ministries and Global Awakening in the countries of North America, Brazil, and Mozambique by

occasions when God does not intervene and encourages Pentecostals to intercede until the prayer is answered or until God instructs the believer to discontinue with that prayer.[92] This suggests that Menzies holds that God hears our prayers even when they are not answered as we had hoped. In essence, the belief is, "Just keep praying until you hear from God."

Similar to early Pentecostals, the research participants mentioned prayer, whether they prayed for themselves, for others, or asked others to pray for them. Joan recounted that at the church she was currently attending, there were two occasions for prayer: after the worship and after the message. At these times, "people can feel free to come forward and have special prayer," and many times the Spirit is moving through healings, words of prophecy, or tongues and interpretation. She also spoke of a church that she had previously attended where every six months the church conducted a "solemn assembly, which was a week of fasting and prayer." She said of this event: "They would have services every night, and there would be praying in the Spirit, and people believing for healing, and so [her husband] was prayed over many times for healing." Christy referenced the existence of a prayer chain, and Kirsten stated she believed her prayers changed things. Kyle spoke of prayer line ministry, or a *prayer tunnel*, where ministers stood in a line at the front of the meeting place, and those who wanted prayer walked by these pastors, allowing each pastor to touch and to pray for them.

Some of the participants mentioned positive and negative aspects concerning prayer. Bob testified about a woman in his current church for whom the church was praying that had cancer with "tumors all over her body and they've all been shrinking." Lindsey spoke of being a part of her church's prayer team, which gave her an opportunity to serve. Kirsten, however, lamented other Pentecostals being critical of her physical disabilities rather than praying for her. While Kirsten also spoke of going to the front during a healing service because she wanted to receive prayer as often as she could, she also experienced pressure to appear to be healed, or one could say, outwardly transformed.

---

conducting pre- / post-conference questionnaires as well as many informal interviews at the conferences. Additionally, respondents in North America filled out a contact card if they were willing to participate in a follow-up phone interview, resulting in sixty-eight interviews being conducted. Brown also concludes that Pentecostals perceive that prayer is "a strategy that should be, and often is, employed repeatedly for the same condition, because prayer appears to be cumulative in its effects"; ibid., 189–90.

92. Menzies, "Reflections on Suffering," 141–49.

Transformation: The Verifiable Evidence of Divine Encounter

Transformation is the fifth aspect, which speaks of verifiable evidence of an encounter with God. In the beginning early Pentecostals placed weight on the need for verifiable evidence concerning the baptism of the Spirit. As *The Apostolic Faith* proclaims when referencing Mark 16:16–17: "Here a belief and baptism are spoken of, and the sign or evidence given to prove that you possess that belief and baptism. This Scripture plainly declares that these signs SHALL follow them that believe" (all caps in original).[93] Thusly, Neumann observes, early Pentecostals held "that the Spirit's activity would be evidenced by observable, physical phenomena."[94] *The Apostolic Faith* continues in the above article to argue from Acts that the sign of Spirit baptism is tongues.[95] Robeck also underscores this point when he writes, "The leaders at the mission agreed that baptism in the Spirit would be recognized when someone spoke in tongues, and not a moment before."[96]

In the beginning, this non-transformational occurrence of tongues was considered to be the evidence. As Robeck highlights, anyone who spoke in tongues was believed to be baptized in the Spirit. Upon reflection, however, Seymour determined tongues was the biblical evidence of Spirit baptism "only if it were also accompanied by divinely-given love." The absence of "this fruit" produced doubt that God had genuinely given the gift.[97] In other words, evidential tongues was not a spiritual ending in and of itself but part of the ongoing spiritual formation. Thus, at the very beginning of Pentecostalism, Seymour stressed the association of transformation with

---

93. "Tongues as a Sign," 2.

94. Neumann, *Pentecostal Experience*, 149.

95. "Tongues as a Sign," 2.

96. Robeck, *The Azusa Street Mission*, 177.

97. Ibid., 177–78. After the revival ended, Seymour published *The Doctrines and Discipline of the Azusa Street Apostolic Faith Mission, Los Angeles, California* in which he spoke of the evidence of Spirit baptism as being love. Scholars propose various reasons that Seymour wrote this particular work. For example, some perceive Seymour abandoned tongues as the evidence of Spirit baptism due to the racism that continued to abound even though individuals spoke in tongues, and others assert Seymour continued to embrace tongues as evidence, but he used this writing to address various issues following the revival. In other words, it is unknown how one is to interpret what Seymour stated. To read excerpts of Seymour's book, see Seymour, "William J. Seymour's Doctrine and Discipline"; see also Espinosa, *William J. Seymour and the Origins of Global Pentecostalism*; Synan and Fox, *William J. Seymour*, 69–84.

Spirit baptism, which accentuated transformation as a necessary result of a genuine encounter with God for Pentecostals.

Blumhofer also connects Spirit baptism with tangible evidence of a perceived change. She comments that early Pentecostals "were empowered to develop certain character traits and a particular spirituality, and to evangelize."[98] Thus, evidence of transformation in addition to speaking in tongues became essential for Spirit baptism. Blumhofer writes that the baptism of the Spirit was "part of the process of spiritual growth and transformation."[99] *The Apostolic Faith* confirms the necessity of other evidence than tongues for the Spirit's baptism:

> If you are baptized with the Holy Ghost, you know it, and everybody else knows it. That is one thing you cannot hide. When you are sanctified, people have to take your testimony and watch your life, but when He comes and covers you over and around and about, people know it. Man may say, it is of the devil and they are drunk, but glory to God, He will shine out Himself, and there is a power back of you that men and women cannot gainsay. It will give you holy boldness to stand up before the world without fear.[100]

The significance of transformation in a Pentecostal's experience with God is demonstrated through the emphasis on verifiable evidence. Neumann underscores verifiable, physical and/or emotional (e.g., tears, laughing, etc.) evidence that the Spirit is working. He writes, "Without this type of 'evidence,' Pentecostals are less confident the Spirit is being experienced."[101] At the same time, the stress on the necessity for transformation to be the tangible evidence means that for a Pentecostal, an experience with God is not just for the sake of the experience.[102] As Warrington perceives, any lack of transformation casts doubt upon the validity of the experience or on the person's willingness to be transformed.[103] Anderson

---

98. Blumhofer, "*Pentecost in My Soul*," 30.

99. Ibid., 17.

100. "A Know-So Salvation," 2.

101. Neumann, *Pentecostal Experience*, 116.

102. Warrington writes, "Such encounters are not merely viewed as self-authenticating or self-oriented; they are deemed to be valuable as motivational forces, leading to personal transformation as a result of the Spirit's involvement in their lives." Warrington, *Pentecostal Theology*, 21.

103. Ibid., 26.

and Mark Cartledge agree that the experience with the divine is to be transformative.[104] Cartledge asserts that the Pentecostal worship service is designed in a "search-encounter-transformation cycle" in which the effect of a divine encounter produces change in a person, such as "edification, cleansing, healing, [or] empowerment."[105] Kärkkäinen, while commenting on the contribution of Pentecostals to pneumatology, indicates the necessity for verifiable evidence when he distinguishes between a Pentecostal's and a non-Pentecostal's emphases on God's presence:

> Whereas for most other Christians the presence of the Spirit is just that, *presence*, for Pentecostals the presence of the Spirit in their midst implies *empowerment*. While this empowerment often manifests itself in spiritual gifts such as speaking in tongues, prophesy, or healings, it is still felt and sought for by Pentecostals even when those manifestations are absent. The main function of the Pentecostal worship service, then, is to provide a setting for an encounter with Jesus, the embodiment of the Full Gospel, to receive the (em)power(ment) of the Spirit. As important as sermon, hymns, and liturgy are, they all take second place to the meeting with the Lord (italics in original).[106]

In the next chapter I will accentuate the research participants' emphasis on the transformations they experienced, but here I simply stress the importance of verifiable evidence of their encounters with God. Hence, the reader is to keep in mind that while the initial, tangible evidence is what is emphasized in the participants' experiences for the purposes of this chapter, Spirit baptism is understood to be for empowerment to be a witness. That is to say, the *initial physical* evidence is not considered its only evidence, but this term implies that transformation will accompany Spirit baptism.[107]

---

104. Anderson, *An Introduction to Pentecostalism*, 188; Cartledge, *Encountering the Spirit*, 25.

105. Cartledge, *Encountering the Spirit*, 25–27.

106. Kärkkäinen, "Pneumatologies," 228.

107. The transformative aspect and the initial physical evidence continue to be central issues of Spirit baptism in contemporary Pentecostalism. Some contemporary Classical Pentecostals have had an encounter with God, which they perceive to be Spirit baptism, that results in transformation without speaking in tongues. Thus, the argument is being made that one does not need to speak in tongues to be baptized in the Spirit. This demonstrates the importance transformation continues to play in Spirit baptism specifically and divine encounters generally.

While all of the participants had indicated having been baptized in the Spirit, five chose to relay their personal accounts of this experience (see also the accounts of Christy and Joan above). Kyle was a teen at a camp meeting when the pastors formed a *prayer tunnel* "for anybody that wanted to receive the baptism of the Holy Spirit." As he stood in line, he observed one minister who applied physical force to each forehead when praying for people, causing Kyle to become anxious; therefore, he began to pray, "Please fill me with the Holy Spirit before I get" to that minister. Kyle laughed when he reported that prior to arriving at the altar: "I had received the baptism. I was speaking in tongues and having a great time in the Lord." Kirsten also was a teenager when she approached the youth sponsors while attending a pool tournament at a coffee house and asked them to pray for her to receive the Spirit. They went to a back room, and when the youth sponsors prayed over her, Kirsten received the Spirit's baptism, which she described as a "very powerful experience" being "born out of a desire to know God." Danielle recalled she experienced Spirit baptism at a time when Reagan was sick in the hospital and she "just didn't know what to pray or how to pray," and she simply started speaking in tongues. She said of that experience, "English was done for me."

Testimony: The Reporting of Divine Encounter

The final aspect is testimony, which I call the reporting of divine encounter. Robeck depicts the testimonies at the Azusa Street Revival as being "not time-worn, tired retreads of something that had happened twenty or thirty years ago. They were new, vital vignettes."[108] For instance, the third edition of *The Apostolic Faith* proclaims:

> Sister Lemon of Whittier, who had been a sufferer for eighteen years and could receive no help from physicians, and had been bed-ridden for fourteen years of that time, has been marvelously healed by the Lord through the laying on of hands and the prayer of faith. She has been walking to meetings. The opposers of the work cannot deny that a notable miracle has been performed through the mighty name of Jesus.[109]

---

108. Robeck, *The Azusa Street Mission*, 154.
109. "Bible Pentecost," 1.

These testimonies were so alive that *The Apostolic Faith* described the giving of testimonies continuing for over two hours with individuals standing in line to declare what God had done.[110] Robeck writes that attendees considered the testimonies "the highlight of the meetings," as evidenced by attendees standing "at the windows outside the mission just to hear the latest tale of God's working."[111] The testimonies were not only told verbally, but they were also declared in written form. For example, *The Apostolic Faith* provides a written testimony of Brother Mead, part of which I share here:

> The first night at the meetings, my heart went out for the baptism. I went forward to be prayed for, and hands were laid on me, and prayer was made, that I might receive the baptism of the Holy Spirit. I continued praying and fasting, in hope and much comfort. One evening, in complete abnegation of self, it was revealed to me that the same power and persecutions that were in the beginning were now to be repeated for the perfecting of the Church. Would I choose it? My heart cried out, Oh, yes Lord, with your smile. And my soul was flooded with Divine love; and I commenced to speak as I would sing a new song.[112]

Testimonies like these are reports of divine encounters that contributed to the formulation of a doctrine of divine encounter, restorational revivalism, as discussed above.

Testimonies have remained a significant part of Pentecostalism. Smith notices, "[M]aking room for testimony is central to pentecostal spirituality precisely because narrative is central to pentecostal identity."[113] As a Pentecostal, I have personally witnessed the significance of testimonies by both hearing and giving them. As a young person, I recall hearing testimonies at a designated time in the service in which individuals stood and declared what God had done for them. While some testimonies were unlike the vibrant testimonies of the Azusa Street Revival in that the proclamations were more general such as, "I thank Jesus for saving and keeping me," nevertheless, others were more particular such as, "I thank Jesus for healing me of the pain in my body this week." These latter testimonies especially affirmed for the congregants that God was involved in the affairs of the people. Car-

---

110. Ibid.
111. Robeck, *The Azusa Street Mission*, 154.
112. Mead, "New-Tongued Missionaries for Africa," 3.
113. Smith, *Thinking in Tongues*, 50.

tledge believes that testimonies provide an avenue in which the Pentecostal "worldview is both legitimated and energised in the community."[114] This means these testimonies that announced a believer's own encounter with God bolstered the hopes and expectations of the listeners; thus, it was only natural that other Christ-followers rose to their feet to request prayer—these testimonies had nurtured hope that God was able to intervene on their behalf, too. Testimonies also were traditionally given following a statewide church camp or a short-term missions trip. Those who had joined in these special activities, such as myself, reported to others what God had accomplished, including baptizing people in the Spirit with the evidence of speaking in tongues or healing persons with various physical ailments, and they rejoiced in having participated in the Spirit's ministry.

Scholars assert that the use of testimony within Pentecostalism is a way in which Pentecostals theologize. Steven Land recognizes that testimony is part of the process of forming theology within Pentecostalism in that a person's experience with God moves "to testimony to doctrine to theology and back again."[115] Frank Macchia similarly states, "Pentecostals have always favored testimonies, choruses, and prayers over intellectual or critical reflection as the means by which to interpret the gospel."[116] Some scholars hold that Pentecostal testimony evolves from a culture that communicates orally to develop theology. Cartledge, for example, remarks that the prominence of testimony in Pentecostalism is due to its roots in oral culture, which is formed through stories, not "abstract propositions."[117] Still, Macchia argues "oral" is "too restrictive" in describing its theology for it does not encompass "written testimony," which early Pentecostals also practiced; thus, Macchia prefers the term "nonacademic theology," a term that embraces the written as well as the oral.[118]

---

114. Cartledge, *Testimony in the Spirit*, 17.

115. Land, *Pentecostal Spirituality*, 36.

116. Macchia, "Theology, Pentecostal," 1120. Smith, in discussing testimony as a narrative, writes, "A narrative makes sense of a life, a series of events, or an experience by a 'logic' that is not deductive but affective"; see Smith, *Thinking in Tongues*, 65. For Smith, testimony is how "pentecostals enact an identity by writing themselves into the larger story of God's redemption"; see ibid., 51.

117. Cartledge, *Testimony in the Spirit*, 17. Similarly, Hollenweger asserts that the Pentecostal tradition's roots are from Black, non-Western heritage that accents oral communication of theology; see Hollenweger, *Pentecostalism*.

118. Macchia, "Theology, Pentecostal," 1120.

Some research participants spoke of testimonies in their interview. Kirsten related how "her dad has a really neat testimony." Her father, who was an alcoholic, drove by an AG church to and from work. Kirsten talked of one occasion where, "he felt like the Holy Spirit was present in the car with him, and the Holy Spirit just whispered to him, 'This is it. This is your last time. This is your last chance.'" Her father walked into the church, and since a service was transpiring, he went to the front and "gave his life back to God." Danielle described how Reagan's family believed him to be "nutso" when he departed the Catholic church; however, after he became sick, his family observed "how positive" their church friends were and how they prayed for Reagan. After Reagan "got well" the first time, they called Danielle and Reagan when they needed prayer. She said of this event: "That was a good testimony of that . . . They didn't think he was crazy anymore." Moreover, the sharing of their stories is a testimony, such as Christy's admission of her telling her story to others, and Jeremy saying he hoped his story "will be helpful to my fellow brothers and sisters in Christ." In fact, the basis of this entire project is constructed on the experiences of the research participants' sharing their testimonies (stories) with me in order to delineate a more nuanced theology of suffering and healing.

CONCLUSION

I have discussed in this chapter that although the Azusa Street Revival did not materialize out of a vacuum, the Pentecostal tradition's beginnings in the United States and Canada did commence with a divine encounter of a person both being healed and receiving the baptism of the Spirit and speaking in tongues. I also stressed that not only has the Pentecostal tradition molded the research participants' hopes and expectations, but participants have also had experiences with God that have contributed to their own belief in divine encounter. Their experiences were mediated by the Pentecostal tradition's emphases on six aspects of divine encounter: restorational revivalism generates the doctrine; worship provides the space; altars supply the place; prayers make the requests; transformation is the verifiable evidence; and testimonies give the reports. In the following chapter I continue the stories, or testimonies, of the participants by portraying the way in which the participants interpreted their experiences with God during the lack of the desired divine intervention to remove their suffering, which moves us toward development of a theological praxis of suffering and healing.

4

Where's God in Suffering?
Absence in Presence and Presence in Absence

My miracle didn't come. God did not part the Red Sea for me and miraculously heal Jason. He did not. He did not. He chose not to. But you know what? He was with Jason. He was with me, and he's still walking with me through this.

—Christy, a participant

THUS FAR THE FORMATION of a theological praxis of suffering and healing has involved apparent absence and presence. I began in chapter 2 by introducing eight Pentecostals who had hoped for and/or expected a divine encounter while experiencing extended suffering, but none came; thus, I invited the reader to enter into the participants' nothingness and sample in a limited way their sense of powerlessness. In the next chapter I emphasized that Pentecostalism's heritage nurtures an expectation of divine encounter that forms a mediated quality in today's Pentecostals' experiences of God as evidenced in the lives of the participants. As such, both the early Pentecostals and the research participants experienced Jesus in revivals, in worship, at the altar, as a result of prayer, and as verified through tangible evidence and reported through testimonies. In essence, they personally experienced God's presence. Via each chapter's chief emphasis, then, I have juxtaposed apparent absence (chapter 2) alongside presence (chapter 3).

Having established the sense of powerlessness within apparent absence while taking into consideration the centrality of experiencing God's presence in Pentecostalism, I now move more deeply into the principal aspects of a theological praxis of suffering and healing by focusing on the main purpose of this study, which is how Pentecostals experience God amidst suffering. I explore here how Classical Pentecostals interpret and/or understand their experiences with God when God does not intervene in the midst of suffering as expected. In the words of Christopraxis, this chapter seeks to answer how Jesus ministers to the participants in their nothingness. It begins with how the research participants experienced God in suffering, which involves two perspectives: ongoing presence and intense presence; these are explored through the lens of Smith's discussion on Pentecostalism's *non-interventionist supernaturalism*. I then turn towards how the participants interpreted their experience with God in suffering, or how they found meaning, which consists of three elements: (1) being transformed in how they relate; (2) making sense out of the suffering; and (3) embracing uncertainty, ambiguity, and mystery. I conclude with conversing with the Fourth Gospel's theme of *presence*, centering on particular characteristics of presence that appear both in the participants' stories and in the Gospel of John.

EXPERIENCING GOD IN SUFFERING

Prior to exploring the participants' experience with God in suffering, I want to reiterate briefly the emphasis placed by Pentecostals on experiencing God. For the research participants, God is viewed as being intimately involved in their lives. This is their worldview.[1] Christy, for example, referenced living in the realm of the supernatural: "Since Jason has passed away,

---

1. Smith writes, "[A] worldview is a passional orientation that governs how one sees, inhabits, and engages the world . . . It is a *framework* of fundamental beliefs . . . through which we 'make sense' of our world . . . [T]hese beliefs . . . are often not beliefs that we consciously, rationally reflect upon . . . They . . . operate subterraneously . . . [W]orldviews are fundamentally *religious* in character, shaping the root commitments of individuals and communities . . . [W]orldviews are *comprehensive*, giving us an account of how the big picture hangs together . . . A worldview tells us something about our *calling*: how we understand our world then determines how we understand our roles *in* it" (italics in original). Smith, *Thinking in Tongues*, 27–28.

it just seems like every step that we take is supernatural. A real thing in our lives." Kirsten recapped her experience as a Pentecostal: "I strongly believe in the gifts of the Spirit . . . and allowing the Spirit to really lead us and guide us in our innermost being. So as a Pentecostal, that's kind of where I operate in everyday . . . So I am very convinced of the ideals behind Pentecostalism because they're real to me." Lindsey also summarized, "[There] has been this sense of the leading and the guiding of the Holy Spirit and . . . trajectories that take place [in my life] because of the sense of God's hand on my life." In essence, God has been and is regularly at work in them. It is this lens through which they understand their suffering, the apparent absence of God (nothingness), and it becomes the mediating quality through which these Pentecostals understand their experience of God in suffering. With the aforementioned in mind, I turn to the two perspectives of how the participants experienced God in suffering and place these perspectives in conversation with concepts from Smith's *Thinking in Tongues*.

Experiencing Apparent Absence in Presence

First, the participants experienced God in suffering by recognizing God's ongoing presence regardless of the circumstances. Although God did not intervene as they had hoped or expected, which chapter 2 calls *apparent absence*, the participants perceived God was there with them. I admit this discovery was a surprise because of my own experience of extended suffering. For me, God had been apparently absent. Period. Cognitively, I understood God to be omnipresent, but my experience of God was one of absence.[2] Since I bring my whole being to this research, I admit that I had expected, and perhaps had hoped, that my own experience would be confirmed through the research; thus, I was ambivalent in my discovery in that I had feelings of disappointment but also of surprise and excitement.

As I reflected on the participants' experience of God's ongoing presence in spite of my ambivalence, I realized they experienced what I now refer to as *apparent absence in presence*. This means that suffering is enveloped in God's presence so that suffering is within the being of God. This

---

2. Pentecostal Denise Peltomaki writes, "[M]any sufferers today also search for God in the darkness and do not find him. This must be acknowledged and taken seriously. To say everyone will find God if they search long enough and have faith ignores the reality that many are exhausted from their search, from crying out to God and receiving no perceivable response. We add to their sufferings by implying that their efforts are insufficient; their faith, inadequate." Peltomaki, "An Afflicted Waiting," 228.

may be illustrated through the use of concentric circles: the smaller circle indicates apparent absence and is placed inside the larger circle of presence so that the smaller circle (apparent absence) is in the foreground while the larger circle is in the background (God's presence). The phrase "apparent absence in presence" emphasizes the reality of the participants' experience of suffering while being upheld by God's omnipresence. This is detected in their general understanding about God, such as Joan's comment, "The Holy Spirit has been a very close friend and very wonderful counselor and guide and ever present." Lindsey, too, has always sensed God's omnipresence, "like [God's] there no matter what." I heard this from Kyle when he spoke of a "pet peeve" of hearing in church, "Lord Jesus, please come among us today"; for him, since God is present in the believer, God is already present in the service. The participants understood that God had remained with them despite their inability to cause God to act by curing the illness, restoring the marriage, providing employment, or completely healing the head injury or the mental illness.

While there was a general grasp of God's omnipresence, several participants specifically remarked how in the midst of God's apparent absence, God provided strength or sustained them, demonstrating God's continuous presence. Both Joan and Danielle spoke of God being the one who was there, enabling them to navigate through the path of suffering. For Kyle, I saw this as he mentioned the poem *Footprints*, which reminded him of God's presence during arduous times. Christy metaphorically described God's ongoing presence in the midst of difficulties: "I have felt him in a way I haven't felt him before. I just always think of my grandma's afghan that she made me. Just so warm. That's just comforting, and it's just there." Thus, while they experienced God's apparent absence, they were sustained by God's ongoing presence. In terms of Christopraxis, the participants perceived in their nothingness that God was continuing to be present, which ministered to them. Thus, as seen in chapter 1, God acts (strengthens them) through God's being (presence).

Experiencing Presence in Apparent Absence

The second perspective of how they experienced God in suffering is that the participants also experienced instances of God's intense presence. Even though the interviewees did not experience the much-desired intervention, they spoke of instances when God was encountered in intense ways, such

Who is Present in Absence?

as clearly speaking to them or intervening in other ways. I refer to these instances of divine encounter in suffering as *presence in apparent absence*. In continuing with the use of the image of concentric circles, here the smaller circle indicates God's presence as being at the forefront, and it is placed inside the larger circle of apparent absence (ongoing suffering) that is in the background. It is likened to God's presence being a lightening bolt that strikes amidst the encompassing suffering and is portrayed when most of the participants spoke of numerous occasions of praying during their suffering and frequently hearing God respond. Namely, God still showed up in spite of their hoped-for-miracle not occurring. In the language of Christopraxis, Jesus intensely came and ministered to the participants while they were in the middle of their nothingness.

For Bob, the image of the desert or the wilderness was helpful as he relayed, "[God's] always dropping manna and quail here and there to remind us that [God's] watching out for us." In Kyle's case, God recently spoke a message of reassurance and comfort through a camp evangelist who prayed for healing for Kyle's back by stating, "It is not a matter of not having faith. It is not a matter of not believing for your healing, but God is walking with you through a journey." Kirsten informed me she was experiencing TIAs, seizures, and taking over ten medications, when "I ended up getting pregnant which was a miracle because I was told I would never get pregnant. God just blessed me with this beautiful boy, and he is a miracle."

Danielle experienced God's healing presence after her grief intensified. As stated in chapter 2, when Danielle returned to work after Reagan's death, she was unable to stop crying. This resulted in Danielle being taken to her own home by her daughter where Danielle slept. On the following day, she turned to the Scriptures, of which she said, "I'd read something, and then I'd turn some place else, and all day it was just awesome." For Danielle, this experience sustained her at a time when she thought she was going crazy.

For Christy, she and some other women had been praying as to how she was to proceed in order to protect both her and the children just prior to Jason's death. This was during the time he had grown increasingly violent, and one day, she clearly received her answer. It was Easter weekend when Jason came out of his room "just crazed" and began "lifting things up and throwing them down" and then returned to his room. Within a little while, Jason again emerged, but he was different in that he said, "Honey." Christy remarked, "He hadn't called me 'honey' forever, and he's always called me 'honey.'" When she looked into his eyes, she saw *his* eyes, which she had not seen in two years. Previously, his eyes had danced, but for the last two years of his life, his eyes had been "hollow and vacant," and she had wondered, "Where are you?" Upon seeing his eyes, she said, "I knew it was the Lord." Jason informed her, "Honey, I don't know who I am. I don't know what's wrong with me . . . but you gotta go. The Lord told me you gotta go, Christy." Jason had already called his sister, who came within fifteen minutes, and Christy's bags were already packed in anticipation of her departure. The family hugged and kissed, and she and the children left and never returned. Christy stated, "The Lord said, 'Christy, just stay the course . . . Don't listen to the voices to the left or the right or behind you. Go and just keep going.'" Jason committed suicide several weeks later.

Sometimes the intense divine encounter transpired before the suffering increased, demonstrating God's preparatory care. Joan spoke of God providing a home that allowed her daughter's family to live downstairs just prior to learning of Craig's diagnosis. Joan did not realize at that point she would soon need them to be living in the same home. Similarly, Lindsey told the account of moving to the same city as her parents just before her grandma passed away and her father contracted a cold and died. She recalled telling her husband that she felt like they were to move, and he responded, "I think you're right." She said, "I knew it was God because [her husband] absolutely hates change. Hates to move." Jeremy reported having the same vision twice while at work the week prior to losing his job. He was in a "deep, dark cave" in which he "walked all around" but without knowing where he was or what he was doing. When he saw a light in the distance and began to move towards it, the vision ended. A couple of years later he understood its meaning: "[W]ork had always been almost like an idol to me. I'd spend hours and hours. I was a workaholic . . . but God showed me that my work was the darkness and out in the light was God, and that's where I had to get. I had to get out to God." To use the words of Christopraxis, then, the above instances demonstrate how Jesus ministered to the participants in their nothingness, whether it was experiencing apparent absence within Jesus's ongoing presence or Jesus's intense presence within apparent absence.

Who is Present in Absence?

Conversing with James K. A. Smith

In light of the research participants' perception of both ongoing presence and intense presence, I direct our attention to Smith's work, who explains and expands on the Pentecostal vernacular surrounding divine encounter. While Smith's expansion is for the purpose of contributing to the science/theology dialogue, I believe it to be of help in cultivating a more robust theological praxis of suffering and healing.

Pentecostals place an emphasis on practices that embody their understanding of divine encounter, such as going to a physical altar to meet with God or offering up prayers of healing for their physical bodies (chapter 3). Smith argues that "embodied practices," such as these, "'carry' within them a tacit understanding . . . an unarticulated, affective understanding that, when articulated, we will describe as a pentecostal 'worldview.'"[3] Concerning the Pentecostal view of experiencing God in the world, Smith asserts, "[P]entecostal worship and practice are characterized by a kind of gritty materiality as space for work of the Spirit," which "contests the natural/supernatural distinction."[4] As evidenced in the last chapter, some of the practices that dispute the natural/supernatural division include the using of the tongue when the person is baptized in the Spirit; the lifting of hands when a person is worshipping; or the anointing with oil when one prays for the other's physical healing. Smith sees such practices as the eroding of a strict dualistic understanding of the natural and supernatural. This erosion of dualism, for Smith, is specifically seen in the prayers of Pentecostals in areas of government, business, and "the arts" (e.g., their praying for a nation's election or for a Christian film's impact in the cinemas on the movie-attendees); thus, as Smith notes, they understand the Spirit to always be at work in creation and in culture.[5] Yet, it is not simply the Holy Spirit alone who is at work in creation and culture, for as Smith observes, Pentecostals believe in the activity of demonic spirits, placing an emphasis on spiritual warfare.[6] The participants supported the concept of Pentecostals' crossing the natural-supernatural distinction, as when Jeremy stated he experienced God's love in nature or Kyle spoke of encountering "some very strong evil

---

3. Smith, *Thinking in Tongues*, 27.

4. Ibid., 99.

5. Ibid., 39–40. Smith explains, "Endemic to a pentecostal worldview is the implicit affirmation of the dynamic, active presence of the Spirit not only in the church, but also in creation." Ibid., 39.

6. Ibid., 41.

spiritual warfare" when he became deathly ill. These perceptions, according to Smith, reveal the erosion of a dualistic understanding between the natural and the supernatural within Pentecostalism.[7] Smith admits Pentecostals have frequently upheld dualistic beliefs, such as the world is bad and thereby to be avoided, but their belief in healing of physical bodies and even God providing for them financially "deconstructs such dualism."[8]

Smith examines the above beliefs and practices of Pentecostalism by placing them within the science/theology dialogue. He recognizes that the Pentecostal vernacular commonly utilizes the language of *interventionist supernaturalism*. This perspective stresses the autonomy of the world, its self-sustainability, into which the divine intervenes; hence, in this view the world is a "closed system," and God is its "visitor" who breaks into its realm.[9] For example, I have frequently heard Pentecostals encourage congregants to worship God to bring God into the service because God inhabits the people's praises. However, Smith believes, despite the common vernacular, implicit within Pentecostalism is *noninterventionist supernaturalism*.[10] This terminology for Smith points to a Pentecostal spirituality that understands the world to be an open system in that God continuously sustains and cares for creation, as demonstrated by the participants' view of God strengthening them.[11] In this view for Smith, matter exists only so far as it is sustained by the Creator who is transcendent. At the same time, the Transcendent One "inheres in immanence." That is, creation is unable to exist without the Creator so that its ontology is a "*gift* from the transcendent Creator such that things exist only insofar they participate in the being of the Creator" (italics in original).[12] Smith's view is incarnational in that when the Word became flesh (John 1:14), God affirmed materiality

---

7. Ibid., 41–42. Smith clarifies, "By dualism I mean a basically Manichean (or Platonic) approach to the world that sees material reality—both bodies and material elements associated with bodies (sexuality, the arts)—as fundamentally bad or evil, and therefore something to be avoided, suppressed, and ultimately escaped." Ibid., 42.

8. Ibid.

9. Ibid., 97.

10. Smith also refers to *noninterventionist supernaturalism* as *enchanted naturalism*.

11. Ibid., 103. Smith also struggles with the word "open" because it suggests the autonomy of nature in which God comes from beyond the boundaries of nature; see ibid., 102. Neumann also describes Pentecostals as viewing nature as an open system; see Neumann, *Pentecostal Experience*, 154.

12. Smith, *Thinking in Tongues*, 100.

(the body).¹³ In his view, then, the autonomy of creation is eschewed for creation participates in God and is sustained by God. This is compatible with the Pentecostal worldview, as Smith writes, "Pentecostal spirituality and practice don't merely expect that God could 'interrupt' the so-called 'order' of nature; rather, they assume that the Spirit is always already at work in creation, animating (and reanimating) bodies, grabbing hold of vocal cords, taking up aspects of creation to manifest the glory of God."¹⁴

Smith addresses this discrepancy between the Pentecostal vernacular and the Pentecostal worldview by proposing terminology that recognizes both God's presence in creation as well as interruptions by the divine; hence, his term *noninterventionist supernaturalism*. Since God is already participating in creation, Smith holds that the world is already "primed" for "special or unique singularities," which are events in which the Spirit uniquely participates in the world. These so-called divine interruptions are referred to by Smith as "more *intense* instances of the Spirit in creation" (italics in original).¹⁵ For instance, Jeremy referred to several occasions when God was present to him during his time of need, such as being able to find things he lost after he prayed. Smith remarks that such language does not speak of God being beyond the boundaries of the world and intervening from outside. Instead, God, who in God's grace is sustaining creation, acts in ways that are uncommonly extraordinary, which are "special or unique singularities."¹⁶

Smith's work is particularly reflected in the understanding of Kirsten and Bob. Kirsten redefined *miracle* as not only being delivered out of suffering but also being sustained in her suffering: "It's just as much of a miracle . . . that he sustains me in suffering as it is that he heals me." Bob broadened the meaning of *intervention* to include both delivering us out of suffering as well as being alongside and comforting us during suffering. In Bob's words, "His deliverance may not be how we think it is. Sometimes he delivers us through the suffering. Sometimes he delivers us out of it." With this in mind, I now sharpen the understanding of divine intervention. Earlier I painted

13. Ibid., 60.
14. Ibid., 101.
15. Ibid., 104.
16. Ibid., 101–5. Smith references Augustine when he writes, "A 'miracle' is not an event that 'breaks' any 'laws' of nature, since nature does not have such a reified character; rather, a miracle is a manifestation of the Spirit's presence that is 'out of the ordinary'; but even the ordinary is a manifestation of the Spirit's presence. Augustine enjoins us to see nature *as* miracle" (italics in original). Ibid., 104–5.

a picture of divine intervention as when God delivers one from extended suffering, as if God is outside of the world and enters into it; however, from this point forward, divine intervention is now expanded to include not only delivering a person out of his suffering but also the concept of sustaining presence, being alongside someone in the midst of his suffering. The importance of this move will become clear as this project progresses.

FINDING MEANING IN SUFFERING

I have argued that the very ethos of Pentecostalism, or the Pentecostal worldview, is a belief in encountering God. While the participants had desired a divine intervention to deliver them from their suffering, they continued to experience God within their suffering through God's ongoing presence and through intense instances of God's presence. With God's presence as a backdrop, I now turn toward how the participants found meaning or interpreted the apparent absence of God, their nothingness, which includes their inability to cause God to intervene (chapter 2).

Defining the Making of Meaning

When my world is no longer operating as it should (see my definition of suffering in chapter 1) and my perception of how the world should work no longer functions within the framework of my worldview, I am forced to make meaning of the experience.[17] In researching the concept "making meaning," I turned to the field of loss and grief because not only did the participants experience real losses (e.g., physical death or personal identity), but their unmet hopes and/or expectations were also losses over which they grieved. It is through their grief they are learning to accept their new path.[18] In turn, this acceptance requires the making of new meaning. Hooyman and Kramer write that in grieving, we seek "for meaning" in order to

---

17. Hooyman and Kramer state, "When faced with a major loss, the world no longer makes sense; there is no comprehensible person-outcome contingency, no guarantee of safety and protection ... A confrontation with death or some other traumatic life event is an attack on our worldview that gives our life meaning and structure ... To rebuild our life, we must again perceive the world and self in positive terms but simultaneously incorporate the loss in our new assumptive world." Hooyman and Kramer, *Living through Loss*, loc. 1270–81.

18. I am dependent on Robert Gonzales for this insight. Gonzales, "Being Present."

"learn how to live in this altered world."[19] In other words, we formulate an interpretation to bring understanding to the internal conflict between our worldview and the events in our lives. This rebuilding of meaning, according to Hooyman and Kramer, is the dominant activity of grief.[20] In the words of Christopraxis, the making of meaning speaks of a reconciliation process. Drawing from Alan Wolfelt's understanding of reconciliation, the participants in their making of meaning entered a process by which they integrated the loss of their hope for a divine intervention from their extended suffering into their life as a whole.[21]

The making of meaning is often accomplished through story. It is part of who we are as humans to ease internal tension by developing some form of understanding through story.[22] Hooyman and Kramer speak of the process of making meaning as being "intensely personal" that involves "weaving an entirely new picture and story about ourselves, our world, and what it means to live."[23] Some use the language of authorship to assist in the process of acceptance by saying, "I'm starting a new chapter."[24] Hooyman and Kramer suggest that through the narration of story, those who experience loss find social validation for their own existence.[25] The narrative is not simply told once but is repeated, which assists in gaining insight and normalizing the loss.[26]

---

19. Hooyman and Kramer, *Living through Loss*, loc. 236–37.

20. Ibid., loc. 680–81.

21. Wolfelt uses the word "reconciliation" to address the process of incorporating a person's loss into his life. Wolfelt, *Understanding Your Grief*, 145–48. Anderson uses the word "reconciliation" to address the ongoing process of a person becoming more whole in Christ (chapter 1). These two usages are complementary, and both speak to the making of meaning in one's life.

22. Brown, in writing about our initial reaction to hurt, speaks of our desire to make meaning by forming a narrative in order to protect ourselves. Brown writes, "Meaning making is in our biology, and our default is often to come up with a story that makes sense, feels familiar, and offers us insight into how best to self-protect." Brown, *Rising Strong*, loc. 1246–47.

23. Hooyman and Kramer, *Living through Loss*, loc. 276–77.

24. Hooyman and Kramer state, "Loss through death, for example, marks the end of one chapter and signifies the beginning of a new one in our lives." Ibid., loc. 277–78.

25. Ibid., loc. 683–84.

26. Hooyman and Kramer comment about those who are experiencing shock or disbelief: "Bereaved individuals may try to gain some control and understanding by gathering information about what happened and telling and retelling the story." Ibid., loc. 761–62.

Since the journey through grief, and thereby acceptance, involves the making of meaning, it is important to explore what this entails. According to Hooyman and Kramer, making meaning is usually defined as including two elements, both of which appear in the stories of the research participants. First, there is the discovery of the loss's "benefits," such as personal development. Second, Hooyman and Kramer state there is "making sense of the loss," such as expanding one's theological perspectives to include this loss. Hooyman and Kramer recognize that these two elements of making meaning may overlap, pointing to permeable boundaries in the categories I outline below.[27] In contrast to their two elements, I perceive three elements surfacing from my research: (1) being transformed in how they relate; (2) making sense out of the suffering; and (3) embracing uncertainty, ambiguity, and mystery. While my first two elements are parallel with the elements of Hooyman and Kramer, I add a third element because it had such a large and strong representation, warranting a separate group.

Being Transformed in How They Relate

One of the ways the participants found meaning in the midst of apparent absence was in their *being transformed in how they relate*. The phrase "being transformed in how they relate" not only speaks of how the participants related to others but also how they related to themselves, to suffering, and to the world around them. I also chose the term "relate" because of my desire to capture the participants' emphasis on *being* over *doing*, or ontology over activity. Growth involves positive changes in one's *being* that yields changes in action, or *doing*. Joan described the difference when she spoke about "performance" and her ability to make others and herself "look good." She said, "I perform. Performance is my bag." For her, there is a difference between *doing* and *being*: "Do. Do. Do. Do. And God's saying, 'I want you to be. And I want you to be so you don't always have to do in order to please me.'" Christy also similarly admitted, "I'm not the same person I used to

---

27. Ibid., loc. 672–75. T. M Luhrmann in her psychological anthropological study of Neocharismatics, which is called *When God Talks Back: Understanding the American Evangelical Relationship with God*, researches how members of the Vineyard hear God. In chapter 9 she draws attention to how Vineyard congregants respond when prayers are not answered, underscoring suffering as an occasion to learn; she writes, "They care about transforming their own suffering, not about explaining why suffering persists. Their faith is practical, not philosophical. Odd as it may seem to a skeptical observer, it can help to have small, specific prayers go wrong"; see Luhrmann, *When God Talks Back*, 299.

be. Most people like me better now because I was always so performance driven . . . I didn't slow down enough . . . to really listen to [people's] needs. It was more like, 'Well, I prayed for that person today. Check it off the list,' instead of like, 'I really wanna pray for your needs.'" Thus, a person may have been doing all the right things, but the actions taken may fail to change who he is; however, when he learns to *be*, it shifts how he relates and interacts with the world around him. As will be discussed more fully below (chapter 6), the participants spoke of adjustments in how they related to others who were suffering, suggesting a change in their ability to be present, which fosters an opportunity for change in others.

Furthermore, *being transformed in how they relate* speaks of the third chapter's discussion of transformation. As previously stated, transformation is a significant element of Pentecostalism, as seen in its juxtaposition to merely experiencing God—namely, a genuine experience with God is authenticated by transformation (chapter 3). For my purposes here, I center on the participants' perception that their suffering generated personal growth, such as changes in perspective and/or character. Contra to the much-desired change in their circumstances, the participants saw transformation in themselves, in their *being*. Christy remarked, "I think that we're taught that we shouldn't suffer as believers . . . but there are benefits to suffering." One benefit for Christy is being able to comfort others with the comfort God has given her since she was unable to offer it previously. Christy genuinely welcomed her transformation: "And would I take it back? I don't know. I've just learned so much through all this . . . If [God] would've brought the miraculous . . . what would our lives look like now? Would I be who I am now? . . . No. (she laughs) No. Maybe I'm kinda liking who I'm becoming." Similarly, Jeremy not only spoke of becoming a better person, but he also implicitly identified transformation as evidence of God's presence in suffering: "In these hard times, I've learned to praise him because his suffering has grown me. I believe he's grown me into making me a better man."

Making Sense out of the Suffering

The second element of the definition of making meaning is *making sense out of the suffering*, which involves forming an interpretation or understanding of the suffering, so it speaks of a cognitive shift. This element of making meaning refers to what Wolfelt describes as a person placing the loss into a frame of reference that she is able to comprehend, which assists her in coping with that loss.[28] As Pentecostals who had expected to experience God, the participants' process of making sense of their suffering focused on their understandings of God. As noted above, making meaning is a very personal process; hence, the research participants varied in how they made sense out of their suffering.

Some of the participants made sense of their suffering by expanding their theological understanding in order to come to terms with their loss. Hooyman and Kramer speak of "need[ing] to change our life's scheme or cognitive representation of our life to be consistent with the loss experience," and provide examples such as rearranging life's priorities or centering on areas of personal control.[29] For the participants, God is seen as intimately involved in their lives; therefore, it is reasonable that the change in how the participants viewed their lives contained a cognitive theological move. For instance, Joan's understanding of God shifted from "if you love me, then this is what you'll do" to "he still loves me even if I don't see an intervention." She said of this modified perception: "[T]hat's a whole new vision of God."

Earlier I wrote of Kirsten and Bob expanding upon the definition of divine intervention. Bob also enlarged his "theology of suffering" when it became a theology of forgiveness during his chronic unemployment. Bob clarified, "We tried our hardest to build relationships with people ... so that we could get to places, and they'd let us down." Bob's expectation of others' assistance in finding employment went unfulfilled; he heard instead apologies for his "falling through the cracks," which meant his circumstances remained unchanged. Since the suffering continued when others disappointed him, Bob discovered he "had to forgive them." Bob said, "The only way to get through the suffering is to forgive." This forgiveness, according to Brown, involves "death and grief," an embracing of the pain.[30] Forgiveness in Bob's situation, then, would include grieving the loss of expected help from others and releasing his unmet expectations in order to embrace

---

28. Wolfelt, *Death and Grief*, 68–69. Hooyman and Kramer similarly write, "In life crises, people are likely to return to their cultural values and beliefs, which they may not use in their daily lives but now help them make sense of their world"; see Hooyman and Kramer, *Living through Loss*, loc. 475–76.

29. Hooyman and Kramer, *Living through Loss*, loc. 1293–94. Wolfelt also speaks of changes in theology to accommodate the loss; see Wolfelt, *Death and Grief*, 68–69.

30. Brown, *Rising Strong*, 2169–78.

his ongoing arduous situation. This expands his theology of suffering to include "one of forgiveness."

A couple of the participants also made sense out of their suffering by becoming aware of their exalting God through their suffering. This may be included in the description of Hooyman and Kramer when they write of "modify[ing] our perception of the loss by reinterpreting the event more positively."[31] This was particularly the case for Joan, who came to embrace exalting God through her suffering with the help of her ongoing reading and studying. After Joan realized she had misinterpreted a personal prophecy concerning "greater things" as being equated to greater status or doing, she made sense out of her suffering when she reinterpreted "greater" as suffering and as "more being instead of doing." For instance, she voiced how her favorite book, *The Making of a Leader* by J. Robert Clinton, recently came alive in a new dimension. By using examples such as the Apostle Paul and Watchman Nee, the author describes different stages of a leader, one of which contains difficult tests for the mature leader that are for God's purpose and glory. She then read to me her journal entry written just days prior to the interview:

> I thought my latter years would be full of rest, enjoyment of grandchildren, and some travel and then enter heaven at the end in a blaze of glory. My idea of retirement was fun and relaxation. It never occurred to me that my greatest struggles would be now at the end of my life, and yet that makes sense. God has been preparing me and training me for the most difficult circumstances and challenges of life.

While some participants trusted in God's will amidst their suffering, a couple of participants made sense out of their suffering by reevaluating their beliefs about the dynamic between God's will and human will. Bob spoke of the interaction between divine and human will in that he now believes that God's will is not necessarily prescribed in every detail of his life. He stated, "I think [God] has a general will, and that's that his Gospel, his salvation, goes to the ends of the earth. And how does that happen? That's gonna be up to you." This means the individual chooses how God's will is accomplished. For Bob, he fulfills God's will by being empowered by the Spirit to be God's witness wherever he is and whatever he does, "whether that's through engineering, ministry, or teaching or whatever."

---

31. Hooyman and Kramer, *Living through Loss*, loc. 1297–98.

Some participants made sense of their experience of suffering by becoming aware of a specific insight. Lindsey spoke of the importance of gaining some understanding about personal suffering when she disagreed with a minister who said, "We don't have to understand. We just need to trust." She asserted, "That always doesn't work for people . . . They wanna understand." Thus, Lindsey had insights about the deaths of both her father and brother. Concerning her father's death, a friend "called and shared the devotional . . . from *Our Daily Bread*, and it was called, 'The Right Time?'" With her father dying on that day; the daily devotion being "The Right Time?"; and her friend being led of the Spirit to call the family, Lindsey was able to say, "I wanted him another thirty years, but maybe this is the right time." She wondered if God was sparing her father from her brother's six-year illness, making her father's death the right time. In the case of her brother, who had not been serving God when he became ill, "he came back to the Lord." It is to be noted, Lindsey's ability to make meaning of her father's death occurred through the ministry of others (chapter 5). Kyle came to terms with his daughter's death when he discovered a Scripture that indicated, "God takes away the young to keep them from trouble." It brought him "tremendous peace" when he perceived that God had allowed his daughter to die in order for her "to avoid something in the future." For Jeremy, although he had been in an accident, he believed that God had protected him in that he had survived. Jeremy was confident God kept him alive because God still has plans for him.

Embracing Uncertainty, Ambiguity, and Mystery

A third element in the making of meaning that emerged from the stories of the participants is *embracing uncertainty, ambiguity, and mystery*. The words "uncertainty, ambiguity, and mystery" suggest limited understanding while being synonymous with unpredictability, obscurity, and incomprehensibility, respectively. Occasionally, when there is the absence of complete understanding, as Hooyman and Kramer claim, "reasons that cannot be understood or questions that cannot be answered have to be integrated as just that: something that cannot be comprehended but must be accepted and tolerated."[32] As Lindsey stated, "I know God can heal. I've seen it. I've been healed. I have no idea why he does what he does. I do know he is loving . . . Sometimes we kind of feel like we get a glimmer of

32. Ibid., loc. 1305–6.

maybe this is why he did a certain thing, but other times we have no idea, but we know he still loves us, and we can still love him." Thus, mystery with its ambiguity is embraced.

The word "embrace" is appropriate in that *embracing* has a connotation of a gentle holding that is willing to release one's grasp.[33] When the participants embraced uncertainty, ambiguity, and mystery, they simultaneously held their ongoing suffering alongside their much-desired removal of suffering, admitting to their own limited insight. As Bob suggested, "Why are we failing to move forward into whatever it is that God has for us . . . unless that's suffering . . . Have we been willing to accept it? Maybe that's what he has for us . . . and are we able to receive that so that we can use that to witness for him? Or do we see it as a bad thing?" At the same time, Bob strove to embrace the uncertainty: "God has always provided for us, and I know he always will provide for us. I know there's something next that he's gonna take us to. And I think the challenge for me has been to remain in the present, not to be holding onto the past or worrying about the future 'cuz we're not there yet." Thus, embracing signifies a gentle holding of uncertainty, ambiguity, and mystery alongside suffering while having a willingness to release the grasp if predictability, clarity, and comprehension should come and/or the specific suffering is removed.

Embracing also allows for a tension to exist between God's presence and apparent absence (nothingness), and one is sustained in this tension by trust. The tension appears in that as one acknowledges absence, one concurrently recognizes presence. Hooyman and Kramer indicate this when they speak of presence and absence in loss: "Loss always contains some ambiguity, even when it is anticipated . . . Part of this ambiguity is being able to hold the opposing ideas of absence and presence in our minds at the same time, to live concurrently with joy and sorrow . . . Life and death each require the other, and without both, neither would be a meaningful concept."[34] That is, one does not know presence without absence and visa versa. For the participants, this embrace was accomplished through trust, not certainty. Certainty involves the concrete, so trust is unnecessary with certainty; however, trust by its definition requires the unknown. Joan reiterated this when she defined faith as "the substance of things hoped for,

---

33. I am grateful for Cynthia Crysdale for this clarification between the words "clinging" and "embracing" in that "clinging" fears loss and separation while "embracing" does not. Crysdale, *Embracing Travail*, 26.

34. Hooyman and Kramer, *Living through Loss*, loc. 263–66.

the evidence of things not seen." She admitted her desire for the "concrete," but she was "having to trust him in the dark." Similarly, Brown defines faith as the "place of mystery, where we find the courage to believe in what we cannot see and the strength to let go of our fear of uncertainty."[35] Kyle supported this, "The pain is in me, but, yes, I embrace the mystery of God's greatness and his almightiness, but down here on earth I don't get the answers necessarily that I think I want. So, yeah, there is a mysteriousness to all of this, but rather than push it away and say, 'God, I don't trust you anymore,' I am gonna trust." The participants' trust was not in their own ability to trust but in their God. This was seen in Kirsten's comment, "Jesus didn't heal every sick person that he was around and neither did the disciples, and they did heal people, and if I become one of those someday, I'll be eternally grateful. I haven't given up on being healed. I still believe God is able, and I trust him, but I also trust him if I'm not healed." Trust, then, centers on God, not on some required measure of personal faith.

This trust implies an embracing of human finitude. For Joan and Kyle, the embracing of finitude appeared as no longer questioning "Why?" and accepting the lack of answers. Kyle explained, "I began to really question the foundations of my own spiritual experience, and that's when I began to really stand up for myself in the sense that I came to the conclusion that for me personally I cannot ask 'Why' questions of God. I have to trust him . . . and that means sometimes letting go of the 'Whys' and saying, 'Okay, Father, I do not understand this . . . but I trust you anyways.'" Similarly, some participants recognized their own finitude when they admitted to not knowing the reasons some are healed and others are not, such as Christy being healed of seizures, but Jason not being healed of mental illness. This recognition expresses humility as one's own limitations are embraced. As Christy said, "[M]y school of thought is: God can. Maybe he would choose not to for other reasons. Reasons that we can't understand. Reasons that are bigger than ourselves"; thus, when praying for others, she currently focuses on God's receiving of the glory whether the miracle occurs now, later, or never.

This embracing of uncertainty, ambiguity and mystery may also provide comfort. Both Lindsey and Danielle were comforted in knowing their loved ones were healed in heaven, indicating a trust in God no matter how God heals. Danielle clarified, "[I]f he healed Reagan on earth, it's kind of

---

35. Brown, *The Gifts of Imperfection*, 90.

like that's great and wonderful, but I believe in the healing in heaven. So you win both ways."

Yet, trust does not always insist on a conclusion to the arduous path, indicating trust is resilient. Joan remarked, "My perception has changed in that it has grown, and I truly, truly trust God. I trust him for the unknown. I know that he's been there before me, and he's going before me. I truly have peace, and it doesn't mean I don't get frustrated or get angry." Jeremy helped me see a connection between presence and trust, and in so doing he linked his making of meaning to how he experienced God in suffering. He said, "Has it been easy? No. But God never said it would be easy. Has he expected me to step out in faith and trust him? Yup. He's asked me to do that. But if we do that, he'll be there." This is not a relationship of *quid pro quo* (i.e., if you do this, I will do this), but I liken it to a discovery. As he trusted God, he discovered God had not abandoned him but was present to him. The image that comes to my mind is the exercise when a person falls backwards in trust and realizes that the friend is present and trustworthy. This means I trust God because I believe God is present, and simultaneously, God's presence with me generates an opportunity for trust (see below). Thus, I have come full circle: the participants experienced God as present in their suffering; one way they made meaning was through trusting God; and this leads to the discovery that God is present and trustworthy. Joan signified this, "I'm learning to trust God more, and my beliefs about God is that he is all knowing and that he has gone ahead of me and been where I'm going to be and that he has prepared the way for me and that I'm learning to lean on him more. And I'm learning that he's a good God even when I'm going through difficult times. And that he will bring me through it and that I will be better as a result."

CONVERSING WITH THE FOURTH GOSPEL

In the background of the above section the participants had an understanding that God was present in their making of meaning. This became clearer for me when I connected the participants' meaning making with their experience of God in suffering through Jeremy's story, creating a link to how one experiences God in suffering to how one interprets his suffering. Through this connection, *presence* becomes the chief theme amidst the experience of apparent absence. Since presence underlines not only how the participants experienced God but also how they made meaning, I now reflect on these experiences through the lens of Scripture, focusing on the Gospel of John's emphasis on presence.

Presence is a major theme in the Fourth Gospel. Given that in chapter 2 I have already examined the apparent absence of Jesus in John and that I have presented that one understands presence through absence, I now seek to portray Jesus's presence in this Gospel. This is accomplished in two phases: (1) by illustrating presence as a major theme of John by exploring the prologue (John 1:1–18) and the cleansing of the Temple (John 2:13–25), two introductory pericopes of John; and (2) by discussing more fully how presence is connected to meaning making as seen in the incarnation. In these phases the reader is to note not only the presence of Jesus but also the elements and sub-themes of making meaning that appear (i.e., transformation, exalting God, God and human wills, uncertainty/ambiguity/mystery, trust, and acknowledgement of suffering). Furthermore, since presence is such a dominating theme of John, I am unable to highlight all the areas that it appears due to space constraints. Therefore, I have chosen to stress two pericopes at the beginning of the Fourth Gospel that establish this theme. This is followed by a discussion on *presence* and *believing*, noticing occasions on how these interact in John.

Introduction of Presence in John

The principal theme of presence in the Fourth Evangelist is implicitly introduced in the Gospel's prologue (1:1–18) by suggesting God is with humanity in two ways: (1) God walking as Jesus among humanity in this suffering world; and (2) God being present with humanity within Jesus's being in the divine and human natures.[36] John speaks of the Creator (1:1–3, 15) coming among those he created and being rejected (1:10–11); this indicates the divine living among us on earth and experiencing suffering. Hence, Jesus embraced this world's suffering through his existence in the world, and he embraced his own suffering, as seen by his endurance of rejection, crucifixion, and death, or the suffering that occurred in his own being. Additionally, verses 10, 11, and 14 reference the divine becoming human,

---

36. Thompson notes that not all the major themes of John are introduced in the prologue, but one theme presented that is germane to my topic is "the embodied Word of God." Thompson, *John*, 26.

which means God is residing with humanity within the one person, Jesus the Christ (known as the hypostatic union).[37]

While there are seven "I am" statements in this Gospel, the prologue points toward four of them that are in the Gospel, indicating God's presence being among us.[38] When John writes in verse 4, "*In him was life*, and the life was the light of mankind" (italics in original), he is referring to these four statements: I am the bread of life (John 6:35); I am the resurrection and the life (John 11:25); I am the way, and the truth, and the life (John 14:6), and I am the light of the world (John 8:12). Thompson writes that "I am" statements that are followed by a "predicate" are "characteristic of divine speech in the Old Testament."[39] Thompson points out that when Jesus states, "I am the bread of life" (John 6:35) or "I am the light of the world" (John 8:12), he is making a declaration that "there is no other bread of life, no other light for the world." By using "the" (definite article), Jesus excludes any others from "these realities."[40] Thompson asserts, "What he offers is himself: he offers the bread of life because he himself is life (John 1:4)."[41] These four "I am" statements mentioned above are juxtaposed to Jesus's absence (two of which were used as illustrations in chapter 2) and are placed alongside

---

37. The hypostatic union refers to Jesus having two natures: being both fully God and fully human. Yong writes that unlike the Synoptic Gospels, which emphasize Jesus's humanity, John begins with the divinity of Jesus. However, it was not until the fifth century that the early church fathers declared at the Council of Chalcedon, "We, then, following the holy Fathers, all with one consent, teach men to confess one and the same Son, our Lord Jesus Christ, the same perfect in Godhead and also perfect in manhood . . . one and the same Christ, Son, Lord, Only-begotten, to be acknowledged in two natures, inconfusedly, unchangeably, indivisibly, inseparably; the distinction of natures being by no means taken away by the union, but rather the property of each nature being preserved, and concurring in one Person and one Subsistence, not parted or divided into two persons, but one and the same Son, and only begotten, God the Word, the Lord Jesus Christ." Yong, *Renewing Christian Theology*, loc. 4757–80, 7103–9.

38. Thompson lists the seven "I am" statements: I am the bread of life (6:35); I am the light of the world (8:12; 9:5); I am the door for the sheep (10:7, 9); I am the good shepherd (10:11, 14); I am the resurrection and the life (11:25); I am the way, the truth, and the life (14:6); and I am the vine (15:1). Thompson comments, "These are statements in which Jesus identifies himself with a particular entity or figure and more specifically, with entities that give life or can be identified as life itself (11:25; 14:6)." Thompson, *John*, 157.

39. Ibid., 158.

40. Ibid., 160.

41. Ibid.

believing, a major theme discussed below. That is, *presence* frequently appears together with *absence* as well as *belief* in John.

The references to the Word being the light in the prologue (1:4–5, 7–9) are linked to another theme that is not mentioned in the prologue but is connected to Jesus's presence, which is the Jewish feasts and festivals. Thompson highlights that John's framework constructs the events of Jesus's life around the occurrence of significant Jewish celebrations.[42] In this way, Jewish institutions become the foci of Jesus's presence in John. Thus, when the prologue speaks of "light," it alludes to Jesus's statement, "I am the light of the world" (John 8:12), which in turn directs our attention to the Feast of Tabernacles.[43] The connection is seen, as Thompson remarks, by this "I am" statement being tied to the traditional practice of "the lighting of the golden candlesticks" at the Feast of Tabernacles.[44] As Thompson asserts, the Jewish rituals, the Law, the festivals, and Abraham in John are not cast off by Jesus, as some might assert, but "he does subordinate them all to himself."[45] He, then, is not their replacement but a superior fulfillment. This means the

---

42. Ibid., 17.

43. The Feast of the Tabernacles (also known as the Festival of Booths) is a fall harvest festival that remembers the Israelites' wanderings in the wilderness after being delivered from Egypt. According to Leviticus 23:33–44, the people are to live in small huts for seven days during the Festival of Tabernacles to remind them of the temporary dwellings in which their ancestors lived. This is to be a festival of rejoicing in which the people on the first day take branches from "majestic trees" and "rejoice before the LORD your God for seven days" (Lev 23:40).

44. Thompson, *John*, 167.

45. Ibid., 229. For example, Gary Burge highlights the theme of presence in the Gospel of John by arguing that Jesus's presence "replaces" Jewish institutions and festivals; Burge, *John*, 41nn32. Thompson explains when writing of Jesus's turning of the water into wine (2:1–11), "[T]he contrast between the 'good wine' . . . and the 'lesser' . . . draws on the biblical portrayal of the coming age of salvation as surpassing all previous eras in both the quality and quantity of God's blessings . . . The blessings of this age follow and surpass the bounty of earlier blessings. The move is not lateral, from the old reality of 'Judaism' to a parallel and new reality in Jesus, outside of Judaism; rather, the move is forward, from Scriptural hope and expectation to the extravagant provision expected in the coming age . . . [B]iblical (and Jewish) eschatology has a built-in expectation of 'replacement' since the coming messianic age surpasses the former in righteousness, justice, purity, and holiness. But this 'replacement' of the old age with the age of abundant blessing in the Messiah is akin to the turning of a page to a new chapter in the narrative, rather than discarding the old story and introducing an entirely new one. Put differently, Jesus does not replace 'Judaism': as Messiah, he fulfills the hopes for God's promised blessed age. The choice wine has been saved until the end and is now offered in abundance. This is the next chapter in the story of scriptural hopes and promises." Thompson, *John*, 62–63.

Who is Present in Absence?

Fourth Evangelist is demonstrating that Jesus's presence is greater than the Jewish institutions and celebrations, not replacing them.

Jesus's cleansing of the Temple (John 2:13–22), the second introductory pericope, accentuates presence in connection to the Jewish feast of Passover and to the Temple. Jesus, similar to other Jews, went to Jerusalem to celebrate the Passover (2:13).[46] Thompson comments that those who are participating in the Passover are required to be purified (John 11:55—12:1; 18:28), which means they must go to the Temple; however, in this pericope the Evangelist is centering on the necessity for "the temple itself" to be cleansed.[47] As Jesus enters the Temple, he is disturbed when he sees those who are selling animals necessary for the various sacrifices and those who are exchanging the monies to provide the appropriate coins for the temple tax.[48] If these activities are in the court of the Gentiles, as some commentators assert, it hinders the ability of the Gentiles to be able to worship God.[49] Thus, Jesus proclaims that they are to stop making his Father's house a house of profiteering.[50] Melissa Archer stresses that when Jesus refers to God as

---

46. The Passover commemorates the night that the Israelites placed the blood of a lamb on the doorposts so that the angel of the Lord would *pass over* their households, sparing their eldest son and delivering them out of slavery in Egypt (Exod 12:1–27). Thompson notes, "Passover had not always been a pilgrimage feast" for there was no command in Exodus 12 to travel to Jerusalem; however, other Scriptures, such as 2 Chronicles 30, command the traveling to Jerusalem for the Passover. Thompson, *John*, 70.

47. Ibid.

48. Travelers needed to purchase animals for sacrifices since it would be too difficult to travel with them. Additionally, a temple tax required a particular coin, which Morris states "Tyrian coinage" was preferred. Morris, *The Gospel of John*, 170. However, the reasons given by scholars for this preference vary. See Morris for a fuller explanation.

49. Melissa Archer writes, "If, as commonly noted by scholars, the selling of sacrificial animals was taking place in the court of the Gentiles, then the central purpose of the Temple as a place of worship *for all people* was being thwarted by commerce!" (italics in original); see Archer, "Worship in Spirit and Truth," 8. Morris also believes the selling occurred in the court of the Gentiles; see Morris, *The Gospel of John*, 169–72. However, Keener holds that while hindering the worship of the Gentiles is a possible reason for Jesus's action, it "is not the reason emphasized" by John, but rather Jesus was challenging "the Jerusalem aristocracy that controlled the temple system"; see Keener, *The Gospel of John*, 524.

50. Thompson references the contrast of the Greek text: "The business of buying and selling had transformed 'my Father's house' (*ho oikos tou patros mou*) into a 'house of trade' (*oikos emporiou*) . . . This contrast indicates what is at stake: either the temple is a house of human commerce, or it is the house of God, a holy place fit for worship of the holy God." Thompson, *John*, 71.

Father, the readers are reminded of the prologue's description (John 1:14) of Jesus being the *one and only* (*monogenēs*), "and they will learn throughout the rest of the Gospel of Jesus' relationship to and identification with the Father."[51] That is to say, in Jesus the divine is walking among us. Since he is the *one and only*, one reason for his driving out the moneychangers, sellers, and the animals is to make a way for all to come into the presence of God, unencumbered by business practices.[52] Later, John will assert that Jesus is that way (John 14:6), the one sent to save the whole world (John 3:16–17; 4:42; 12:47–52).

When Jesus is questioned by which authority he commits such acts, Jesus not only links himself to being God's temple but also predicts his death and resurrection (2:19, 21–22). For the initial audience, as Archer remarks, the prologue (1:14) has already indicated that Jesus "tabernacled amongst humanity," which "transfers Israel's most sacred liturgical symbol—the tabernacle/tent of meeting/Temple—to Jesus." As the "glory of God" (*Shekinah*) appeared "in the tabernacle," so now the glory of God appears "in Jesus."[53] Archer notices Jesus has not only stated this is God's dwelling and God is his Father, but he is also making "a claim about himself."[54] That is, he is the Temple. Archer perceives that the readers have already heard that Jesus is the Lamb of God (John 1:29, 36).[55] Therefore, during the first Passover mentioned in this Gospel, Jesus implies he is the Lamb who is the tabernacle of the Holy God who will be the only necessary sacrifice by dying and rising again.[56] Moreover, this Temple does not need to be cleansed for he is divine. As Thompson comments, "In John, the risen Jesus is the new, purified, and indestructible Temple that is truly the dwelling of God."[57] As

---

51. Archer, "Worship in Spirit and Truth," 8.

52. Archer proposes that through the clearing of the temple Jesus eliminates any way to make sacrifices to God, leaving only himself as God's Lamb, as the remaining sacrifice, and she connects this to John the Baptist's statement in John 1 as the one who takes away the sins of the world. Ibid., 7.

53. Ibid., 3.

54. Ibid., 8.

55. Ibid., 4.

56. Archer states, "Given the emphasis throughout the Fourth Gospel on the Jewish feasts—Passover in particular, it seems plausible that the hearers of the Gospel would understand the designation of Jesus as the Lamb of God to refer primarily to Jesus as the paschal lamb, a point that will be reinforced in the description of Jesus' passion." Ibid., 4–5.

57. Thompson, *John*, 69.

an additional note, verses 22 and 23 of this pericope connect *presence* to *believing* (see below).

Characteristics of Presence in John

Having explored presence as a major theme in John, I now turn to characteristics of presence as portrayed in the Fourth Gospel. As humans, we may have a tendency to associate mere presence as being impractical in comparison to an overt action of deliverance. This is illustrated in a current television commercial on protection against identity theft in which robbers enter a bank and command everyone to lay on the ground. The security guard, who is present in the lobby, simply stands by the patrons who are lying on the floor, causing one customer to insist that the guard takes care of the situation. The so-called guard replies that he is not a guard but "a security *monitor*." His job is to inform others only when there is a robbery. He pauses and calmly states, "There's a robbery." Thus, the failure to visibly act and intervene in the midst of clear and present danger is portrayed in the commercial as being useless, in effect leaving the customer abandoned. However, contrary to this portrayal by American advertising, presence contains some necessary and essential characteristics that may be overlooked by a pragmatically oriented Pentecostal, such as myself. These characteristics, which are in John's Gospel, not only illuminate and expand on the significance of divine presence in the research participants' lives, but they also support and enhance how the participants made meaning out of their suffering.

A fundamental characteristic of presence is its communication of worth and value. This communication occurs in two ways. First, when John says the Word enters the world that the Word had created (John 1:10) and physically lives among humanity on earth, this embodied action communicates the world's worth. Second, God also demonstrates the worth of humanity in Jesus's ontological essence of divinity being present (united) with humanity (John 1:14). This worth to God is evidenced in God's sending of the Son, which flows out of God's love for the world (John 3:16). Thus, it is God's love for humanity that causes God to be present with human beings (both physically and ontologically), conveying the existential worth and value of humans.[58] Therefore, through these embodied actions in the

---

58. That worth is also communicated through the physical aspect of embodiment. Smith observes that when God became human flesh, God is implicitly declaring the

person of Jesus, the divine is eternally saying to humanity, "You matter to me." In the words of Christopraxis, when Jesus enters humanity's nothingness, humanity finds its worth.

The Fourth Evangelist also exemplifies worth through the divine being present as the good shepherd as seen in Jesus's statement, "I am the good shepherd" (see John 10:11–18). The good shepherd is unlike the hired hands who are not the owners of the sheep, implying the sheep are of little worth to them. The hired hands' own lives are of more value to themselves than the lives of the sheep they oversee. This is in stark contrast to the good shepherd who values the lives of the sheep over his own life, as seen in the words, "I lay down my life for the sheep" (John 10:15). The good shepherd's presence is seen in Thompson's comment that this shepherd "sustains his flock" and provides life for the sheep.[59] In Thompson's words, "Jesus' death brings life" to the world.[60] Thompson, noting this pericope follows the healing of the man born blind who was thrown out of the synagogue, perceives how this may encourage other disciples. She writes, "And even as the good shepherd calls together, guards, and sustains his flock, so Jesus calls together, guards, and sustains his people who no longer have a sure place within the synagogue, but who hear and respond to the voice of this good shepherd."[61] In similar fashion, the original audience may have also experienced being thrown out of the synagogue and faced persecution; thus, they were being reminded that Jesus was sustaining them, demonstrating their value. Similarly, when the participants spoke of being sustained by God in their suffering, they were implicitly stating God was validating their worth.

The foundational characteristic of worth inherent within presence also leads to other characteristics of presence. That is, by communicating worth, presence honors the human will and fosters opportunities for transformation, forgiveness, and trust. While each characteristic is intricately connected to the other, I will speak of each one separately. To begin,

---

goodness of creation, and when Jesus was resurrected with a physical body, God reinforced the value and the goodness that the divine has placed on human bodies, specifically, and creation, generally. In speaking of the dualistic understanding that some Pentecostals have held in which physical bodies are wicked and are to be shunned, Smith writes, "This runs counter to God's own affirmation of the goodness of material creation (including bodies, Gen. 1:27), as well as the reaffirmation of the body in the incarnation (John 1:14) and resurrection." Smith, *Thinking in Tongues*, 42.

59. Thompson, *John*, 220.
60. Ibid., 226.
61. Ibid., 220.

Who is Present in Absence?

presence honors the human will, refusing to force one's own will on the other. When Jesus was bodily present in this suffering world, individuals physically encountered the embodied Word of God. As Thompson comments, in these encounters in John "none of them remains unchanged," pointing toward the opportunity for transformation.[62] These changes occur as Jesus respects the human will, allowing for a variety of human responses. Thompson explains that some encounters result in the individuals becoming Jesus's followers; some wrestle with Jesus's "claims and challenges"; others doubt Jesus's "authority"; and some appear to believe but waver in their belief.[63] The respect for the human will, then, is portrayed as the people are free to respond to Jesus with belief or unbelief in the Fourth Gospel.

The above discussion leads to the second characteristic of presence in that presence fosters an opportunity for transformation. This means that the transformation may or may not occur, but the occasion for it is provided through presence.[64] When one communicates worth to the other and respects the other's will through presence, an opportunity is created for change without forcing the change. Such a presence that refuses to force transformation is evidenced in the Fourth Gospel by Jesus being present on this earth without the removal of all its suffering. For example, not only did Jesus refrain from keeping Lazarus from dying, which generated loss and grief for Mary and Martha (John 11), but he also refused to eradicate his own suffering, enduring rejection, beatings, crucifixion, and death (John 18, 19). Jesus, instead, enters into the suffering of this world as one of us, permitting the suffering world to continue while he remains present to it. Kirsten indirectly articulated this type of presence when she noted Jesus's words in John 12:8, "For you will always have the poor with you." Kirsten found meaning in these words in that they indicated the lasting quality of suffering; thus, she asserted, "[W]hy shouldn't I be the one that suffers instead of somebody else?" While presence does not demand change, transformation may transpire in the midst of it. This was evidenced in the story of Kyle, who illustrated the power of Jesus's presence to foster an opportunity for change when he spoke of "theophostic prayer." *Theophostic prayer* refers to "a type of prayer where the individual that's praying with you leads you in prayer with the direction of the Holy Spirit to the place of

---

62. Ibid., 42.

63. Ibid.

64. I am indebted to Gonzales for this understanding of presence. Gonzales, "Living Compassion."

your pain and then invites Jesus into that." Kyle described a powerful healing experience when he saw that he was not alone while being abused as a child, but Jesus was present with him.

Since presence respects human will and thereby offers an opportunity for transformation, it also creates occasions for forgiveness when necessary. This is forcefully illustrated in one of Jesus's personal relationships: Jesus's refusal to stop Peter from denying him. Although Jesus forewarns Peter (John 13:36–38), Peter is allowed to fail when he disowns Jesus. Such a denial points towards Peter's lack of presence alongside Jesus in Jesus's suffering, which would have offered support to Jesus, but instead the absence of support contributed to Jesus's own suffering. Jesus, however, embraces this suffering as seen in the forgiveness and restoration of Peter (John 21:7–19). Thus, while presence upholds the human will in John's Gospel, it also supports an opportunity for forgiveness and reconciliation. By respecting the human will, presence accepts that humans inflict suffering for which forgiveness is necessary. Forgiveness goes into the offender's world, grieves, accepts, and releases the pain. In other words, forgiveness enters the nothingness, the hurt that should not have been, and embraces and releases it. Thus, the human will is upheld in this Gospel while concurrently holding out an opportunity for forgiveness.

Kirsten made sense of her suffering by understanding the reality of human will. Kirsten, in speaking of her abuse as a child, said bluntly, "It was never God's will for it to happen, but it did." She then pointed to humanity's free will that is able to choose to respond to God's love. Kirsten explained, "God has never done anything to stop me from sinning except invite me to respond to his wooing. But for people who aren't even aware of the Holy Spirit . . . how much less are they gonna respond, and . . . I was in the hands of cruel people who . . . weren't responding to God." Similarly, Kirsten perceived that people are also free to intervene because God expects "us to be his hands and feet in a very literal way." This means for her, "we fail to operate in the opportunities that God gives us to be like him" when we allow suffering to continue. It is at this point when people fail to intervene, that a theology of suffering moves to one of forgiveness (see Bob's comments above). As discussed in the next chapter, the members of the body of Christ have a free will to enter into the other's nothingness and participate in Christ's ministry to the sufferer, cultivating opportunities for change in the midst of uncertainty.

Who is Present in Absence?

Not only does Jesus's presence generate an opportunity for transformation by respecting human will and inviting forgiveness, it also fosters an opportunity for trust, as demonstrated in the previous paragraphs when some responded to Jesus's presence with belief. An occasion for nurturing trust is not unexpected when one recalls that the Gospel of John's purpose (as explained in chapter 2 above) is so that the readers "may believe" or "continue to believe" (John 20:31), making *believing* a chief theme.[65] John's understanding of *believe* is not simply equated to Western culture's usage of it (e.g., an expression of an opinion as in "I believe such and such a team will win" or intellectually holding to certain doctrines such as "I believe Jesus Christ is the Son of God"). According to Thompson, the Fourth Gospel connects those who believe to those who are followers of Jesus; thus, people are invited both to initially believe and "to continue in faith." When *believe* is used without an object, as Thompson notes, it basically denotes "commitment or trust," pointing toward a faith that endures.[66] Additionally, Thompson perceives *believe* for John includes knowing information about Jesus that involves "also understanding who he is." Yet, knowing and understanding Jesus are not "separated from the actual practice" of being his disciple.[67] In other words, cognitive beliefs are not disconnected from one's being and one's actions. Keener agrees, "'Believe' . . . is a conviction of truth on which one stakes one's life and actions, not merely passive assent to a fact."[68]

Belief and unbelief are also juxtaposed to the pericopes of the absence of Jesus, as mentioned in chapter 2 of this project. One such instance occurs in John 20 in which Jesus's body is expected to be in the tomb, but it is not

---

65. Keener comments, "John employs the verb [*pisteuō*] 98 times, whereas the three Synoptics employ it 30 times, and Paul 54 times (by contrast, Paul employs the noun 142 times, the Synoptics 24 times, and John never). Viewed from another angle, cognates of this term appear on the average page of the Greek text of the NT according to the following distribution: 0.09 in Revelation; 0.24 in the Synoptics; 0.55 in Acts; 1.10 in the Catholic Epistles; 1.25 in Paul; 1.31 in Hebrews; and 1.48 in John. That John emphasizes faith heavily cannot be disputed." Keener, *The Gospel of John*, 326.

66. Thompson, *John*, 304. Keener also observes that John underscores a faith that perseveres; see Keener, *The Gospel of John*, 327.

67. Thompson, *John*, 304. Rudolph Bultmann also writes, "Knowledge is . . . a constitutive element in genuine faith"; see Bultmann and Weiser, "πιστεύω," 227.

68. Keener, *The Gospel of John*, 327. Bultmann also sees that John's usage of *believe* involves a turning away from the world "to the invisible and sovereign" (20:29; see also 15:19; 17:14) as well as abiding in Jesus (8:31–32); see Bultmann and Weiser, "πιστεύω," 223–26.

there. In the midst of this apparent absence and the uncertainty, ambiguity, and mystery that it generates, belief is evident but only in the beloved disciple (20:8). Mary is so convinced Jesus's body is stolen (20:2, 13, 15) that she fails to recognize Jesus but assumes him to be the gardener (20:14–15). When Jesus appears to the disciples who are in a locked room because they fear the Jewish leaders (20:19), Thomas is not among them; hence, when the other disciples report of Jesus's appearance, Thomas boldly proclaims (20:25), "Unless I see the wounds . . . I will never believe it!" Thompson remarks, "Thomas simply wants what the others have been granted: an encounter with the risen Jesus."[69] Thus, Thomas is similar to many Pentecostals: he desires an encounter with Jesus.[70]

Within a few days Jesus again appears to the disciples along with Thomas, and Thomas now sees and believes. When Jesus invites Thomas to touch the wounds, Thomas exclaims (20:28), "My Lord and my God!" This declaration, Thompson remarks, "acknowledges the inclusion of Jesus, the Word made flesh, in the identity of that one called 'the only true God' (1:1, 14)," thereby forming the other bookend of the confession of faith in the prologue (1:1, 14).[71] Thomas believes in that he now knows Jesus is alive, and he understands who Jesus is. It is unfortunate that Thomas has been labeled as the one who doubts since Mary and the other disciples also did not believe until they saw Jesus.[72] The disciples and Mary are similar to others in the Fourth Gospel who see and then believe; thus, they are included in the repetitive pattern of *seeing is believing* in John.[73] In other words, while Jesus's physical presence fosters an opportunity for trust, Jesus takes special notice of those who *believe without seeing* in his response to Thomas, "Have you believed because you have seen me? Blessed are the people who have not seen and yet have believed" (20:29). According to

---

69. Thompson, *John*, 424.

70. Thompson writes, "No doubt he [Thomas] gives voice to the desires, the longings, of many believers since his day, who simply want to see Jesus." Ibid.

71. Ibid., 425.

72. Thompson states, "Thomas's adamant refusal ought not to be very surprising. Up to this point, only the beloved disciple has believed without seeing the risen Lord (20:8)." Ibid., 424.

73. For example, in John 4:46–54 in the healing of the official's son, the official's household saw the son was healed, and they believed; in 11:45, after Lazarus is raised from the dead, John states, "Then many of the people, who had come with Mary and had seen the things Jesus did, believed in him." The reader is to also note that both of these cases contain the absence of Jesus as well.

Who is Present in Absence?

Thompson, Jesus is not criticizing Thomas for seeing and then believing and neither is Jesus stating that one is "*more* blessed" if one believes without seeing (italics in original). For Thompson, "Such faith simply arises in different circumstances or is catalyzed by different experiences."[74] That is, this trust surfaces amidst uncertainty and ambiguity. Ambiguity exists when one does not physically *see* Jesus today but still experiences his presence. Such an encounter with Jesus fosters an opportunity for trust in him. As previously noted in chapter 2 above, John is encouraging his readers to have encounters with Jesus similar to those in his Gospel. These encounters with Jesus nurture occasions for trust such as seen in the lives of the research participants. As Jeremy said, "The truth is there's been some really tough times, but God's been there. We have to trust him." Jeremy, like the original audience, couples presence with trust amidst his experience of uncertainty, ambiguity, and mystery.

CONCLUSION

Having discussed how the participants experienced God in their suffering and how they interpreted their suffering, I have stressed how divine presence connects both of these aspects. The participants experienced both God's ongoing presence (apparent absence in presence) and intense instances of God's presence in their suffering (presence in apparent absence). Moreover, they made meaning of their suffering, which included being changed in relating, making sense out of their suffering, and embracing uncertainty, ambiguity, and mystery. By conversing with the Gospel of John, I pointed out that when Jesus ministered through his presence to the participants, they were valued, which included honoring their will. Through Jesus's presence there are also opportunities to be transformed, to be forgiven, and to trust. As I move into the next chapter, I will seek to show how presence is experienced in apparent absence through the ministry of others. In the words of Christopraxis, Jesus also ministers to sufferers in their nothingness through person-to-person ministry. It is to this subject to which I now turn.

---

74. Thompson, *John*, 427–28.

5

Where Are Others in Suffering?
Suffering As an Opportunity for Relationality

Reality is: suffering hurts, and suffering takes a lot of time, and suffering takes people coming alongside you to help you through it, and that's what I've learned.

—CHRISTY, A PARTICIPANT

IN THE PREVIOUS CHAPTER I sought to establish that even though there was the apparent absence of God (nothingness), Jesus sustained the participants with his ongoing presence. I additionally stressed how Jesus's intense presence appeared and ministered to the research participants amidst Jesus's prolonged apparent absence; I reflected on the participants' experiences of suffering with extensive help from Scripture and theology. In this chapter I again emphasize the unique instances of presence amidst apparent absence by highlighting believers' participation in Christ's ministry to those who are suffering, and I will examine the participants' experiences with considerable attention given to culture and psychology. In the words of Christopraxis, I will underscore acts of ministry that reveal God to the participants and reconcile (heal) the participants to God.

Who is Present in Absence?

To recap using Christopraxis, the participants are in an impossible situation in that they are unable to cause God to deliver them out of their extended suffering (chapter 2). Some persons have prayed and some have also fasted, but suffering, such as illness, continues. Some have exerted much effort, doing what they could to alleviate their suffering but with little change in their circumstances. This was seen in Bob's attempts at networking, but full-time employment continued to remain elusive, or in Jeremy's endeavors to return to work after a head injury, but his new limitations rendered him inadequate for the task. In the midst of impossibilities (nothingness) Jesus came to the participants and ministered to them through his presence, which revealed God and brought healing to them. In the same way Jesus came and ministered in his very being to the participants in their nothingness, this chapter highlights how Christ-followers joined Jesus's being through their acts of ministry, revealing God and bringing wholeness and healing to the participants, which resulted in God being encountered. That is to say, Pentecostals experience divine presence in the midst of apparent absence through person-to-person ministry.[1]

While the last chapter discussed how the participants understood their experience with God in their suffering, this chapter centers on how the participants perceived their experiences with both Pentecostals and non-Pentecostals. I have classified these experiences as being unhelpful or helpful. In keeping with Christopraxis, the unhelpful responses comprise those that neglected to resonate with the sufferer so that either God was not revealed and/or liberation or comfort failed to occur, and thereby God was not encountered. This reflects back to the third chapter's assertion that human elements may hinder a divine-human encounter. I argue that when the much-desired instantaneous divine intervention does not occur, the unhelpful responses not only neglect to encounter God, but they increase isolation that reinforces individualism, a recognized trait of Pentecostalism. This discussion on the lack of support is followed by an exploration of the helpful responses, which include those that connected with the participant in that God was revealed and healing transpired in some fashion; in this case, the human element encouraged a divine-human encounter. I assert that the individualism that arose in the unhelpful responses is contrary to the relational nature of humanity, which is conveyed by exploring

---

1. Root writes, "A practical theology of Christopraxis seeks to examine human relationships of shared humanity as places where the ministry of God as event is occurring." Root, *Christopraxis*, loc. 2432–33.

John Bowlby's attachment theory. The relationality of humanity is then supported by considering the Fourth Gospel's emphasis on loving each other in the story of Jesus's washing the disciples feet (John 13). As I aim to demonstrate, suffering becomes an opportunity for relationality with others and an encounter with God. As will be seen, when the body of Christ participates in Christ's ministry to the sufferer through acts of ministry in the Spirit's power, God is encountered amidst nothingness, but first I examine acts of isolation that fail to join others in their nothingness.

UNHELPFUL RESPONSES: ACTS OF ISOLATION

While all eight of the research participants spoke of those who were helpful to them (see below), six out of the eight recounted instances when they perceived others to respond in an unbeneficial way. The unhelpful responses ranged from ignoring the suffering to articulating reasons for, or solutions to, the participants' pain. I offer a disclaimer in that I do not believe any of these responses were intentionally malicious, but rather they suggest an uncomfortableness with suffering and perhaps a lack of knowledge on how to appropriately respond. I am not suggesting that I know the caregivers' motives, but I do place these responses in conversation with concepts such as individualism, vulnerability, connection, and Christopraxis to illuminate what such responses may communicate. After introducing this section, I outline six types of unhelpful responses, which is followed by a discussion on individualism.

Unlike Christopraxis, which speaks of entering into nothingness, the unhelpful responses indicate how others distance themselves from the participants and their nothingness, leaving them alone in their pain. While Christopraxis, as Root explains, sees the impossibility (nothingness) and accepts the need for another minister, the unhelpful actions point toward a belief that "human action can create an actuality for itself that eliminates nothingness."[2] In other words, these responses disregard the prospect of impossibilities and ignore the common human traits of vulnerability and weakness, thereby neglecting to enter into the participants' nothingness.

---

2. Ibid., loc. 2890–98. This is particularly emphasized by Root in his discussion of Adam and Eve, who took the tree's fruit (human action) in order to create "an actuality" that no longer requires "God's possibility." They are choosing "to live in the actuality of their own power rather than in and through the possibility of God's act of ministry, which comes out of nothingness." Ibid., loc. 2866–67.

Thus, they foster a rugged individualism that insists for the other "to pick herself up by her own bootstraps," a slogan referenced by some of the participants.

These responses to the participants are classified as unhelpful in that they failed to connect with the participants. When I refer to *connection* I am not only pointing towards revealing God and generating healing but also to an energy Brown defines as feeling "seen, heard, and valued" in that one can "give and receive without judgment."[3] The path of suffering is one in which there is a longing for connection. When one comes face to face with his finitude in suffering, the need for the other intensifies.

While sufferers yearn to connect with others, regrettably, no other person can fully grasp the sufferer's pain.[4] In fact, this is the very nature of suffering: it creates an existential experience that no other person is completely able to apprehend while it also simultaneously generates a longing within the sufferer for connection.[5] It reminds me of Emmanuel Levinas's comparison of the experience of suffering to the experience of color or sound in that this sensation cannot be described. It loathes any particular quality or appearance—it is "unassumable." It goes beyond meaning and rejects the placing of itself into a "meaningful whole."[6] As such, suffering eludes apprehension, leaving its prey isolated since others are unable to fully enter the sufferer's experience. Suffering's isolating quality becomes magnified in the expression of unbeneficial responses in that they build barriers rather than bridges and create absence rather than presence.

This absence is particularly portrayed in the first type of unhelpful responses in that some participants failed to receive any response at all from those who were expected to act. Instead, these potential caregivers were physically absent. Kyle explained:

> When she [his daughter] actually died, the pastor only spent a matter of minutes with us, but that is the only experience we had with our pastor or any representative of our church during that

---

3. Brown, *Daring Greatly*, 145.

4. Root writes that a human being requires someone or something outside of himself who is distinct from him in order to be a person (a subject). The human being is "bound in time" and requires "ontologically what it is not for it to be." This is a distinction between the created and the Creator and is "why *ex nihilo* is [a] gift, for it reminds the creature of the need for others, of being made to be free for others to need a minister" (italics mine). Root, *Christopraxis*, loc. 3639–43.

5. I am grateful to Dr. John J. Gowins for this insight.

6. Levinas, *On Thinking-of-the-Other*, 91.

whole year and a half of illness leading to death . . . It was very grievous to us that very few of our very close friends had hardly the time of day for us until she died, and then they swarmed us, which is always the situation. They swarm you with meals. They swarm you with love for a few weeks, and then you're left alone.

Bob, too, commented that Pentecostal ministers did not reach out to them when they were forced to leave the company housing due to mold: "They didn't call and check on us. That was it. The ropes were cut." Such a lack of presence may contribute to how a person develops an unhealthy theology about God and suffering.[7] As Kyle indicated, "Most sufferers feel like they've been abandoned by God because the church doesn't do anything for them, so therefore that means God isn't doing anything for them." In short, apparent absence on the horizontal plane points to apparent absence on the vertical plane.

Another type of an unbeneficial response focused on a better future for the participant rather than entering into the participant's current suffering. Such was the case for Bob, who heard, "God's got something for you just around the corner," which Bob interpreted to mean, "He's got something he's preparing you now for something greater later." Similarly, people said to Danielle: "With time you will feel better," or "You will find someone else." Occasionally, the belief in a better future is couched within spiritual language, not unlike a response Christy received, "Sometimes God has to get someone out of the way in order to bring about his plan for your life." By looking ahead, this response did not enter into Christy's current grief. The above comments clung to a belief in betterment and failed to embrace the immediate moment of impossibility. By looking towards a better future, these caregivers avoided joining in the current uncertainty of the participant, which implicitly circumvented their own embracing of human vulnerability, a common trait of all humans. In essence, they ignored their own human finitude by focusing on an assumption that the participant's life will improve. As Bob asserted, "And his [God's] deliverance isn't necessarily

---

7. Anderson speaks of this: "Whether we realize it or not, every act of ministry reveals something of God . . . What we may intend as a very practical application of a biblical principle or church rule says something about who God is . . . [W]hen we speak and act as a Christian we give others reason to conclude that we are speaking on behalf of Christ. When we speak and act out of the authority of the church, we give others reason to think that God's nature and character, as well as his will for persons, is embodied in our words and actions." Anderson then gives an example of not permitting children to partake of communion, which may communicate that God "does not want children to taste and touch of his own grace." Anderson, *The Soul of Ministry*, 7–8.

to betterment, but his deliverance is to his presence in and with us and through us to shape us."

A third kind of unhelpful response neglected to be present in the here and now through minimization. This appeared when believers informed Bob: "Everyone goes through that." Similar to above, this response tacitly communicated a belief in a better future in that the extended suffering became merely a season through which all believers traveled, diminishing the other's suffering in the caregiver's eyes. Consequently, the sufferer's voice was lost in a sea of people who have previously had this arduous experience, signaling that her own experience did not matter. Through this response, caregivers reduced the impact of the actuality of the participant's suffering for themselves, lessening their awareness of the sufferer's vulnerability and thereby their own. The end result in this type of response is an increase in the sufferer's isolation and a lost opportunity for an authentic relationship.

In the fourth type of unbeneficial responses, some caregivers became unavailable to the sufferer when their own pain was triggered, resulting in a shift in focus from the carereceiver to the caregiver. This is seen in the caregiver's attempt to one-up the participant's suffering, a response that irritated Danielle: "It's just like, 'Oh, they're telling that story. Well, I'll tell my story,' or you can up it. I hear people upping things, and it just, oh, my gosh, it just drives me crazy." Such a response is competitive in nature, revealing individualism in that it seeks to be on top by having a worse experience than the sufferer rather than joining alongside the sufferer in the pain. Respondents also appeared to be triggered as they told Kirsten, "At your age? You know, you shouldn't have all these things wrong with you." The speaker seemed to be trying to make sense out of Kirsten's suffering about which Kirsten noted, "It upsets people more, I have found, that I'm not healed than it upsets me." In this case, persons are reacting to Kirsten's struggles due to their own preconceived expectations of how a younger person's life is to be. Since their own expectations are unmet, they are triggered and fail to respond in a way that connects with Kirsten's current situation.

In the fifth type, some caregivers looked at the sufferer's own action or inaction as causing the lack of an instantaneous divine intervention. This was seen in placing blame on the participant by concentrating on what the participant was to do or not to do rather than being present with the hurting individual.[8] For instance, a couple conveyed to Danielle that if she truly

---

8. The importance of providing a *space to* simply *be* rather than *blaming* is seen in a study by Rebecca Walker and Glynis Clacherty at a Pentecostal-based women's shelter;

believed, then her husband's leukemia would not return. Kyle and Christy spoke of being asked about the nature of some sin that was committed to hinder healing. Christy explained, "I would hear things like . . . 'What sin [did] Jason commit? What things are Jason doing wrong for him to be in the situation that he is in right now? Is he fasting enough? Is he praying enough? Is he this? Is he that?'"

The final type of response attributes the suffering to Satan and/or demonic powers. This type of response can contain both unbeneficial and/or beneficial characteristics. In the case of Christy, she was informed that Jason had a demon, a response that failed to connect with her. Research demonstrates demonization to be a common belief among Pentecostals in relation to not only suffering in general but also mental illness specifically.[9]

---

through the use of a twelve-month action-research project called the Wardrobe Project, the researchers connected with the women from the shelter in a less structured space through artwork. The authors conclude "an emphasis on sin in relation to suffering and healing creates a context where the women feel responsible for the abuse they have suffered" while the centering on the women's "abuse and violence . . . creates a labeling of victimhood that some of the women feel they must perform in order to effectively fit into the life of the shelter." Walker and Clacherty, "Shaping New Spaces," 33. As a result, the authors stress the need for a space in which "there is less judgement or need for corrected behavior." Ibid., 57. For a fuller explanation, see 31–58.

9. Jean Mercer asserts that Pentecostals hold the causes of mental illnesses as being the result of demons, making deliverance for mental illness a necessary treatment; see Mercer, "Deliverance, Demonic Possession, and Mental Illness," 595–611. The equating of demons to psychological and physical problems is detected globally among Pentecostals. In a study by Lethabo Mabitsela, five Pentecostal South African pastors underscored the necessity for a safe and trusting relationship in which empathy was expressed to cope with psychological distress, sharing a similarity with psychology; this study also revealed that these pastors were different from the field of psychology by occasionally equating psychological distress to demon possession. This study encourages collaboration between psychologists and Pentecostal pastors to assist in meeting the mental health needs of people within a community as well as the offering of increased training to assist in an awareness of one's limitations and to provide coping strategies; see Mabitsela, "Exploratory Study of Psychological Distress as Understood by Pentecostal Pastors." Afe Adogame, by drawing from official documents, accounts, and testimonies of the Redeemed Church of God's literature as well as two interviews of its members, concluded that within this Pentecostal group HIV/AIDS was associated with a demon from which a person was to seek deliverance; however, other programs within the church were preventive in nature in that they provided spiritual and social care; see Adogame, "HIV/AIDS Support and African Pentecostalism," 475–84. The subject of demons has been addressed by Pentcostal E. Janet Warren. Based on her dissertation, she focuses on developing a biblical model of boundaires and cleansing for understanding and acting against evil spiritual forces and offers applications for ministry in *Cleansing the Cosmos* (see also her non-academic re-write, *Holy Housekeeping*).

Who is Present in Absence?

For instance, Jeffrey Bjorck and Pamela Trice surveyed 230 students at a Charismatic Bible institute concerning the subject of depression in which the students rated thirty-two causes and twenty-five treatments for depression. While recognizing diverse causes for depression, the fourth highest cause was demonic oppression and/or possession, following rape, abuse, and loss of a spouse. Correspondingly, faith-based cures were believed to be most efficacious, with the reading of Scripture as the most highly supported remedy, indicating believers' responsibility to treat their own depression.[10] Similarly, Gerard Leavey uncovered that Pentecostal ministers in his study believe psychological problems to be a result of the devil

---

10. Bjorck and Trice, "Pentecostal Perspectives on Causes and Cures of Depression," 283–94. When examining other studies within global Pentecostalism, the results are diverse concerning the causes and treatments for suffering. Katherine Attanasi interviewed over fifty Pentecostal women and conducted follow-up interviews with twelve of those women who were from one of two communities in South Africa. One of the benefits of Pentecostal theology, according to Attanasi, was the increased flourishing of the women. Through the belief in divine healing women may be healed of HIV/AIDS, find support for HIV/AIDS through prayer groups, and be encouraged to seek medical treatment for HIV/AIDS. Attanasi also identifies a drawback in Pentecostalism that was, paradoxically, the impairment of the flourishing of women; this was seen in the women being blamed for a lack of faith for not being healed of HIV/AIDS and using prayer as a strategy to prevent the wife from contracting HIV/AIDS from an unfaithful husband. The latter demonstrates the gender inequality between men and women; see Attanasi, "Pentecostal Theologies of Healing, HIV/AIDS, and Women's Agency in South Africa," 7–20. George Wanje in a qualitative study reports mixed perceptions of HIV testing in Mombasa, Kenya among Pentecostals. On the one hand, barriers surfaced for advocating HIV testing. For instance, since holiness is important, receiving the HIV test is interpreted as a sign of not being a believer; since one depends on faith to receive healing, one demonstrates a lack of faith by receiving the HIV test; and since disease is sexually transmitted, an indication of sinful behavior, it is difficult for Pentecostals to discuss HIV. On the other hand, Pentecostal leaders saw the importance of stressing HIV testing. For instance, some Pentecostals understand that Scripture does not command one to abstain from the HIV test. Furthermore, if pastoral leadership advocated it, congregants sought HIV testing; see Wanje, "'It Is Not a Sin Going for the Test.'" Steven Rasmussen, using ethnographic action research, studied the way in which Northwestern Tanzanian Pentecostal pastors responded to sickness and death while also seeking a way in which the pastors could "contextualize" the gospel to suffering and death. In interviewing over one hundred ministers, Rasmussen concluded that Pentecostals perceived a variety of causes to sickness and death (e.g., natural, demonic, sin); however, they struggled when prayers to Jesus did not result in healing for all. During the course of this research, Rasmussen noted that the ministers "came to a greater appreciation . . . of the need to show that faith in Jesus brings perseverance and victory" even in the absence of healing (317); see Rasmussen, "Illness and Death Experiences in Northwestern Tanzania."

and/or demons.¹¹ Some studies note that moving blame to the devil and/or demons is helpful to the sufferer. It eliminates a sense of culpability from the individual and creates an active resistance to evil. For example, Susan Dunlap's ethnographic study of a Pentecostal congregation writes about "casting out the devil":

> [I]t loosens the grip of self-blame when illness strikes. Many who are ill labor under the burden of guilt in addition to the burden of their poor health. In an atomized society that teaches that one's lot in life is individually determined according to one's willpower, hard work, and personal morality, those who are sick often assume that it is personal failure or sin that has caused this illness. Blaming the devil for one's illness shifts the blame for illness from the individual to an external, malevolent force.¹²

My concern is not whether demons may inflict suffering, but the all-encompassing categorization by Pentecostals that suffering, particularly

---

11. Leavey interviewed nineteen clergy in the UK from a variety of religious backgrounds, six of whom were Pentecostal, and of the Pentecostals five were from Africa and one was a Caucasian who was originally from the UK. Contrary to the non-Pentecostals, the Pentecostals held that mental illness has a supernatural connection, namely, demons; see Leavey, "The Appreciation of the Spiritual in Mental Illness," 571–90. In another study, Leavey interviews thirty-two clergy, seven of whom were Pentecostal, about mental illness. Leavey notices among the Pentecostals a strong correlation between sin and being unhealthy as well as a belief that a person is spiritually vulnerable to demonization through openings in her life, such as sin and unbelief; see Leavey, "U.K. Clergy and People in Mental Distress," 79–104. Jennifer Payne noticed in studying African American Pentecostal ministers that in their sermons these ministers perceived depression to be a weakness in that they encouraged their congregants to "go to Jesus" and "praise and worship Jesus" rather than cry; see Payne, "Saints Don't Cry," 215–28. In another survey by Payne, Pentecostal ministers were more likely than non-Pentecostals to hold that the causes of depression are spiritual or moral rather than biological, and depression was strongly affected by spiritual elements; see Payne, "Variations in Pastors' Perceptions of the Etiology of Depression," 355–65. Joseph Quayesi-Amakye sees a tension in beliefs about suffering and evil between the leadership and the laity of Gahanaian Pentecostals. The laity emphasize demonic powers, and the leadership view evil as not necessarily inconsistent with the goodness of God; see Quayesi-Amakye, "Coping with Evil in Ghanaian Pentecostalism," 254–72.

12. Dunlap also perceives there is a downfall to placing blame on the devil in that one does not accept one's part in the suffering; see Dunlap, *Caring Cultures*, 53. In a study by Maringira et al. of former soldiers who are in exile in South Africa, the authors state that the soldiers found relief in the Pentecostal setting from their distress and troubling nightmares from the war by talking to the pastor; by transferring blame away from themselves to the devil and evil spirits; and by fighting the devil through praying and fasting; see Maringira et al., "Between Remorse and Nostalgia," 79–100.

mental illness, is the result of demons. Such an uncompromising response does not allow space in which one hears the voice of the sufferer, listens to the Spirit, and cultivates self-awareness. This neglect misses the opportunity to hear how to participate in the Christ's ministry and opens the door for judgment and blame if the sufferer is not delivered. Bjorck and Trice seem to concur when they conclude that while Pentecostals may not believe that "initially becoming depressed" is an indication of "spiritual failure," the inability to rapidly put a stop to the depression is likely to generate the assumption among Pentecostals "that the sufferer is not practicing her/his faith with sufficient devotion, given that spiritual treatments (e.g., Bible reading, scripture memorization, fasting, confessing sin) are . . . viewed as the most effective solutions."[13] In other words, it is put upon the sufferer to change the situation, which points toward individualism as it isolates.

INDIVIDUALISM IN PENTECOSTALISM

As seen in many of the above responses, Pentecostals may frequently foster individualism when extended suffering is not alleviated. These responses demonstrate that in the face of a lack of a desired divine intervention, individualism rises to the surface; the isolating quality of suffering is amplified; and a move towards relationality is thwarted. To better appreciate this move towards individualism, I offer here a very abbreviated description of life prior to the industrial revolution in order to gain understanding of the landscape from which North American Pentecostalism emerged. Prior to the era of industrialization, Western culture was less about the self and more about community. Clinical psychologist Robert Karen comments that even though preindustrialized society had its own issues, relationality was one of its major attributes. Extended families and the greater surrounding community were tightly woven into the everyday fabric of a person's

---

13. Bjorck and Trice, "Pentecostal Perspectives on Causes and Cures of Depression," 288. In a similar study, Justin Harley evalutes the beliefs of 255 Pentecostals from three communities in respect to the causes and treatments of mental health disorders. Harley determined that Pentecostals were not any more likely to hold that the root of a mental health disorder was from the individual's "bad character" or from the way the individual was raised than the general population. However, Pentecostals were unlike the general population in their preference to seek help through spiritual means, such as petitioning God, reading the Bible, or talking with their minister, rather than the taking of medications; see Harley, "Pentecostal Christian View toward Causes and Treatment of Mental Health Disorders."

life. People labored, worshipped, rejoiced, and played together, creating a sense of belonging, identity, and mutuality. In essence, there were attachments in every aspect of life.[14] Karen writes, "People lived in such close daily proximity and were so mutually dependent that little of what one was could be hidden."[15]

This slowly changed with the onset of the industrial revolution. Karen writes that the world was altered from one in which people had plainly defined "roles and duties, to one in which they had to make their place."[16] Competition, from Karen's perspective, became the central feature, and with it dependency became an unwanted characteristic in men and eventually in women in that emotional needs were not to be acknowledged. The familial and communal relationships that had been primary to a person's life dissipated, and the close attachments that had enveloped each person, withered.[17] Judith Jordan makes similar observations about today's society: "In Western industrialized nations, the self is encouraged to be mobile and free of constraining bonds of community. It is competitive and achieves safety and a sense of well-being by successfully competing with and beating others. Gaining ascendant power over others is seen as the route to safety and maturity."[18] It is out of this environment that Pentecostalism was birthed, engendering its individualistic traits.

Various scholars acknowledge Pentecostalism's individualistic characteristics. Kärkkäinen recognizes that Pentecostals "speak of the church as a fellowship," but "much of Pentecostalism especially in the Global North and as a result of missions work from therein, has tended to foster the hyper-individualism of the post-Enlightenment mentality."[19] Simon Chan in his contribution to a Pentecostal ecclesiology laments, "Traditionally evangelicals and Pentecostals have been plagued by excessive emphasis on an individualistic conception of the Christian life which they are only beginning to correct by a more communal understanding."[20] Although Albrecht underscores the communal aspect of Pentecostal spirituality, he too admits its individualistic nature when he writes, "The essential mystical quality of

---

14. Karen, *Becoming Attached*, 412.
15. Ibid.
16. Ibid., 413.
17. Ibid.
18. Jordan, *Relational-Cultural Therapy*, loc. 132–34.
19. Kärkkäinen, "The Pentecostal Understanding of Mission," 39.
20. Chan, *Pentecostal Ecclesiology*, 10.

their experience lends itself to a certain focus on the personal/individual dimension of spirituality."[21]

Some writers connect Pentecostalism's individualism to modernity and/or to a shift in a non-Western culture's practices.[22] Gerardo Marti, who writes about the growing individualism in an increasingly globalized world, regards Pentecostal believers who hold to prosperity theology as being able to adapt quite well to a modern globalized system and theorizes how this occurs. In his ethnographic study of a Los Angeles based Pentecostal church that practices prosperity doctrine, Marti believes that they are well-suited to "the individualization processes experienced" by the contemporary workforce within capitalism.[23] For instance, a Pentecostal perceives himself as belonging to God's primary mission within his own setting so that he makes personal choices in his work and home that are aligned with this identity, which means he exerts his "own 'self'" in egocentric ways." This, according to Marti, "resonates . . . with workers in globalized capitalistic structures."[24] A Pentecostal, who holds to the prosperity doctrine, is viewed as being empowered to be ambitious and increase in her wealth and social status while also maintaining Christian morals, and this affirms the individualization of "global capitalism."[25] Joel Robbins, in his essay on the ways in which Pentecostalism shares elements with Western modernity outside the West, observes, "Pentecostalism generally introduces some form of individualism into the cultures of its converts." This may include separating from the familial group or being responsible for his own salvation.[26]

Gwyneth McClendon and Rachel Beatty Riedl in their study determined the chief, shared trait among Pentecostal churches in Nairobi, Kenya was "an individualistic theme." In their study, they randomly selected Pentecostal churches in Nairobi from which they listened to sermons as well as carefully read some of the sermons and found that 82 percent of the sermons clearly communicated individualistic tones. Such individualism was detected when the sermons upheld the self, supported expressions of

---

21. Albrecht, *Rites in the Spirit*, 243.

22. While my project conducts research in North America, I include research from other parts of the world in this chapter because the emphasis on Pentecostalism's individualism globally demonstrates individualism's impact as being more noticeable in societies that are more communal than the West.

23. Marti, "The Adaptability of Pentecostalism," 5–25.

24. Ibid., 23.

25. Ibid., 24–25.

26. Robbins, "Anthropology of Religion," 168.

a person's autonomy, and called for the person to separate from traditional collective ties. For example, the individual was encouraged to fight the devil in her own life, to trust in God for her life, and to conquer her own victim mentality. The authors observe that their results are in contrast to their assumption that religion highlights the communal aspect. For instance, the results imply that Pentecostalism's strategy to battle poverty centers on transforming the person rather than fighting poverty through the church's structured programs.[27]

Pentecostalism's individualism also may be compromising Pentecostalism's original purpose for Spirit baptism, which has been empowerment for service.[28] Contra to the belief of many Classical Pentecostals that the reason for Spirit baptism is to be empowered to serve (e.g., AG, PAOC, Four Square), Adam Stewart uncovered that many of his study's participants stressed Spirit baptism's personal benefits, failing to see it as primarily empowerment for ministry. For example, Stewart notes that a PAOC minister highlighted the Spirit being "ultimately concerned with the immanent, relational task of helping individuals navigate the difficult aspects of their lives" rather than for ministry.[29] This change suggests that an experience of Spirit baptism, which is already individualistic, is becoming increasingly focused on the self, a movement that is apparent in the surrounding Western culture.[30] When Spirit baptism is not seen as empowerment for

---

27. McClendon and Riedl, "Individualism and Empowerment in Pentecostal Sermons," 119–44.

28. Albrecht confirms this in his study, which found that, in Spirit baptism, "Pentecostals experience God as empowering Spirit and commissioning Lord," as they see God as being able "to assist them in the mundane matters of life as well as the opportunities for service"; see Albrecht, *Rites in the Spirit*, 248–49. Aaron Friesen's study on 531 classical Pentecostal ministers from three denominations also found that ministers agreed that Spirit baptism empowers them for service; see Friesen, *Norming the Abnormal*.

29. Stewart, *The New Canadian Pentecostals*, 132. Stewart conducted ethnographic research of three churches of the PAOC that included forty-two interviews and 158 responses to a survey. Stewart recounts that only one-third of those interviewed perceived Spirit baptism to be for empowerment to minister. See 125–36 for a fuller explanation.

30. Jean M. Twenge asserts that from the time GenMe'ers (those born in 70s, 80s, and 90s) entered the world, they were instructed to place themselves above all others. She writes, "Unlike the Baby Boomers, GenMe didn't have to march in a protest or to attend a group session to realize that our own needs and desires were paramount"; see Twenge, *Generation Me*, 4. She continues, "The growing primacy of the individual appears in data I gathered on 81,384 high school and college students. These young people completed questionnaires measuring what psychologists call agency—a personality trait involving assertiveness, dominance, independence, and self-promotion. Between the 1970s and

ministry, it no longer contains the relational emphasis in person-to-person ministry. Instead, it fuels the individualistic proclivity of Pentecostalism, leading Pentecostals to perceive the Spirit as merely an aid for the self.

Thus far I have explored the unhelpful types of responses heard by the participants and placed them alongside individualism. In reflecting not only on the discussion immediately above but also on the earlier exploration of Pentecostalism's desire for a divine encounter (chapter 3), the unhelpful responses amidst ongoing suffering are not a surprise. In the face of a longing for a divine encounter that does not appear, the ongoing extended suffering is a threat to a Pentecostal worldview; thus, these caregivers may tell themselves a story to protect themselves (chapter 4). This story is then verbalized through unbeneficial responses that reinforce individualism. Their responses imply the existence of their uneasiness with vulnerability amidst suffering when the divine is slow to eradicate the extended suffering. Their uneasiness with vulnerability indicates a desire for certainty rather than embracing the ambiguity of loss and the mystery of a lack of an instantaneous deliverance.[31] In their search for predictability in the chaos, they informed the participants that their lives will eventually improve or that they were culpable for the ongoing suffering. Thus, individual human action through self-agency, rather than divine action, becomes the way out of the nothingness, and this denies the need for ministry from the other. As a result, there is a disconnection from instead of a connection to the other, the Spirit, and the self, which reflects culture's individualism instead of humanity's relationality. Unfortunately, these unhelpful responses neglected to minister healing to the participants, which could have been accomplished by joining them in their nothingness and thereby participating in the ministry of Christ. In short, the human element of the unhelpful

---

the 1990s, both young men's and women's agency increased markedly, with the average 1990s college student scoring higher than 75% of college Boomers from the 1970s"; see ibid., 74. She notes that there is an increase in narcissism in those who belong to GenMe than previous generations; see ibid., 68–71. Twenge also perceives that increased individualism is demonstrated in the large range of personal choices from individualized cell phone ring tones to a person's personalized playlists on her iPod to the large array of combinations one may purchase at Starbucks (she says 19,000 combinations are possible); see ibid., 101.

31. Brown, speaking of religion when it stresses social disengagement, writes "When religious leaders leverage our fear and need for more certainty by extracting vulnerability from spirituality and turning faith into 'compliance and consequences,' rather than teaching and modeling how to wrestle with the unknown and how to embrace mystery, the entire concept of faith is bankrupt on its own terms." Brown, *Daring Greatly*, 176–77.

response that isolates hinders the divine-human encounter. However, not all of the participants' experiences with others were acts of isolation; some were acts of relationality, acts of person-to-person ministry. After relating responses that were helpful to the participants, I place them in dialogue with Bowlby's attachment theory, a psychological theory that defied individualism by embracing relationality.

HELPFUL RESPONSES: ACTS OF CONNECTION

While earlier I highlighted the individualistic trait of Pentecostalism, the existence of the communal aspect is not to be ignored.[32] Pentecostal communities, according to Albrecht, traditionally avoid formal "catechesis," such as confirmation; instead, believers are incorporated into Pentecostalism through their inclusion in the Pentecostal community. This means for Albrecht that "the transmission of the tradition" is less about formal teaching and more about living out and experiencing the Pentecostal tradition within the community.[33] Thus, Albrecht asserts that shared experiences, such as Spirit baptism and healing, "bind them [Pentecostals] together

---

32. Hansjorg Dilger in studying a Neo-Pentecostal church in Tanzania discovered how a closely connected church community offers support for those who are suffering; see Dilger, "Healing the Wounds of Modernity," 59–83. Lorena Núñez, in a qualitative study of two Pentecostal churches in Johannesburg, perceived the church communities provided migrants a worldview that generated healing, deliverance, and meaning to their suffering as well as a place to belong in the midst of the suffering; see Núñez, "Faith Healing, Migration and Gendered Conversions in Pentecostal Churches in Johannesburg," 149–68. Based on interviews, Marian Tankink sees how the Pentecostal community assists in bringing healing to those who are suffering from horrific memories from the war; see Tankink, "'The Moment I Became Born-Again the Pain Disappeared,'" 203–31. Richard Eves highlights the individualistic and communal aspects of Pentecostalism (the latter of which is discussed below) in the event that illness or death occurs among the Lelet of New Ireland in this ethnographic study. Besides using biomedicine in order to become well, the sick one also seeks God for healing, and the congregation joins in these prayers. While there is an emphasis on human agency in Pentecostalism (as seen in the individual choosing to believe God for salvation and/or healing while seeking to be free of sin), the Pentecostal community also examines the sick one for signals that it is her sin that generates the illness; see Eves, "'In God's Hands,'" 496–514. In her study Catharina J. Beijer perceived Pentecostals provided the coping strategies of Ghanaian Pentecostals living in the Netherlands, such as praying, fasting, deliverance, worshipping God, operating in the gifts of the Spirit, hearing sermons of comfort, sharing emotions with other believers, and belonging to the church community; see Beijer, "'Although 90% of the System is against Us, We are Able to Survive.'"

33. Albrecht, *Rites in the Spirit*, 205.

while reinforcing and relaying their beliefs and tradition."[34] In other words, a horizontal connection transpires as Pentecostals experience a vertical connection with the divine. To put this in terms of Christopraxis, as God ministers (revealing/reconciling) to Pentecostals through similar experiences, Pentecostals experience a connection, a sense of community, with each other. As Christopraxis argues, the reverse is also true. When Pentecostals connect with each other through acts of ministry (God is revealed, and people are restored), God is experienced.[35] That is to say, a vertical connection with God occurs during horizontal acts of ministry.[36]

One of the more profound ways this transpires in Pentecostalism is in the emphasis on prayer (chapter 3). Several of those interviewed referenced the receiving of prayers from others as being beneficial to them. Joan made mention throughout her interview of the Pentecostal community praying for Craig and her, and Kyle spoke of going to the front and receiving prayers for healing.[37] Praying for one another within a Pentecostal congregation

---

34. Ibid., 206.

35. Pentecostalism shares a similarity with Christopraxis in its underscoring of ministry between persons, or the importance of relationships. This is demonstrated when Dostin Lakika et al. examined the counseling services that Pentecostal and non-Pentecostal Congolese refugees in Johannesburg received; while the article does not delineate between those who are Pentecostal and those who are not, it notes that the refugees perceived the counselors to be used of God, "divinely sent helpers." Counseling alone was not seen as being able to heal unless God intervened. Lakika et al., "Violence, Suffering and Support," 101–19.

36. Root writes, "The Spirit's work rests in the same paradigm of Christopraxis. The Spirit unveils God's ministry as God's being in Jesus Christ (revelation) to and through human experience (encounter), calling the human agent into ontological union with God, through Christ, connecting the human spirit with God's own Spirit (reconciliation). Yet, this connection comes not through a magical transcendental state but by a calling of the human agent into ministry (as mission)—to swing open the doors and preach (Acts 2), to feed the widows (Acts 6) and orphans, to go to a friend with a word of comfort, to feed the homeless, to listen and not talk, to leave the kitchens of the powerful and cook comfort food for campers. Union with God comes to us through the act of ministry itself that takes us into divine encounter." Root, *Christopraxis*, loc. 2233–38.

37. This supports Poloma's study of congregants from twenty-one AG congregations. She writes, "The belief and practice of healing in this AG sample is supported by the common availability of simple healing rituals that are part of most Pentecostal congregations. Eighty-five percent (85%) of the respondents in our AG survey at least on occasion were involved in prayer for healing with others in their church, with 28 percent reporting a regular participation in this congregational ritual"; see Poloma, "Pentecostal Prayer within the Assemblies of God," 54. In a previously mentioned study of C. G. Brown (chapter 3), Brown similarly highlights the importance of repetitive prayer, "Respondents did not understand healing as an all-or-nothing phenomenon but as a

often involves going forward to the front (the altar) and requesting that the minister, a prayer team, and/or other congregants intercede on the behalf of the sufferer. Such a practice of praying includes physically placing hands on the sufferer and/or anointing him with oil, and seeking God to intervene on the sufferer's behalf. As Courtney Jones Andrews acknowledges in an ethnomedical study of a Pentecostal church in the Southern United States, these experiences clearly demonstrate a way in which "the whole church community shares in the pain and the suffering of each of its individual members, offering support and encouragement to anyone in distress."[38] In regards to attachment theory (see below), the church community can provide a safe place and a felt sense of security for one who is in need through prayer.[39]

The Pentecostal practice of prayer corresponds in several ways to Christopraxis. First, believers in this type of relational ministry are participating in the ministry of Christ, who intercedes for his followers (John 17:13–26; Heb 7:25). Second, this type of ministry for Pentecostals also includes a dependence on God, calling for the necessity to be empowered by the Spirit in one's weakness.[40] An observer of Pentecostals praying for each other often witnesses Pentecostals quietly praying in tongues in addition to praying in their native language. As illustrated by their praying in tongues, Pentecostals accept that they do not know how they should pray (Rom 8:26).[41] However, as Smith asserts, this practice is not simply to assist

---

process that often takes time and repeated prayers to complete, especially for more serious conditions; even dramatic improvements are understood as the result of previously laid groundwork"; see Brown, *Testing Prayer*, 280.

38. Andrews, "Health and Salvation," 65.

39. Mario Mikulincer and Phillip Shaver write, "A person can seek proximity to a group and use the group as a source of comfort, support, and safety in times of need (i.e., a safe haven), and as a secure base for exploration and growth." Mikulincer and Shaver, *Attachment in Adulthood*, loc. 11545–46.

40. Root's view of Christopraxis highlights humanity's weakness when he stresses it as an opportunity for ministry and an encounter with the divine. Root asserts, "[T]his ministry that we do with God is born not in our strength, but in our weakness ... Weakness as the core component both allows eternity to enter time and keeps those in time from thinking they can possess eternity, yet through weakness those in time can join eternity! Our weakness, our deaths, become the field of ministry, for these places of weakness are where God's being is released in becoming"; see Root *Christopraxis*, loc. 2301–8.

41. Smith writes, "[T]he person praying in tongues is, first and foremost, doing just that—*praying*, and praying *to God*, and thus seeking to express a desire to God 'in groans too deep for words' (Rom. 8:26). Such a prayer is not intended to communicate

intercessors as they minister to the sufferer, but it also has an intended effect on the one receiving prayer. This practice informs the sufferer that God hears and heals, and it seeks to foster in her faith, hope, and receptiveness to the supernatural, a miracle.[42] Herein, then, lies evidence of an encounter with God in this act of ministry: believers are not only joining with Christ's act of intercession by praying in their native language for each other, but they are also connecting with the divine while desiring to bond with the sufferer in helping her to experience the divine through their praying in tongues, the language of the Spirit.

While prayer is a common way in which ministry occurred among the participants, all of the participants also referenced other ways in which believers responded through acts of ministry, which being translated into the terms of Christopraxis: God was revealed, and restoration took place. Some participants spoke of help and support in more general terms, such as Joan stating she received practical help from the church members. Several participants specifically defined the practical help they received, which included actions such as: counseling; praying; organizing; and making provisions.[43] Practical help reaches out to connect with someone by meeting a need through an act of compassion, taking a risk by moving towards the other while being uncertain of the response. It also recognizes the caregiver's own need and vulnerability if he was placed in a similar situation to the carereceiver. An explicit compassionate act not only suggests the embracing of the other's suffering, but it also implies that relationships are necessary in suffering. As Kirsten asserted (chapter 4), we are God's "hands and feet." Thus, these horizontal, practical acts of ministry are means by

---

propositional content, but rather to express the depth of a desire when 'we do not know how to pray as we should' (Rom. 8:26). Such a glossolalic prayer expresses a depth of dependency upon God, and thus a humility before the divine. It also indicates a dependence upon the Holy Spirit in particular since the Spirit is thought to be the one who 'intercedes' through such groans (Rom. 8:26) that do not conform to the conventions of a given language." This is, for Smith, "an *illocutionary* act of *praying*" (italics in original). Smith, *Thinking in Tongues*, 144.

42. This is the perlocutionary element. Ibid., 144–45.

43. Since several participants underscored the prayers of others, I chose to categorize *praying* (in contrast to providing a *space to be*) as a practical help because it seeks a change by inviting God to meet the unmet need as well as praying for others when they may struggle to pray for themselves. I want to thank Lincoln Engelbert for the insight that providing a *space to be* is different from offering prayer. A *space to be* is created and then prayer becomes the practical outcome.

Where Are Others in Suffering?

which God intervenes in concrete ways, and as such, they communicate worth (chapter 4).

Christy spoke of both non-Pentecostals and Pentecostals providing practical assistance when she had a clear need. The non-Pentecostal church where she and Jason had most recently been attending, reached out everyday to Jason in the weeks prior to his death, including a visit by a counselor. Immediately following Jason's death, that church entered into Christy's nothingness by being present in the house where Jason died, cleaning it, and assisting Christy in organizing, pricing, boxing, and selling Jason's possessions. For example, a gun expert and an owner of a construction company, both who attended the church, appraised Jason's guns and tools, respectively. One Pentecostal man in another city informed Christy: "The Lord told me the day of Jason's funeral that I was supposed to take care of your guys' transportation." Speaking in the terms of Christopraxis, this man encountered God, entered Christy's nothingness, and joined God's act of ministry by providing her a car as well as by paying for its maintenance, and this act of ministry was continuing at the time of the interview.

Not only were there practical helps of support, seven out of the eight participants spoke of helpful responses that pointed towards an experience of a *space to be*, which I see as an act of compassion that centers on *presence*. According to the revised definition of *intervention* (chapter 4), this, too, is a horizontal intervention that participates in Christ's ministry to the sufferer. Joan experienced this type of support when congregants invited Craig and her into their home, "accepting of the fact that he would hug and kiss the wife probably two or three times and the husband, too." Such presence communicates worth; it says, "You matter to me" (chapter 4). Providing a *space to be* includes the embracing of the path of suffering on which the person is journeying. Kirsten agreed, "I think it's so valuable to make a place for them even when they're depressed or whatever." By using the word "embrace," I am saying that a provision of a *space to be* does not perceive ongoing suffering as evidence of God's absence. Instead, a *space to be* is willing to wait while embracing the person and her journey on the path of suffering. As explained previously (chapter 4), an embrace does not cling to the suffering but tacitly believes God to be at work and implicitly invites the Spirit to transform the situation. In other words, presence respects both God's will and human will, which offers an opportunity for transformation (chapter 4). Such was the case for Bob in that he believed he was rescued through others being present to him. He commented, "They weren't trying to tell me what to do, how to do it. They just listened." The *space to be*, then, includes the idea of walking with or being alongside without attempting to fix it but allowing the person and the suffering to exist. Kirsten confirmed, "Talk to them like they're human, like you don't have to fix them."

A *space to be* permits the person to talk, to contemplate, and to feel—to be who he is in the moment, which honors the other's will. A *space to be* has an absence of condemnation, such as "you should not," "you must," or "you ought." Christy confessed to attending a non-Pentecostal church for a season to find emotional security due to the judgment Jason and she had experienced among Pentecostals. Jeremy remarked that being in a group of three other couples implicitly helped him as they ate together and played cards once a month. He reported, "They were there, I mean, every month we'd go, and I saw their love. I saw their support." This also alludes to a *space to be* as possibly including a reciprocal relationship, which Kyle experienced in a friendship that contained mutuality and reciprocity as they were present to each other. Danielle spoke of a grief support group in which she connected with other members through similar suffering, and she bonded with others through sharing. Thus, presence creates an opportunity for trust.

A *space to be* not only acknowledges the believer is united with Christ in the divine life but also perceives the person's sufferings are in Christ, recognizing Christ's presence in the suffering. This was the case for Christy when a Charismatic Catholic aunt walked with her during the last months of Jason's life. Christy said, "I learned so much from her because she talked about suffering in a way that the Pentecostals don't talk about suffering." Christy heard her aunt repeatedly say, "Your sufferings are united with Christ." The aunt joined the presence of Jesus in Christy's nothingness through an act of being present to Christy, and in this *space to be*, God was revealed and restoration occurred in Christy. This exemplifies Christopraxis's person-to-person ministry. It embraces relationality over individualism and sees suffering not as a path to isolation but as an opportunity for relationality, as demonstrated by Bowlby's attachment theory.

ATTACHMENT: A THEORY OF RELATIONALITY

At the time Bowlby introduced attachment theory to the discipline of psychology, Western psychological theories tended to mirror the milieu of the individualistic culture. Jordan observes that humanity's growth was portrayed "as a trajectory from dependence to independence" so that the goal of being a parent was to help the dependent child to become autonomous and independent.[44] When Bowlby's attachment theory was emerging, Karen describes psychoanalysis as being the dominating theory, reflecting the culture's individualistic nature by focusing mostly on the individual's inner psychological constructions and secret desires, not the relationships within the family.[45]

Contra to psychoanalysis's focus on the internal self, Bowlby concentrated on a person's relational experiences. Mario Mikulincer and Phillip Shaver write that Bowlby perceived attachment as being necessary throughout a human's life, not only early in life. For Bowlby, humans are "inherently relationship seeking," and he asserted that no matter the age of the person, the need for others is not infantile; when adults are suffering, it is advantageous for them to pursue and obtain support from others.[46] Lindsey depicted the need for others one week after her father's death when she journaled, "We are sustained, upheld, loved, supported, cared for, and we must go on. We have each other."

Bowlby believed in an innate attachment behavioral system in which when one is threatened, she seeks the proximity of an attachment figure for support.[47] For example, when a child hears a sudden loud noise or encounters a stranger, the attachment behavioral system is activated: the child voices her distress through crying, clutching tightly to the caregiver, and/or seeking to be close to the caregiver. When the child receives support and is near the caregiver, the child is able to relax, and the attachment behavioral system is deactivated. In the absence of any threat, the attachment behavioral system is not activated; therefore, as Bowlby held, it is unnecessary at those moments to pursue others' support and care, but one is able to center on other pursuits, such as exploring one's world or being creative.

A threat is seen as that which the person considers dangerous, endangering the person's survival and engendering a need for protection. Such threats not only include pain, loneliness, being demoralized, or some other perceived endangerment but also involve those dangers that may not be intrinsically threatening but intensify the prospect of peril, such as the absence

---

44. Jordan, *Relational-Cultural Therapy*, loc. 105–6.

45. Karen, *Becoming Attached*, 27–35.

46. Mikulincer and Shaver, *Attachment in Adulthood*, loc. 406–21.

47. My description of Bowlby's attachment theory is drawn from the writings of Mikulincer and Shaver in *Attachment in Adulthood: Structure, Dynamics, and Change*.

of light, an unidentified noise, or being secluded.[48] When the attachment system is activated by a threat, according to Mikulincer and Shaver, the goal is to gain a sense of "felt security" in which the person feels protected and secure. When this goal is achieved, the person is able to attend further to issues other than self-protection and be more willing to take risks; thus, when the goal is reached, the attachment system is disengaged.[49]

Mikulincer and Shaver clarify that attachment figures are not simply anyone with whom one has a close relationship, but instead they provide three distinct functions. First, attachment figures are pursued "for proximity seeking," which means they are sought when a person has a need. Second, attachment figures provide a "safe haven" when a person needs "protection, comfort, support, and relief." Third, attachment figures supply a "secure base," which permits the person "to pursue nonattachment goals in a safe environment."[50] With these three functions in mind, Mikulincer and Shaver state, "[A] close relationship partner becomes such a figure only when he or she provides (or is perceived as providing) a safe haven and secure base in times of threat or danger."[51] In the words of Bowlby, when one feels threatened, he goes to one who is "stronger and wiser."[52]

Mikulincer and Shaver add an additional attribute of attachment figures: the attachment figure's absence that is actual or anticipated, which brings about "separation distress." Children who are separated from their caregivers may protest the separation by crying or searching; if they are unable to be gain proximity, this leads to despair, as seen in depression and a loss of appetite and sleep. If children are reunited with the caregiver after an extended period of time, they demonstrate detachment through anger or withdrawal. This last characteristic is significant for Bowlby because he held that this progression of searching, despairing, and detaching only occurs with attachment figures.[53] Mikulincer and Shaver notice that such emotional reactions to the attachment figures' absence occur in adults as well. Adults may become "anxious, preoccupied, and hypersensitive to signs of love or its absence, to approval or rejection."[54]

48. Mikulincer and Shaver, *Attachment in Adulthood*, loc. 422–32.
49. Ibid., loc. 463–71.
50. Ibid., loc. 564–70.
51. Ibid., loc. 570–71.
52. Ibid., loc. 391.
53. Ibid., loc. 572–82.
54. Ibid., loc. 642–43. Mikulincer and Shaver note that the person who is seeking an

Where Are Others in Suffering?

So far I have centered upon the attachment behavioral system, demonstrating humanity's longing for relationships in suffering. When humanity is in distress, they yearn for a felt sense of security by seeking out an attachment figure. This theory defies the individualism of Western culture and embraces the need for relationships. Joan indicated this when she spoke of her personal move from individualism to connection:

> And I'm gonna allow the body of Christ to minister to me, and I'm gonna share my need, and I'm not going to hold it all in or isolate myself. And that is a tendency that I would've had, and I have had, just isolate myself. You know. I'll go through this by myself. No. I need to be more public. I need to allow people to help me, come around beside me, and not be so private. It says bear one another's burdens so that's what I have been doing, and the church family here has gathered around me, and I'm very grateful.

Thus, Bowlby's theory challenges the *pick-yourself-up-by-your-own-bootstraps* mentality by accepting the finitude and vulnerability of humanity. Yet, there is an additional element of Bowlby's that is germane to this project—the caregiving behavioral system.

Besides the attachment behavioral system, Mikulincer and Shaver discuss Bowlby's caregiving behavioral system. The authors write that Bowlby described the caregiving behavioral system as a capability of all humans to be able to offer "protection and support to others who are either chronically dependent or temporarily in need."[55] While the caregiving system originally denoted supplying care to one's relatives, currently it includes "genuine concern for anyone in need."[56] Mikulincer and Shaver describe

---

attachment figure also has an attachment style that is either secure or insecure, which influences the person's perception of the threat, the availability of the attachment figure, and their choice of strategy. Mikulincer and Shaver explain the concept of attachment style: "A person's attachment style reflects his or her most chronically accessible working models and the typical functioning of his or her attachment system in a specific relationship (relationship-specific attachment style) or across relationships (global or general attachment style). As such, each attachment style is closely tied to working models and reflects the underlying, organizing action of a particular attachment strategy (primary or secondary, hyperactivating or deactivating)." See loc. 802–6. An insecure attachment style includes one of three possibilities: anxious, avoidant, or disorganized. An anxious attached style tends toward hyperactivating strategies and avoidant attached style uses deactivating strategies. A disorganized attached style involves both anxious and avoidant characteristics, using both strategies.

55. Ibid., loc. 8608–9.
56. Ibid., loc. 8619.

two purposes of the caregiving system: (1) to satisfy the other's "needs for protection and support in times of danger or distress," and (2) to encourage the other's desired "exploration, autonomy, and growth when exploration is safe."[57] When the caregiving system is activated, Mikulincer and Shaver comment that the caregiving person is changed momentarily into an attachment figure who is "stronger and wiser." In that moment, the aims of the caregiver and carereceiver become one—both desiring that the carereceiver's need for "safety and security" be satisfied.[58] For instance, when a Pentecostal couple opened their home to Christy and her children on Friday nights, providing a meal and playing games with her kids, Christy stated she felt safe enough to fall asleep during those visits. The safety enabled her to express her autonomy by sleeping rather than joining in the playing of games.

Research indicates, as Mikulincer and Shaver point out, there are two basic occasions when the caregiving behavioral system is initiated. First, the caregiving desire is prompted when the other is dealing with a threat, anxiety, or uneasiness and requests help or could plainly use assistance.[59] This is evident in Christy's description of church members' supportive responses to Christy's moments of "grief bursts" (grief unexpectedly erupting). Second, caregiving responses are activated when the other is offered an occasion to explore or learn and is in need of support in order to pursue this opportunity or because she has chosen to take advantage of it and desires to discuss it.[60] In both cases, the prospective caregiver offers care and comfort because of his own "*appraisal* of the other's need for assistance or encouragement" (italics in original).[61] For instance, Danielle spoke of receiving encouragement from another Christian patient at the hospital. This is also seen in the instances of people finding meaning (chapter 4) with the aid of others, such as Lindsey's friend calling and mentioning the devotional "The Right Time?"

Once the caregiving system is activated, Mikulincer and Shaver emphasize that empathy is viewed as a major strategy of the caregiving system. For the authors, empathy involves two elements: "sensitivity and responsiveness." Sensitivity denotes "attunement to, and accurate interpretation

57. Ibid., loc. 8633–35.
58. Ibid., loc. 8636–39.
59. Ibid., loc. 8639–41.
60. Ibid., loc. 8641–43.
61. Ibid., loc. 8643–44.

of, another person's signals of distress, worry, or need, and responding in synchrony with the person's proximity- and support-seeking behavior." Responsiveness involves "generous intentions; validating the troubled person's needs and feelings; respecting his or her beliefs, attitudes, and values; and helping him or her feel loved, cared for, and understood."[62] This caregiving may be mutual. Kyle recounted support in the form of connection with others after his daughter died. He illustrated an experience of sensitivity and responsiveness in this connection, when he said, "After our experience, all the sudden we became more aware of other people that have lost their children, and we began to be community with them. We could relate." That is, Kyle related to others in mutuality at the place of vulnerability.

While caregiving may be hindered by the needful person's inability to express her needs, it may also be hindered by the caregiver's sensations, views, convictions, and apprehensions that interfere "with sensitivity and responsiveness."[63] Hence, when a prospective caregiver neglects the signs of a person in need through disregarding or misreading the cues or sidestepping the job as caregiver, the caregiving system's aim of providing for the sufferer's need is not met.[64] Mikulincer and Shaver believe that, the sufferer may "feel misunderstood, disrespected, or burdensome" when there is a scarcity of sensitivity and responsiveness, which only serves to heighten the sufferer's anguish.[65] For Kirsten, the lack of responsiveness spilled over into her relationship with God—when others were unavailable, she believed God was unavailable.

Taking into consideration attachment theory's behavioral and caregiving systems, I argue that suffering is an opportunity for relationships. When an adult is disturbed and unable to cope with anxiety or a threat, he may seek out the other, or even a group, for support in order to find comfort, to be soothed, and/or to be encouraged. When a potential caregiver perceives the other is suffering, her own caregiving system may be activated, and she may intervene through empathy and/or practical acts of support. Bowlby's attachment theory indicates that no matter the age, suffering generates in each of us a desire to connect with others—either to

---

62. Ibid., loc. 8661–66.

63 Ibid., loc. 8692–93. Mikulincer and Shaver also discuss attachment processes in leadership, underscoring that followers look to leaders for care and support during difficult periods; see Mikulincer and Shaver, *Attachment in Adulthood*, chapter 15.

64. Ibid., loc. 8667–70.

65. Ibid., loc. 8670–71.

receive care or to give care. Such caregiving is depicted in Christopraxis: just as Christ has entered our nothingness, believers now enter the other's nothingness and participate in Christ's ministry through acts of ministry in which God is revealed and people are restored; thus, Jesus is experienced in Christopraxis.[66] This means rather than individualism surfacing during a lack of a desired, divine intervention, humanity's relationality is embraced and love is expressed as Jesus both demonstrated to and commanded his followers as portrayed in John 13.

LOVE ON DISPLAY

From the outset of reading John 13, the reader may note three connected elements: presence, absence, and believing. This pericope begins with *presence* (Passover Feast) alongside *absence* (Jesus's departure), which is followed by *presence* ("I am" statement) that is connected to *believing* (13:19). Thus far in this project I have stressed that God is present with humanity in the Son. Such presence communicates humanity's worth as Jesus enters humanity's nothingness (the suffering world). Now, John 13 initiates a shift in this Gospel. Leon Morris perceives this shift involves not only the completion of Jesus's public ministry but also, more importantly for this project, the footwashing "is a significant action, setting the tone for all that follows," which includes Jesus's Passion and departure.[67] Prior to this, Jesus speaks of God's love for the world (3:16) and that the Father has sent him (e.g., 3:16–17; 4:34; 5:30, 37; 8:16, 18); however, in these verses Jesus begins to also talk of the disciples' loving each other (13:34–35) and his disciples' being sent (13:16, 20).[68] This implies that *loving* and *sending* are intimately

---

66. Root writes, "Human action is bound in impossibility; it sits in the framework of possibility through nothingness. But because the divine is the action of ministry, which comes out and goes into *nihilo*, human action that does the same—that is, *confesses its nihilo* for the sake of participating in the hypostasis, participating in subjects as persons—is bound in the fellowship of ministerial act with God" (italics in original). Root, *Christopraxis*, loc. 3705–8.

67. Morris, *The Gospel of John*, 542–44. Morris sees the rest of John as containing discourse with his disciples and the events of his crucifixion, death, and resurrection. Thomas perceives the footwashing as preparation as in preparing the disciples for Jesus's soon departure; see Thomas, *Footwashing in John 13 and the Johannine Community*, chapter 4.

68. Thompson remarks that prior to this, Jesus has spoken of the Father sending him; however, "now, anticipating the time when he will send out his disciples, Jesus makes the same point about the relationship of the disciples to him: he will send them

connected in this Gospel, which will be discussed more fully in the next chapter.⁶⁹

A dominant theme in this pericope is portrayed when Jesus gets up from the table and prepares himself to wash the disciples' feet. Such an act by Jesus is to display not only his love for his disciples but also to demonstrate how they are to love each other.⁷⁰ As Morris writes, the washing of feet was normally completed before the meal, not during the meal, making Jesus's action more significant.⁷¹ Thompson comments that footwashing points toward the numerous washings of the extremities since they require it more often. She also notes it is "an act of hospitality" that is completed by either a servant or a guest, which allows guests the occasion to conduct themselves in a similar manner to their conduct at home by washing their feet after their journey.⁷² Thus, it is an ordinary ritual of antiquity. However, when Jesus, who is one in authority (13:3), washes his disciples' feet, he is positioning himself as a slave (13:12–17).⁷³ Such a position is a place of vulnerability, and for Jesus, it is an expression of love. In this position of vulnerability others may not accept or understand the demonstration of love, as seen in the lack of understanding in Peter's comments (13:6–10). Thompson notes, however, "Jesus is resolutely determined to carry out *this* act that demonstrates his love for his own, portraying it in the form

---

and tell them what to do and say; therefore, a response to them will actually be a response to Jesus, and hence to the Father who sent him." Thompson, *John*, 291.

69. I saw this as a result of reading Moloney's *Love in the Gospel of John*.

70. An emphasis on his love for the disciples may be implied in the Greek text in 13:1, which, Thompson states, contains one long sentence with phrases and clauses that modify "the main verb and its object: 'he loved them [his own]'"; see Thompson, *John*, 284. My purpose in exploring this account is not to argue whether or not this is to be a church sacrament or if it is an embodied parable. For example, see Thomas, *Footwashing in John 13 and the Johannine Community*; see also Morris, *The Gospel of John*, 542–45. As Keener comments, "John includes a summons to foot washing (whether symbolically or literally), by which believers are called to exemplify the same pattern of self-sacrificial service to the death"; see Keener, *The Gospel of John*, 902. Thus, part of this pericope's purpose (but not its only purpose) is to call Christ-followers to love as Jesus's loves, sacrificially.

71. Morris, *The Gospel of John*, 544.

72. Thompson, *John*, 281.

73. Keener writes, "John prefaces the scene by emphasizing Jesus' authority, source, and destination, which heightens the significance of his service to the disciples that immediately follows (13:3)"; see Keener, *The Gospel of John*, 900. Thompson notes, "Here Jesus performs an act of service typically rendered by a slave: he will soon die a death suffered by slaves, death by crucifixion"; see Thompson, *John*, 282.

of service that overturns human categories of judging (7:24) and human standards of glory or honor" (italics in original).[74]

While Jesus's embodied action of love for his disciples appears in a routine custom of antiquity, it also calls them to love each other in a similar manner (13:15–17). Thompson convincingly captures this:

> Similarly, in the community of Jesus' followers, conduct toward the other is to be governed by love rather than the preservation of one's own status or honor. Jesus' disciples are to think not of what is due to them—in Jesus' case, proper regard for him as Teacher and Lord—but instead to serve one another in the mundane practices of life. Washing someone's feet is neither heroic nor remarkable. The love and service to which Jesus calls his disciples will work itself out primarily in the routines of daily living.[75]

These mundane practices were seen in the lives of the participants, as in Lindsey's family receiving food after her father died and assistance with the funeral after her brother died, or Jeremy's wife being provided a place to stay when she traveled to visit him in the hospital. In the words of Christopraxis, the washing of feet symbolizes entering the pit, expressing love by entering another's nothingness. Yet, as Jesus's action in the Passion reminds us, Jesus's love is one that goes beyond practicing a familiar custom but goes all the way to the death; so also is to be the disciples' love for each other (15:12–13).[76]

The concept of loving each other in this pericope is positioned alongside the theme of betrayal and denial (13:2, 21–30, 37–38). This is fitting because love is vulnerable in that it embraces uncertainty, risk, and emotional exposure. It is willing to take a chance on being hurt, indicating one cannot be betrayed unless one loves. Unlike humans, the divine-human one knows Judas will betray him (13:26–30) and Peter will deny him (13:37–38), yet he continues to love them, as seen in the embodied action of washing their feet. Such an action illustrates how his foreknowledge does not diminish his love for them. As Thompson also notes, his foreknowledge of Judas's

---

74. Thompson, *John*, 287.

75. Ibid., 289.

76. Thompson remarks that the "footwashing and crucifixion become mutually interpretative. Jesus' death, interpreted as a selfless act of service and sacrifice, provides a model for the disciples to emulate (John 15:13; 21:17–19). The disciples are to love one another as Jesus has loved them (13:34–35). Such love will include acts of service, such as washing another's feet; and it may be manifested supremely, as Jesus' love was, in death (15:13; 1 John 3:16)." Ibid., 286.

betrayal does not stifle his anguish (13:21).[77] Thus, Jesus demonstrates by washing the disciples' feet that love embraces vulnerability, which may include being aware of the impending pain. Thompson comments that Jesus informs his disciples that they, too, may experience betrayal (15:20) from close companions.[78] Yet, such knowledge, as Jesus compellingly exemplifies, is not to deter them from embracing their vulnerability by loving each other. By continuing to be present to Judas and Peter, Jesus communicates their worth and respects their human will and provides opportunities for trust and transformation while inviting his followers to do the same. According to Kirsten, there is beauty in service:

> If all of us were all healed, even in a Pentecostal church, how would we operate as a church? You don't have to do anything if everybody's 100 percent functional. You don't have to rely on God, but if somebody's there (A) to remind you that you have to rely on God, and (B) you have to operate as his hands and feet, then that's when you can become the most effective and beautiful as a church as really serving each other.

This love among the disciples, which embraces uncertainty, risk, and emotional exposure, is an indication to the world that they are Jesus's disciples (13:35;15:8). Thompson writes, "If the disciples are to bear witness to the world, they must emulate and embody the pattern of Jesus' life (15:13–17) as the one sent by God."[79] That is, the Sent One's love for the world is an embodied action that includes laying down his life for humanity, and so are the disciples to do the same for each other as Jesus's sent ones into the world. In this manner, the presence of Jesus is experienced through the disciples' love for each other in light of Jesus's physical absence.

CONCLUSION

I have stressed in this chapter that the helpful responses from members of the body of Christ made a connection with the participant and participated in Christ's ministry through acts of ministry that both revealed God and generated healing in some form. These helpful individuals indirectly perceived the isolation and the longing for connection in suffering as they

---

77. Ibid., 293.
78. Ibid., 292.
79. Ibid., 291.

entered into the participant's nothingness, the apparent absence of God, welcoming the participant's vulnerability as well as their own. They took a risk by reaching out to the sufferer, being uncertain of the sufferer's response and/or God's, and also in reaching out, they were tacitly recognizing their own vulnerability if they should happen to journey along a similar path. By entering into the participant's nothingness, they implicitly joined the sufferer in embracing humanity's finitude, acknowledging uncertainty, ambiguity, and mystery as being part and parcel of life. In loving the other, they were letting go of the certainty that pious platitudes proffer. Loving another, then, involves entering a pit (nothingness), which may be unpleasant, such as entering a home in which a husband has committed suicide. When loving another, the Christ-follower indirectly trusts God is present by entering into this apparent absence of God. It is here that a powerful connection is made as worth is communicated; human and divine wills are honored; and opportunities for trust and transformation are engendered. As they enter into the other's nothingness, there is recognition of the need for the power of the Spirit, an implicit acknowledgement of weakness. In this act of ministry, Jesus is encountered as God is revealed and healing flows. Thus, presence is experienced in apparent absence. In the next chapter, I discuss how believers may be pragmatically present to others in suffering, expressing love through empathy.

6

How to Be Present in Apparent Absence

Empathy

I feel like my level of empathy has just exploded, and I like that because we're all hurting in some way. We are.

—Christy, a participant

IN THE PREVIOUS CHAPTERS I have used the practical theological methodology of Christopraxis whereby I reflected on the experiences of extended suffering of Classical Pentecostals with the aid of Scripture, theology, culture, and psychology. Through this method, I have also embraced a Pentecostal methodology to form a more robust theology of suffering and healing by combining experience with Scripture. In so doing, a Pentecostal theological praxis of suffering and healing is emerging, which involves:

* revealing God to humanity and reconciling (healing) humanity to God;
* cultivating an ability to hold both presence and apparent absence concurrently;

- embracing, which includes holding the pain while being willing to release it;
- perceiving that suffering is an opportunity for relationality;
- participating in Christ's ministry to the sufferer through an intervention of presence and/or practical assistance;
- offering opportunities to make meaning (reconciliation) of the suffering;
- generating occasions for the sufferer to be transformed in how he relates to his context;
- creating opportunities for others to make sense of their suffering;
- giving occasions for trust, which may result in the embracing of uncertainty, ambiguity, and mystery;
- communicating worth, respect for the other's will, and fostering occasions for transformation and forgiveness.

I now narrow my focus to a specific praxis, namely empathy, as a way in which believers may be present to others. By concentrating on a specific action that reveals truth (praxis), this chapter answers the questions of Christopraxis, "How then should we live?" and "What should we do?" I seek to demonstrate that through the expression of empathy believers are participating in Christ's ministry so that God is being revealed and humans are being healed. This means, God is experienced through this act of compassion. Taking this into consideration, then, I assert that empathy is an appropriate response or act of ministry to members of the body of Christ who are suffering. I will argue in four movements that the expression of empathy is a theological praxis of suffering and healing: (1) by presenting the experiences of the participants in how they would now minister to others; (2) by clarifying the meaning of empathy, sympathy, pity, and compassion; (3) by asserting that Jesus is God's expression of empathy to humanity, God's love in action, as demonstrated in John's Gospel; and (4) by offering Marshall Rosenberg's Nonviolent Communication (Compassionate Communication) as a way to participate in Christ's ministry through the expression of empathy.

HOW WOULD THE PARTICIPANTS NOW RESPOND?

As in the pattern set forth in previous chapters, I begin this chapter with the experiences of the participants. All of the participants pointed towards the importance of *being with others* when speaking about how they would now respond to individuals who are suffering. This response corresponds with what I have underscored concerning Christopraxis: In chapters 4 and 5 the participants encountered God in that Jesus came and ministered to them through ongoing presence and intense instances as well as through person-to-person ministry; thus, the participants, who have experienced Christ's ministry, now desire to minister to others who are suffering by *being with others*. Kyle particularly highlights this: "It would be hypocritical of me to say I am aware of God's presence in my own suffering and not understand and not be ready to help others in theirs." In other words, experiencing God's presence in their own suffering moves sufferers to be present to others in their suffering.

While all of the participants spoke of being alongside the other in response to another's suffering, many of the participants also informed me that their understanding of the importance of *being with others* was a shift from their previous responses in that they are now more compassionate or empathic. While a couple of participants stated this change occurred naturally as they matured, other participants indicated this change was a direct outcome of their own suffering. Joan believed her response would now be completely different from how she had reacted previously and illustrated this with a story about a friend who had believed her adult daughter would be healed. When the daughter died, Joan attempted to educate her friend by giving her books, of which Joan said, "Oh my goodness, talk about lack of comfort! I would definitely not approach it that way again. I could've destroyed my friend by total insensitivity." In responding to those who were suffering, Joan would now point to God being present even while persons may feel very weak, broken, and unsure of where God is in the moment. Christy, as indicated previously (chapter 4), spoke of her move from *doing* to *being with others* when they are suffering. When remarking about being more empathic, she said, "I like that God's changed that in me because I was always the kind of person [who thought], 'Pull yourself up by your bootstraps.' [I was] like my dad, 'Cowboy up-kind-of-thing. Let's just plow through this. Let's just go.' And that's not reality." Jeremy, too, referred to being more relational by being more present than absent when others are suffering. He stated, "There's been a real shift. Because if I had a friend going through what I've gone through and then going through, I would be there for him. I would love him. I would want to counsel and be with him."

I discovered six ways, or what may be referred to as *interventions* (chapter 4), from the participants' stories of how they would *be with others* who were in the midst of suffering. The first three ways that I mention were examined in previous chapters, which are presence, practical action/being available to act, and praying for others. Due to the previous discussion, I simply express here Lindsey's comments about presence, Kirsten's brief remarks about availability, and Kyle's perspective on prayer. For Lindsey, being present does not involve helping people find an answer. Instead, being present includes praying for strength and comfort and affirming God's ability to heal if God chooses to do so. She said of presence: "If somebody says, 'I fully believe that God's gonna heal,' I will encourage them, and I wouldn't hinder their faith. I also wouldn't say to somebody who doesn't have faith, 'Well, you just need to pray harder or have more faith' [because] I think we wound people that way." Concerning availability and practical action, Kirsten sees it as important to follow through when saying, "We will help you out if you need it." This means one is to be intentional about meeting the needs of the other by making plans, providing time, and enlisting others, if necessary. Several participants also discussed *being with others* who are suffering through intercession. Kyle explains, "I would not say, . . . 'I'm praying for you,' if I'm not praying because that was part of our experience, too. So many people said, 'We're praying for you,' and I don't really think they were. Maybe in the first week after [my daughter] died, they were praying, but then life goes back to the normal pace, and you don't."

The three remaining ways to *be with others* who are suffering are: inclusivity, listening, and encouragement. Kirsten spoke of the significance of inclusivity in being with someone who is suffering. For Kirsten, it is not enough to simply invite a sufferer to a church gathering. Instead, congregants are encouraged to deliberately include the sufferer in activities outside the context of church functions, making an effort to extend hospitality to the one who is suffering. In Kirsten's words, "If you're gonna invite them over, invite them over, and make 'em a part." Some participants spoke of listening to the sufferer as a way to *be with the other*. Both Christy and Danielle indicated that listening involves hearing the other's story. Christy stated, "I just am more in tune to people, and I take time for people because I really want to take time for people. I wanna hear their story." Danielle similarly said, "I'd be that listener that everyone needs after they lose someone." Several participants raised the importance of encouraging the sufferer that God is present. For instance, Danielle spoke of her desire to "always encourage" those who are suffering "that God is with them." The word "encourage" is key, and to help us understand its significance, I look to its antonym, "discourage." When we are discouraged, it points to a longing that is either not coming to pass or we do not believe it will come to pass. Thus, the participants' desire to encourage sufferers by stating, "God is present," implicitly indicates that people who are in the midst of suffering commonly sense that God is absent—God has abandoned them. That is to say, sufferers are often discouraged because they long for God but believe God is not with them while they are suffering. Christy expressed her desire to encourage others: "I wanna show them that through the hardest thing in life God is good, and he's there."

However, *being with others* in their suffering is not merely a matter of saying the proper words, acting appropriately, or simply showing up. Although these actions are good, they may be completed without thought and in a mechanical manner. Instead, a few of the participants indicated that *being with others* involved what I refer to as sensitivity, which is being sensitive to the Spirit, to self, and to others. Kirsten specifically underscored being sensitive to the Spirit when she believed that being with others began with praying for a spirit of compassion. She particularly asserted that "you need God's help to be compassionate" when ministering to someone whose experience of suffering is unfamiliar to you, the caregiver.[1] Yet, Kirsten was clear that one's lack of familiarity with another's type of suffering does not negate the possibility of ministering to him simply because the caregiver has not experienced that particular kind of suffering. For Kirsten, God can give us the compassion we need "because Jesus has been through every kind of suffering." Being sensitive to the Spirit not only involves praying for God to give us compassion but to pray for the sufferer "until you get just this understanding." Kirsten said, "Pray for whatever's in their life because sometimes they can't pray for it themselves."

Sensitivity also involves being attentive to one's self, particularly to one's own unhealed wounds. Both Bob and Kirsten remarked about being triggered due to their own pain, which hindered their ability to be compassionate and helpful to those who were suffering. Kirsten clarified, "If you're

---

1. As Deborah van Deusen Hunsinger and Theresa Latini mention, all compassion comes from God for "God's love is the wellspring from which we draw when we need compassion for ourselves or another." Hunsinger and Latini, *Transforming Church Conflict*, loc. 1655–56.

too close to something, that's not probably the best thing to get involved with because you'll damage yourself."[2] Thus, self-awareness includes an acknowledgment of a need for boundaries in order to take care of one's self. Kirsten also linked self-awareness to discernment as to whom one is being called to help or the type of person one is more gifted to help; this discernment assists in avoiding the trap of attempting to help anyone in need, which may result in resentment.

Finally, *being with the other* involves sensitivity to others and their pain. Danielle highlighted this sensitivity when she spoke of recognizing where the other person is in her journey. This type of sensitivity focuses on the carereceiver. Danielle's words succinctly caution future caregivers: "It's not about me now; it's about that person." Thus, being sensitive to others for Danielle includes eschewing any attempts to "trump" the sufferer's experience by the caregiver sharing his own experience. Danielle also emphasized the significance of avoiding insensitive platitudes such as, "With time it's gonna get better." Danielle admitted that while such an adage may be true and while it may also sound positive, it is not what the person longs to hear; instead, the other person yearns for empathy.

HOW TO DEFINE THE TERMS

As seen above, several of the participants spoke of *empathy*; however, the words "empathy," "sympathy," "pity," and "compassion" are used variously by people with different connotations. For instance, several of the research participants indicated that empathy only occurs when an individual experienced an identical form of suffering as another. While an identical experience of suffering may increase our capacity for empathy, I do not hold to this opinion. Believing that I may only have empathy for those who

2. Mikulincer and Shaver write of being triggered: "Dealing with another person's suffering can evoke two different kinds of emotional reactions in a potential caregiver (Batson, 1991): empathic compassion and personal distress. The two are often commingled, making it difficult for some people to tell whether the optimal response is to help the other person or to turn away to avoid one's own negative feelings. Although both compassion and personal distress are signs that one person's distress has triggered potentially caring reactions in another, the two states are quite different in attentional focus and motivational implications. The main focus of compassion is the other person's needs or suffering, and the natural implication is that the distress should be alleviated for the sufferer's benefit. In contrast, the main focus of personal distress is the self's own discomfort, which might be alleviated either by helping or by ignoring, or fleeing, the situation." Mikulincer and Shaver, *Attachment in Adulthood*, loc. 8672–79.

experience the same suffering as I have experienced limits the number of occasions I may be used by the Spirit to express empathy. Instead, I believe I can tap into my feelings and experiences while listening to the other (being with), which will assist me in identifying in a limited capacity with the other's feelings and enable me to possibly perceive the other's needs. For example, even though I have never experienced the death of a spouse or a child, I have felt sadness concerning other losses, which allows me to access that feeling and enable me to connect to the possible needs of that person.[3] With that being said, I have chosen in this section to clarify how I am using *empathy, sympathy, pity,* and *compassion* due to the variety of understandings connected to these terms.

Jean Baker Miller and Irene Pierce Stiver define empathy as "the capacity to feel and think something similar to the feelings and thoughts of another person."[4] For Patricia DeYoung empathy includes being able to feel "the darkest and most painful moments" of the carereceiver as well as communicate those feelings. At the same time, DeYoung notes that empathy is able to differentiate between the carereceiver's and the caregiver's feelings.[5] Jordan offers both a definition and description of the impact of empathy in therapy:

> Empathy is a complex cognitive affective skill; it is the ability to put oneself in the others' [sic] shoes, to "feel with" the other, to understand the other's experience. It is crucial to the felt experience of connectedness . . . for empathy to "make a difference," to create healing and lessen isolation, the client must be able to see, know, and feel the therapist's empathic response. Chronic disconnection

---

3. Brown also argues, "The bottom line is this: If we want to build connection networks . . . we cannot reserve empathy for the select few who have had experiences that mirror our own. We must learn how to move past the situations and events that people are describing in order to move toward the feelings and the emotions they're experiencing." Brown offers an example of an experience of an African-American medical school student who straddles a "very white, male world of medicine and black family life." Although Brown is "not an African-American medical school student," she has "had similar experiences in terms of trying to balance two worlds that often seem mutually exclusive." Brown writes, "For me, this experience makes me feel lonely, unworthy and like something is wrong with me." Therefore, while Brown does "not want to project" her own experiences onto the African-American medical school student, she wants "to be able to touch," in herself, "some of the emotions that [the student] might be feeling so that [Brown] can try to connect with what [the student] is saying." Brown, *I Thought It Was Just Me,* 56–58.

4. Miller and Stiver, *The Healing Connection,* 27.

5. DeYoung, *Relational Psychotherapy,* 51–55.

leads to demoralization and a loss of hope for empathic responsiveness from the other person, indeed, from all others.[6]

Hence, empathy includes both the cognitive and affective aspects in that it involves a skill as well as one's emotions in which a caregiver identifies similar feelings and/or experiences within herself to the one receiving care but knows that her feelings and experiences are different from the carereceiver's. This on-the-ground skill of empathy is not only for the professional counselor or clergy, but it is also necessary for those sitting in the pew.[7]

In light of these considerations as well as the discussion of empathy in Charlene Burns's *Divine Becoming: Rethinking Jesus and the Incarnation*, I define empathy in the following manner: a potential within humanity that may be refined and/or developed through skills and practice in which a person listens and identifies feelings and possible needs that the other may be experiencing. This identification may initially produce a temporary affective response in the caregiver towards the carereceiver. In this process of identification the caregiver may imagine herself in similar instances to that of the carereceiver or call to mind her own similar experiences and/or feelings while recognizing that her imaginings or actual experiences/feelings are different from the carereceiver. That is to say, empathy may occur naturally and/or by choice. When it is natural, it is an "unconscious physical and psychological event" in which the body and the emotions respond first by matching the current state of the other person followed by a sense of feeling with the other, a "felt comprehension" of the other's experience. When empathy is a choice, it begins with using the imagination to identify with the carereceiver, which generates a feeling response that is experienced psychologically and physically. Yet, there is an awareness in these responses, whether it is natural or by choice, that the caregiver's affective experience is being generated by the carereceiver, which means it is differentiated from that of the carereceiver.[8]

---

6. Jordan, *Relational-Cultural Therapy*, loc. 784–95.

7. Highlighting empathy as a skill may produce questions as to its passion and earnestness, but it is not simply a skill without emotion. It is an expression of compassion that emanates from love. It is a way in which one enters into solidarity with the sufferer. In developing the skill that expresses empathy, it may at first appear mechanical and without feeling; however, the expression of empathy becomes more natural as one becomes more proficient at communicating empathy within a certain skill set.

8. Burns writes, "*Empathy* is a somewhat removed way of responding to others. It seems to be an innate capacity for some and more a learned skill for others. Empathy is

Empathy is distinct from *sympathy*, *pity*, and *compassion*. Sympathy is similar to empathy in that the caregiver shares similar feelings as the carereceiver; however, *sympathy* holds that the experiences of both the caregiver and the carereceiver are the same. In other words, there is a lack of differentiation between the affective responses of the caregiver and the carereceiver. An example may be observed when someone loses a parent and a well-meaning relative states, "I know how you feel. I felt the same way when my mother passed away." The caregiver's own pain is being triggered so that it becomes more about the caregiver than the carereceiver, which is common in sympathy. *Pity* also is not to be confused with empathy. Andrea Hollingsworth notes that pity suggests "that the sufferer is inferior."[9] In empathy, however, there is an absence of a *power over*, and there is, instead, the presence of a *power with* the one suffering.

An important and related word to empathy is *compassion*, which means "to suffer with." While compassion has feelings of empathy for another, it has an additional feature in that it is moved to action. I am drawing from Hollingsworth, who writes, "I define compassion as *being empathically connected with others in their suffering and taking action to ease their distress*" (italics in original).[10] I agree with Hollingsworth who sees a "helping behavior," or an action, as not only providing things like food, clothes, or shelter but also "empathically bearing witness to another's pain."[11] Empathy, then, in and of itself, is a helping act of compassion. This additionally means that whether one is providing practical assistance or

---

the more conscious and linguistic aspect of sharing in the lifeworld of another. When it occurs as a natural response, entrainment, attunement, and sympathy all come into play in a kind of sequential flow of unconscious physical and psychological events that culminate in felt comprehension of the other's experience. But because it is a cognitive event, it is possible to generate empathy by choice. In this case, the sequence is to some extent reversed. The decision to relate empathically can be made fully consciously, as when a therapist enters into counseling with a client, or quasi-consciously, as when a parent 'steps back' from the urge to solve her children's problems for them. When the decision for empathic relating is conscious, the first step in the process becomes imaginative projection. Through the imagination, the emotional responses of sympathy and psychophysiological responses of attunement and entrainment are stimulated. Sympathy does not require imaginative projection. In sympathetic responding, one is with the object of sympathy. Sympathy is an innate and somewhat automatic response, and as such can result in confusing one's own needs with those of the other" (italics in original). Burns, *Divine Becoming*, 104–5.

9. Hollingsworth, "Implications of Interpersonal Neurobiology," 840.
10. Ibid., 839.
11. Ibid., 856n3.

expressing empathy, either act of compassion is an intervention in accordance with the revised definition of *intervention* (chapter 4), and I see this compassionate act, an intervention, when God, from whom all compassion flows, sends the Son into the world as it is presented in the Fourth Gospel.

HOW DOES GOD RESPOND?

Having portrayed how the participants would respond to others who are suffering, I now turn to God's response and God's instruction to those who follow Jesus Christ. I have attempted to show so far in chapters 2 and 4 of this project that both absence and presence are major themes in the Gospel of John, respectively. In the last chapter I discussed a specific vulnerable act of Jesus's love, the washing of the disciples' feet, while introducing the concept of the disciples being sent into the world. I continue the discussion in this chapter as I explore the theme of love in action in John's Gospel by particularly drawing from the writing of Francis Moloney. This will be accomplished by (1) asserting God is a major figure in the Fourth Gospel; (2) highlighting the connection between loving and sending in the Gospel of John; and (3) underscoring John's emphasis on the disciples' love for each other which reveals God to the world.

I begin with the assertion that the Fourth Gospel has God the Father as a central character. Although some perceive that describing God's character in John is difficult because God does not appear and articulates very few words (i.e., 12:28), Thompson believes God is a "literary figure" (a character) in the Gospel of John.[12] Moloney goes further by asserting, "[An] intense focus upon the human-divine person of Jesus undervalues an important element at the heart of the Johannine story: the Gospel is *ultimately* about God, and not Jesus" (italics in original).[13] Moloney argues that if Jesus is the only one who has seen God (1:18), the chief concern of the Gospel is that Jesus reveals God.[14] Thompson similarly reminds her readers, it is not that Jesus describes God in what he says "*about* God," but it is Jesus's "words and deeds" that reveal God (italics in original).[15] In

---

12. Thompson, "God's Voice You Have Never Heard," 186.

13. Moloney, *Love in the Gospel of John*, 38. Moloney also writes, "The Gospel may be about Jesus, but Jesus is about God's business." Ibid., 51.

14. Ibid., 3.

15. Thompson, "God's Voice You Have Never Heard," 188. Thompson also notes, "The actions attributed to God in the Gospel are either implied or assumed, or else understood

other words, Jesus reveals God to the reader, making the character of God a central feature of the narrative.

As the central character in John, God acts by loving. For Moloney, the central theme of John is love in action, particularly in its emphasis on God's actions "in and through the Son."[16] Such prominence placed on action in John correlates with Christopraxis, which holds that we know God by God's actions. Moloney asserts that John does not focus only on words to communicate God's love (i.e., *agapē* and *phileō*) but also God's actions. This love in the Fourth Gospel for Moloney is particularly expressed in the actions of Jesus's life, death, resurrection, and ascension as well as in the believers' love for one another.[17] Keener likewise writes, "Nowhere in this Gospel does God say, 'I love you'; rather, he demonstrates his love for humanity by self-sacrifice (13:34; 14:31), and demands the same practical demonstration of love from his followers (e.g., 14:15, 21–24; 21:15–17).[18]

This demonstration of love is characterized as another major topic in John which, according to Moloney, is God's act of sending. This is particularly observed in the act of sending Jesus, which is highlighted twenty times in the Fourth Gospel (3:16–17; 5:23, 30, 36; 10:36; 12:49; 14:24; 17:3, 18, 21, 23, 25; 20:21; 7:28–29; 8:16, 18, 26, 28–29).[19] Thompson remarks that the act of sending makes God and/or "the Father the subject and initiator of the Son's activity." For her, *sending* speaks of an agent who is completing a mission for another so that the sent one exemplifies the one who is doing the act of sending while also focusing the readers' attention on the one who sends.[20] The connection between loving and sending is especially apparent in 3:16–17. For Moloney, this first statement in John of using the word "sending" not only establishes the theme of God's sending of the Son but

---

indirectly through the actions of Jesus. The actions that are 'assumed' actually fall under the category of comments by another character (usually Jesus) or comments by the narrator." Ibid., 189.

16. Moloney, *Love in the Gospel of John*, x–xi.

17. Ibid.

18. Keener, *The Gospel of John*, 566–67. Thompson also remarks about the actions of God in John, "[M]ost of the statements about God are sentences with active verbs, rather than predications of virtues ('God is good') or essence ('God is omnipotent'). Although some of the verbs refer to past action and some to future, many refer to present action, and almost all the verbs have Jesus as the object (loves, knows, sends, gives) or agent of the action, or the believer as the object (keeps, sanctifies, loves)"; see Thompson, "God's Voice You Have Never Heard," 190.

19. Moloney, *Love in the Gospel of John*, 57.

20. Thompson, "The Living Father," 27–28.

also links it to love.[21] Moloney summarizes these two verses: "God's act of loving the world initiates the cycle of the sending of the Son that culminates in his crucifixion and exaltation. There the heavenly is revealed so that the believer might have eternal life. God's love makes the gift of eternal life possible, and the mission of Jesus is to make that love known."[22] In the words of Christopraxis, it is the very being (person) of Jesus that is God's action, which is particularly seen in 3:16–17, and Christ-followers participate in the very being of God through acts of ministry to one another.

In the Fourth Gospel Jesus not only reveals God to the world, but Jesus also continues to be revealed to the world through the love that the believers have one for another. Moloney notes that the command to love one's neighbor is absent from John's Gospel; instead, there is the theme of the disciples loving each other.[23] As seen in this project's previous chapter, when Jesus washes the disciples' feet, he commands his disciples to love each other, which displays to the world that they are Jesus's disciples (13:34–35). Yet, this is not the only place we read of Jesus's commanding the disciples to love one another. We also read this in John 15:12–17 in which two times the disciples are instructed to love each other in the same manner Jesus has loved them. That is, his love for them is an embodied action in that he lays down his life for them. Jesus, however, does not only instruct his followers to love each other, but he also prays for them to be unified (John 17). Moloney stresses that the reason Jesus prays for unity is so that the world may believe that God sent Jesus.[24] He comments, "As Jesus was sent, 'given' so that the world may have life (3:16–17), so the disciples are sent into the world (17:18) that it may believe and know that Jesus is the Sent One of God who loved the world (17:21, 23; 3:16–17)."[25]

One way the disciples' love may be expressed is in the way the church responds to those who are suffering within their midst. In the same way that God ministers to this fallen world through an act of love by sending and giving the Son to rescue humanity, so Christ-followers are to respond in loving action toward those who are experiencing suffering.[26] As God

21. Moloney, *Love in the Gospel of John*, 57–58.
22. Ibid., 61.
23. Ibid., x.
24. Ibid., 207–8.
25. Ibid., 208.
26. I am using here the idea of attachment theory's caregiving system (chapter 5) in which Mikulincer and Shaver describe the caregiving system as a capacity of all persons

came in the person of Jesus and lived in this fallen world, Christ-followers reflect the *imago Dei* by being with the sufferers within their ranks through loving acts of ministry in which God is revealed and people are healed. Yet, these acts are not simply to benefit the church. As Thompson comments, "Love moves from the household of faith outward, from the community to the world. In commanding the disciples to love one another, Jesus does not envision a love that shrinks from risk, rejection, and suffering, or that is limited to only each other. Love for one another impels love for the world."[27] However, as Thompson also cautions, as Jesus's love for the world did not always produce belief in Jesus (chapter 4), neither will the disciples' love for each other guarantee that the world will believe in Jesus.[28] Nevertheless, the love that the disciples have for one another serves a greater purpose: that the world may see Jesus. Moloney writes, "[A]ll the love commands directed to the disciples in the Gospel and to the readers/hearers of the Gospel are missionary."[29] To quote Anderson, "Mission is the praxis of God through the power and presence of the Spirit of Christ. As a result of this mission, the church comes into being as the sign of the kingdom of God in the world."[30] Thus, I am saying, by loving each other in God's power and presence, the church bears witness to God's sending of Christ to save the world, a sign of God's reign. I now turn to a specific act of love, the expression of empathy, which is a way to be present in suffering while revealing God to others and reconciling others to God.

HOW ARE WE TO RESPOND?

I discussed in chapters 4 and 5 the importance of presence amidst suffering whether it was the presence of Jesus Christ or of other Christ-followers. Expressing empathy is a particular way one may participate in being present, and Marshall Rosenberg's *Nonviolent Communication* (NVC), which is also

---

to provide safety or security and help to those individuals who are temporarily in need or who are chronically dependent. Because of our encounter with God in Jesus when God responded to our plight by providing a need for a savior, we reflect the image of God as we respond with empathy to those who are suffering in our midst when our caregiving system is activated.

27. Thompson, *John*, 301.
28. Ibid., 302.
29. Moloney, *Love in the Gospel of John*, 206.
30. Anderson, *The Shape of Practical Theology*, 30–31.

called *Compassionate Communication*, offers a specific approach by which empathy may be expressed.[31] Rosenberg witnessed race riots in Detroit, Michigan during the 1940s in his inner-city neighborhood, resulting in his becoming a psychologist to work against the tide of such violence. As a result of the chaotic 1960s' demonstrations and violence, Rosenberg desired to take the compassionate training that he received as a psychologist and share it with the culture at large to transform conflict through empathy; thus, he developed four components that comprise a way to communicate and listen compassionately: observation, feeling, need, and request (OFNR). With this in mind, I will draw from OFNR by briefly explaining observations, feelings, and needs, which are the three components I use in expressing empathy, and this will be followed by the relational and theological natures of empathy.[32]

How to Communicate Compassionately

The first component of NVC is observation, which is distinguished from evaluation. Unlike an evaluation that leans toward generalities, an observation is very specific in describing what a person hears, sees, smells, tastes,

31. Many now refer to NVC as *Compassionate Communication*, and when speaking in Christian circles, I particularly prefer using *Compassionate Communication*; however, for the sake of brevity in this project I will be using the shorthand form "NVC." In describing NVC, I am drawing from Hunsinger and Latini, *Transforming Church Conflict*.

32. NVC references modes of communication: offering empathy towards the self (inner mode); listening to the other through empathy (outer mode); and expressing honestly one's own OFNR to another (outer mode). Each of these modes consists of OFNR. Facilitators in NVC teach that in empathy the caregiver listens to the other's observation, feeling, need, and request. Gill et al., *Nonviolent Communication (NVC) Toolkit for Facilitators*, 273. It is essential to point out that in the expression of empathy the caregiver makes observations while identifying feelings and needs that the caregiver hears; however, the caregiver does not make a request but *hears* one if it is stated. A request is a strategy to meet a need in NVC whereas empathy seeks to be present with the person without designing a plan of action. Thus, for the purpose of this project I am stressing the hearing of observations, feelings, and needs in expressing empathy. Unlike needs, requests are specific, centering on a strategy that includes a person, location, time, object, and action. There are three types of requests: (1) a connecting request—for example, "What do you hear me saying?"; (2); a strategizing request in which a request is made to brainstorm about a strategy—for example, "Would you like to brainstorm over the next fifteen minutes for possible ideas as to how I can meet my need for support?"; and (3) an action request that proposes a certain action to meet the need(s)—for example, "Would you like to meet again next week at noon for two hours to listen, be present, and pray with me in order to help meet my need for support?"

or touches within a certain time and setting. Observations are likened to a movie camera that films an event as it occurs without any explanations as to what is transpiring. An evaluation, however, expresses blame and judgment through such ways as: making interpretations (You are not praying and fasting enough); forming labels (You are conceited); and providing diagnoses (You have a demon of depression). It utilizes all-or-nothing terms like "never" or "always," and all-inclusive words such as "everybody" (Everybody goes through that). Evaluations may be an indication that caregivers are being triggered so that the focus turns to the caregivers rather than the carereceiver; in this sense, an evaluation becomes a way for caregivers to tell themselves stories about the carereceiver's suffering in order to protect themselves and avoid entering the carereceiver's nothingness. Evaluations, then, fail to make a connection, which further isolates the sufferer. Empathy's chief characteristic is to make a connection by letting the sufferer know someone is accompanying her on the path of suffering.[33] As Brown comments, "Empathy seeking is driven by the need to know that we are not alone."[34]

By using the empathic skill of observation, the caregiver reflects back the content of what has been communicated to him by the carereceiver. This response, as Deborah van Deusen Hunsinger and Theresa Latini note, demonstrates the caregiver's understanding of the words that have been spoken.[35] For instance, in responding to a carereceiver who is experiencing ongoing physical ailments and has just voiced her anger as well as her questions about God and God's interaction in the world, the caregiver may express empathy by reflecting back content: "I understood you to say that in light of the fact that you still struggle with sickness, you wonder about God's provision of care for you." Such mirroring communicates to the sufferer understanding, validation, and normalization of her experience.

---

33. Hunsinger and Latini write, "The overall purpose of compassionate communication is interpersonal connection. NVC assumes that a trustworthy connection between people is the precondition for finding *any* satisfactory way to transform conflict because it is the basis for any kind of cooperative human activity or fulfilling emotional relationship. In order to achieve mutual understanding and connection, NVC aims for three things: authentic connection with oneself; empathic reception of the other; and honest expression toward the other" (italics in original). Hunsinger and Latini, *Transforming Church Conflict*, loc. 283–86.

34. Brown, *I Thought It Was Just Me*, 50.

35. Hunsinger and Latini, *Transforming Church Conflict*, loc. 1853.

The second component of Rosenberg's NVC is feelings. Feelings are an affective experience that is often sensed physically within one's body. For instance, one may clench his fists and grit his teeth when feeling angry, or wiggle her foot when she is anxious. NVC believes feelings are generated by our needs. When I experience positive feelings such as contentment, peace, or joy, my needs have been met. When I experience negative feelings such as frustration, discouragement, or worry, my needs are not being met. In this way, the identification of feelings is linked to the identification of needs. Feelings may also be a product of one's thoughts, such as an evaluation. For example, if I see a person with his eyes closed while I am teaching, I may believe the person is sleeping, prompting me to judge myself as boring, which leads to feelings of dejection. However, if I learn the individual had a horrible headache and was simply resting his eyes while he listened to the lecture, my feelings change to relief as well as concern for the individual.

Hunsinger and Latini make an important distinction between thoughts or evaluations and feelings. While thoughts may trigger feelings, feelings are not the same as our thoughts or our evaluations. Americans may experience confusion in this regard because they use the word "feel" in place of the word "think." For instance, I may say, "I feel that she is hurting," which means, "I think she is hurting." Thus, when we use the word "feel" with the word "that" or with words such as "like," "he/she/it," "you," or a proper name, we are not expressing a feeling but a thought. We also commonly convey *faux feelings* within American culture, which are actually evaluations of actions done to us. For instance, a person may say, "I feel abandoned"; "I feel misunderstood"; or "I feel betrayed." Therefore, rather than saying a *faux feeling* such as, "I feel abandoned," the voicing of true feelings may include stating, "I feel lonely, depressed, or hurt" because one interprets another's behavior as abandonment.[36] While NVC differentiates feelings from thoughts and needs, Hunsinger and Latini caution that we are to avoid believing that identifying true feelings is simply a vehicle to discover our needs. Instead, they perceive that "emotion moves us toward encounter with others and, when considered theologically, emotion moves us toward encounter with God."[37]

According to Hunsinger and Latini, when the caregiver mirrors the carereceiver's feelings, he makes a connection as he demonstrates his

---

36. Ibid., loc. 965–1002.
37. Ibid., loc. 961–64.

understanding of the carereceiver's emotions.[38] Using the above illustration of a person who experiences ongoing illness, the caregiver might say, "So when you do not see God intervening in your life by the removal of your illness, you feel confused and frustrated, not understanding God's lack of provision in your life." If the carereceiver does not specifically name her feelings (e.g., she expresses *faux feelings* instead), the caregiver may offer conjectures as to what the carereceiver may be feeling. For instance, "When you say you are abandoned by God and others, I wonder if you feel lonely, frustrated, and helpless." By using *wonder*, the caregiver is expressing curiosity and offering the carereceiver the opportunity to agree or disagree, which respects her will. Such curiosity also indicates the caregiver is distinguishing his own experience from that of the carereceiver's experience, which is important in empathy.

The third component is needs, the lynchpin of NVC in that persons are viewed as regularly attempting to meet needs through everything they do. Needs are defined as universal qualities that enable humans to flourish. It is only when our needs are met that we are able to grow and thrive. As such, our universal needs indicate our finitude. As Hunsinger and Latini remark, it is through the embracing of our needs as finite humans that we also signify our dependence on God.[39] Joan suggested this when she stated, "It is important that I allow Jesus to meet my needs everyday and find joy in his presence." Thus, she accepted that she was not complete without God. At the same time, while we recognize that our needs are met in Christ, the church as the body of Christ participates in Christ's ministry by meeting each other's needs. This is how we acknowledge our interdependence.[40] Such interdependence was evidenced in the lives of the research participants. Christy spoke of needing assistance, healthy guidance, and a *space to be*. Several participants indicated the importance of needing others in their lives during their suffering to support them, such as Bob wanting a

38. Ibid., loc. 1856–57.

39. Hunsinger and Latini write, "Ultimately, then, our 'neediness' is one of the most basic signs of our dependence on God and one another, and is therefore to be affirmed. It is a sign of our sin when we pretend to have no need of God or of our fellow human beings." Ibid., loc. 918–20.

40. Hunsinger and Latini state, "When we live in a steady awareness of our true needs, we become acutely aware of our interdependence and rejoice in it . . . We recognize that we are made in the image of God in order to love one another, pray for one another, uphold and support one another, and encourage one another in the life of faith. Because the image of God is relational by definition, we glorify God whenever we acknowledge our basic interdependence." Ibid., loc. 907–10.

secure space to talk and Kyle longing for community and a sense of belonging. Kirsten said, "I needed somebody who would just: (A) believe me, and (B) be there for me." Lindsey not only spoke of the need for a relationship but also of wanting a reprieve from the steadiness of her sorrow. Danielle needed someone to physically embrace her and hear her. It is important to note that each of these tacitly communicates how the identification of needs points to the body of Christ's opportunity to be God's hands and feet.

The caregiver demonstrates this interdependence when a connection is made through the expression of empathy. As Hunsinger and Latini remind their readers, the caregiver uses observation and feelings to speculate as to the current underlying needs of the carereceiver.[41] Using the above illustration, the caregiver might say, "So when you do not see God intervening in your life by the removal of the sickness, I wonder if you feel confused, frustrated, and disappointed because of your desire for security in your relationship with God." As an expression of curiosity, the carereceiver in this instance is given the freedom to agree or disagree with the wondering about her need for security. If she disagrees with it, the carereceiver may identify a different need that may make sense to her.

When the caregiver connects the feelings to the person's needs and the carereceiver identifies with the underlying need(s), it results in both healing and empowerment. When the need is made known, the carereceiver experiences a stinging relief. This is what NVC calls "sweet pain," which is an *aha* accompanied by an *ouch*. It brings an awareness of a vacuum or a hurt in one's life that simultaneously generates healing. That is, a healing-pain occurs at the recognition of one's need, which may bring the relief that is needed so that no other action is necessary. It is also here at the identification of a need that a connection between the caregiver and carereceiver occurs. In other words, we connect at the place of our needs—our common humanity.

Moreover, Hunsinger and Latini comment that the carereceiver is also energized as she sees her underlying desires when the feelings are linked to the needs.[42] They explain:

> When we empathize with feelings or simply reflect the content [observation] of someone's story, the connection with the other is not as sturdy or deep. Nor does the [carereceiver] get the clarity she needs about what is really at stake for her. Only when we

41. Ibid., loc. 1858–61.
42. Ibid., loc. 1894–95.

plumb the depths of the need underneath the feeling do we assist the other in getting the kind of self-understanding that will enable her to take action.[43]

This attention to needs in NVC, then, is what provides the opportunity for change. As Hunsinger and Latini write, while it is important to specify the feelings, such identification is unable to generate transformation. Hunsinger and Latini point out the person often remains "stuck repeating the same feelings over and over without being able to work through them to some kind of action" when the need(s) associated with the feeling(s) is (are) not named.[44] Such an emphasis on change corresponds with the weight Pentecostals place on transformation as seen in previous chapters. In light of the above discussion, then, the recognition of the need alone may at times be all that is necessary to bring relief and generate healing (sweet pain); however, on other occasions the identification of the need emboldens the carereceiver to act accordingly to meet the need in a healthy way. Therefore, the caregiver's loving act of empathy not only makes a connection with the carereceiver but also assists in the carereceiver's own understanding and empowerment. The caregiver's act of love, then, is distinct from the previously mentioned unhelpful comments (chapter 5) that stressed self-agency by blaming the sufferer for his failure to act, which fostered isolation, thereby cultivating a disconnection that did not empower the carereceiver.[45]

In using the above three skills of observation, feeling, and need, a caregiver mirrors to the carereceiver what he heard the carereceiver communicating, which demonstrates his understanding while validating and normalizing the carereceiver's experience. Hunsinger and Latini highlight that when these three components are used in expressing empathy, each component builds on the previous one.[46] They write, "As we gain more skill,

---

43. Ibid., loc. 1898–901.

44. Ibid., loc. 719–21.

45. This empowerment to act is also supported by relational-cultural theory (RCT). In RCT, mutual empathy generates growth in relationships, which produces a more authentic connection. The result of these types of relationships is: zest, which is an aliveness; clarity or knowledge, which is a better understanding of self, other, and the relationship; sense of worth, which reminds the person she matters; productivity or action, which is being empowered to act inside and outside the relationship; and a desire for more connection. Miller and Stiver, *The Healing Connection*, 30–34. See also Jordan, *Relational-Cultural Therapy*, loc. 459–61.

46. Hunsinger and Latini, *Transforming Church Conflict*, loc. 1837–913.

we can practice the deeper forms of empathy, which means keeping our focus almost exclusively on the other's needs."[47]

In light of the abovementioned three components, I offer a word of caution. While these components have been presented in a linear fashion, the expression of empathy is more like learning to ride rolling waves. In this analogy the caregiver, as he listens to the carereceiver, matches a wave's speed and rides it by offering an observation, and as he continues to move with the flow, he may speculate as to the carereceiver's feeling by using the word "wonder," which may be followed by inquiring, "Is that what you are saying?" As the carereceiver responds, the caregiver understands more about the carereceiver's experience. As the caregiver continues to listen, he voices observations with occasional feelings while periodically inquiring if he has understood correctly, and all the while he is mirroring the rhythm and course of the carereceiver's expressed experience. In other words, there may be several instances in which the caregiver articulates observations and/or feelings prior to suggesting a need. Thus, empathy moves with the flow of the conversation, moving back and forth, up and down, finding its way toward a connection with the other.

What Is the Relational Nature of Empathy?

While one may walk through these three components of NVC in a mechanical manner, genuine empathy is relational by nature in that it has a sense of presence, a willingness to wait, and respect for the other's experience and will. To begin, the expression of empathy involves a sense of presence, which embraces not only being with the other but also being attuned to the other. Such attunement inherently conveys that the other person matters in this moment more than any other concern of the caregiver. Being attuned to the other parallels with Pentecostals sensing the Spirit's presence in that they have a deep knowing that the Spirit is attuned to them—they matter. Being attuned to the other implies sensitivity to timing in how to express empathy: with words or with silence. This sensitivity suggests, then, the Pentecostal caregiver is attuned both to the carereceiver and to the Spirit for direction and discernment as to when to speak or to remain silent.

Empathy also communicates an inherent desire to wait, to remain with a person. It listens, hearing the sufferer's feelings and needs. While a Pentecostal who advises may insist on transformation, which hinders

47. Ibid., loc. 1837–38.

a connection, the Pentecostal who empathizes is willing to foster an opportunity for change by waiting. This means it does not advise, educate, minimize, diagnose, one-up, or analyze. According to Bob, a temptation for caregivers is declaring how they view the other's suffering rather than allowing the sufferer to express his own perspective. This relates to Wolfelt's assertion that a person who is grieving is an expert in her own loss.[48] Unfortunately, so-called helpers too often assume that they are the experts in the other person's pain. Hunsinger and Latini also write, "What we need when we ask for empathy is not someone to solve our problems or even to make us feel differently, but rather to give us the opportunity to be heard by someone who cares about us."[49] It is when the Pentecostal caregiver is willing to wait that he is providing an opportunity for the Spirit to move while also trusting in the carereceiver's ability to hear the Spirit speak. Since being with the other (empathy) involves being sensitive to the Spirit, the other, and the self (as seen above), the caregiver remains open to hear not only from the carereceiver but also from the Comforter.

Additionally, inherent within empathy is the acknowledgement that each person's experience is unique, generating respect for the other's experience and will. Such awareness accentuates a caregiver's dependence on the Spirit in order that the caregiver may cultivate a more heightened understanding to the carereceiver's situation. As stated above, empathy recognizes that the caregiver's own similar experiences are unreliable to guide him in giving empathy; his experiences provide only a partial contribution in informing his grasp of the carereceiver's experience. This cultivates an acknowledgement of our need for God when expressing empathy and serves as a reminder that all compassion comes from God, not ourselves. This means that empathy, for a Pentecostal, embraces a dependency on the Spirit so that the Pentecostal caregiver experiences the Spirit's empowerment to minister through insight and understanding.

---

48. Wolfelt writes, "One third of the people in your life will turn out to be truly empathetic helpers. They will have a desire to understand you and your unique thoughts and feelings about the death. They will demonstrate a willingness to be taught by you and a recognition that you are the expert of your experience, not them. They will be willing to be involved in your pain and suffering without feeling the need to take it away from you. They will believe in your capacity to heal." Wolfelt, *Understanding Your Grief*, 127.

49. Hunsinger and Latini, *Transforming Church Conflict*, loc. 375–76.

What Is the Theological Nature of Empathy?

In light of the immediate above discussion as well as the previous chapters, I argue that empathy also is theological in nature in that Jesus Christ is God's embodied expression of empathy, and believers may participate in Christ's ministry through the presence and power of the Spirit through the offering of empathy. Just as the sending of Jesus is God's love in action, empathy is an act of compassion, an act of love that suffers alongside. Correspondingly, as empathy is present with the other amidst suffering, so Jesus is also present with humanity, as seen in his divine and human natures as well as his living in this suffering world. In such presence, as communicated through God's embodied empathy in the person of Jesus, God conveys humanity's worth and respects humanity's will. Through this act of love, God fosters a connection with humanity, a central characteristic of empathy. That is to say, we know that we matter to God and are seen and heard by God in the very being of Jesus. As an embodied statement of God's empathy, God identifies with us while also being differentiated from us; thus, there is the similarity as well as the difference that is part of the expression of empathy.

God also validates humanity when the divine one embodies humanity in the same way that the mirroring of content, feelings, and needs validates the other's experience. When Christ embodied humanity, he became vulnerable by entering into our nothingness (suffering), a risk that empathy takes by coming alongside the sufferer. Because empathy fosters a connection, normalizes and validates another's experience, and communicates worth, empathy is healing—it reconciles. As the expression of empathy enters into the other's suffering, which is healing, so Jesus, who enters into our suffering (nothingness), brings healing. Kazoh Kitamori posits, "*God in pain is the God who resolves our human pain by his own. Jesus Christ is the Lord who heals our human wounds by his own*" (italics in original).[50] Speaking of this healing that occurs as being *in* Christ not just *through* Christ, James Torrance similarly writes:

> Christ does not heal us by standing over against us, diagnosing our sickness, prescribing medicine for us to take, and then going away, to leave us to get better by obeying his instructions—as an ordinary doctor might. No, He becomes the patient! He assumes that very humanity which is in need of redemption, and by being anointed by the Spirit in our humanity, by a life of perfect obedience, by

---

50. Kitamori, *Theology of the Pain of God*, 20.

> dying and rising again, for us, our humanity is healed *in him*. We are not just healed "through Christ" because of the work of Christ but "in and through Christ" (italics in original).[51]

Thus, God says, "I am with you" by sending Jesus, an act of empathy, an act of love.

Since Jesus is God's expression of empathy, God's act of ministry, Christ-followers participate in Christ's ministry through the expression of empathy in the power of the Spirit and contribute to a theological praxis of suffering and healing. The expression of empathy is a theological *praxis* in that it is an action that reveals God. Empathy expressed in person-to-person ministry in the power of the Spirit demonstrates that God is with the sufferer in the same way Jesus is with humanity in his very being as the human-divine one. As previously mentioned by some participants, they believed God had abandoned them when the body of Christ failed to come alongside them; thus, when we are present with the sufferers, God is revealed as being with present with them. This praxis is also a theological praxis of *suffering*. In the same way Christ has entered into humanity's nothingness, the expression of empathy through the power of the Spirit in person-to-person ministry enters into the nothingness of the sufferer; thus, it is an act of compassion that suffers alongside. It embraces the suffering in that it is willing to hold it. This praxis is also simultaneously a movement towards *healing* and *wholeness*. In a similar fashion that Jesus Christ reconciles humanity with God, empathy assists in reconciling the unmet expectations and/or the suffering into the person's understanding, and that is healing. Hunsinger and Latini confirm that an "empathic connection with those we serve supports our capacity to participate in Christ's ongoing ministry of compassion and healing."[52] As portrayed in the word "embrace," empathy is willing to release the suffering. This loving act of empathy through the power of the Holy Spirit, then, not only generates a revelation of God who suffers with us but also produces reconciliation so that Jesus is encountered through the Spirit.

Empathy expressed, not through our own strength but through the power of the Spirit, is particularly salient for the Pentecostal who experiences an unmet expectation of an instantaneous divine intervention to relieve her suffering. This unmet expectation produces an apparent absence of God. It is precisely here, within such an experience of apparent absence,

---

51. Torrance, "The Vicarious Humanity of Christ," 141.
52. Hunsinger and Latini, *Transforming Church Conflict*, loc. 3910–11.

that God's presence may be experienced through the community's love for each other as the community participates in God's own compassion. The ultimate purpose of this compassionate love within the community, as previously stated, is to reveal God to the world. It is the loving action *within* the Christian community that is the prerequisite for God to be revealed *through* the community. God can be encountered in acts of love as expressed through empathy through the power of the Holy Spirit even when a Pentecostal does not experience an instantaneous intervention by God amidst suffering. Through empathy, God's compassion flows through the community to the Pentecostal who is suffering, revealing God as compassionate. Such acts are missional—their ultimate purpose realized in the revelation of God to the world through love between Christians, expressed in empathy. This is an important understanding in light of the danger previously expressed of Pentecostalism reducing the Spirit baptism from missional empowerment to being personally beneficial.

CONCLUSION

In the previous chapters I have discussed the path of suffering on which some experienced the apparent absence of God. Christopraxis refers to this as nothingness, and I have added to Christopraxis's understanding of nothingness by including in the discussion the impossibility of being able to cause God to instantaneously eradicate suffering. Suffering places us face to face with our vulnerability, which involves risk, uncertainty, and emotional exposure. When we, as children, are afraid and filled with anxiety and we cry, typically the caregiver comes, holds, and soothes us until we are comforted and find the place of security, as attachment theory explains. As adults, this longing for security does not cease when suffering disrupts our secure base; instead, suffering remains as we yearn for someone to rescue and protect us. Unfortunately, life is no longer as simple as when we were small children in that there is no longer any human who is able to pick us up and take away our suffering. In the absence of a desired instantaneous divine intervention amidst extended suffering, we come face to face with our vulnerability, our finitude, and/or our mortality. It is here on this path of suffering that empathy becomes a powerful tool to assist in revealing God and reconciling (healing) humanity. Human empathy does not eradicate pain or solve the problem, but it enters into the suffering in a limited fashion, joining the person in her nothingness, providing opportunities for healing.

In some ways, a person who is suffering is similar to one standing in an area that is enclosed by a barbed wire fence. Other humans can see the person who is hurting, but it is impossible for them to completely join the person in his experience of suffering. As a result, the existential nature of suffering is loneliness. The suffering person cries out for relationships with others, as portrayed through attachment theory. She cries out for a connection, which Western individualism in its extreme form, resists. Yet, we are able to enter into the other's nothingness in a limited fashion by reaching through the isolating fence through the expression of empathy. Through empathy we connect with the person, providing a measure of community, comfort, and healing. In some cases, we may be able to ameliorate some of the suffering on the other side of the fence by providing food, clothing, and shelter; however, we are incapable of fully removing the pain within the person's very being. Christ is the one who has completely entered into nothingness, and he alone is the one who is capable of fully removing the pain within a person's being. In his very person, Christ fully reveals God and wholly heals the person. We participate in this ministry of revelation and reconciliation by offering the hurting person empathy in the power and presence of the Spirit. In the final chapter, I discuss further research to explore ways in which Christ-followers may participate in Christ's ministry.

7

Where to Go from Here
The Conclusion

I think Pentecostals need to understand suffering a little bit better than they do. There needs to be more out there.

—Christy, a participant

The preceding pages put forth a theological praxis of suffering and healing that involves four elements: the path of suffering; God's presence; relationality with others; and the making of meaning. I liken these four elements to spheres that are interconnected, providing a fuller understanding of experiences of suffering, experiences with God, and experiences with others (see figure 1). Through the combination of these four elements, I assert through this project that being on a path of suffering is an occasion for Pentecostals to experience the presence of God and to connect with others through relationality and eventually to make meaning out of the experience. Such an assertion is this project's contribution to a Pentecostal theological understanding of suffering and healing by means of praxis.

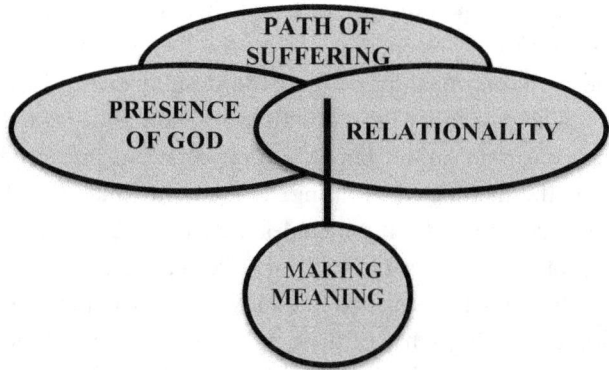

Figure 1. Four elements of a theological praxis of suffering and healing

To begin, this project demonstrates that the path of suffering is an opportunity to experience the presence of God, and such presence is an act of ministry. Pentecostals are known to expect God to miraculously and instantaneously deliver them from their suffering; through this expectation suffering becomes an implicit opportunity for the glory of God to be displayed through immediate deliverance. However, when expected deliverance from the suffering does not occur and the apparent absence of God prevails, this project demonstrates that God is still present. That is, a divine intervention is expanded to include God being present in suffering in two ways. First, God is present through ongoing presence so that while the apparent absence of God is in the foreground, God's sustaining and constant presence is in the background. Second, God is also present through intense instances of presence even when the suffering is not removed; namely, God's special presence is at the forefront while God's apparent absence is in the background. In both cases, Pentecostals are able to say, suffering is not devoid of God's presence.

This project additionally argues that God's presence, or intervention, may occur through acts of ministry through other persons. In this way, suffering becomes an opportunity for relationality. Suffering is an occasion whereby Pentecostals may participate in God's ministry to the sufferer through an intervention—practical acts and/or a *space to be* (presence). When God is revealed to the person and the person is moved towards wholeness (reconciled), this is an act of ministry that is participating in the Christ's ministry through the power of the Spirit. It is here that God is encountered.

Who is Present in Absence?

While being in the presence of God, whether it is while being alone or while being in the presence of others, the Pentecostal on the path of suffering also makes meaning. When the desired divine instantaneous deliverance fails to occur, a Pentecostal's worldview is disrupted, and it is necessary to integrate unmet hopes and expectations into a new framework. This is the making of meaning. The way in which the Pentecostal makes meaning of her suffering includes the telling of her story to others. The making of meaning on the path of suffering for Pentecostals entails three elements: being transformed in their very being in how they relate to their world; the making sense of their suffering; and the embracing of the uncertainty, ambiguity, and mystery of their ongoing suffering.

Since the path of suffering is an opportunity to experience both God's presence and relationships with others out of which comes meaning, this project then moves to answer the question as to how Pentecostals are now to respond or what Pentecostals are now to do. In keeping with Pentecostals' emphasis on praxis, I put forth that the expression of empathy is a theological praxis of suffering and healing. It is a concrete act of ministry (an act of ministry of revelation/reconciliation), specifically an act of compassion, that participates in God's ministry of love in action. God's love in action is expressed through embodied empathy in the person of Jesus, who is the divine-human one who reveals God while also reconciling humanity to God. God's act, then, is not separate from God's being. As God's expression of empathy, Jesus enters humanity's nothingness and is present to humanity. Such presence not only suffers alongside persons, but it also heals them. In Jesus, humanity is affirmed, normalized, and validated, which communicates humanity's worth. Through Jesus, God connects with us by meeting us at our place of need—our need for God. The expression of empathy by others, then, is a means by which God is encountered in person-to-person ministry amidst apparent absence. The expression of empathy conveys presence, thereby communicating that God is present. It listens, through the making of observations, naming feelings, and identifying needs, which encourages the telling of the person's story; thus, a healing connection is made. The Pentecostal caregiver through the expression of empathy, then, enters the sufferer's nothingness in a limited way, and in so doing, God is revealed and the sufferer is healed. Through this act of love, the world will then know we are Jesus's disciples. This is Christopraxis.

WHERE TO GO FROM HERE

HOW TO ADVANCE THIS PROJECT

After considering this project, I now invite the reader to reflect how it may be advanced beyond these pages. This project's expansion of a theological praxis of suffering and healing for Pentecostals may move forward by three means. First is the call for the further development of a theology of suffering and healing among Pentecostals through additional research. I have interviewed only eight Classical Pentecostals in my effort to include experience alongside Scripture in this contribution to a theology of suffering and healing. I propose opening a research study with broader parameters that are not limited to Classical Pentecostals but include Charismatics and Neocharismatics. Moreover, I believe it would be beneficial to complete a study involving those who had been practicing Pentecostals at one time, but they moved away from this tradition and/or their faith as a result of suffering. Such a study may illuminate an expanded praxis of suffering and healing that would inform our acts of ministry among those who are suffering while instructively revealing our beliefs about suffering.

Second, increased training among current Pentecostals would contribute to advancing this project beyond its pages. Half of the research participants spontaneously spoke of their desire to see more education in the area of suffering among Pentecostals. The participants' remarks on increased training included formal education in colleges and seminaries for those pursuing ministry as well as informal training via books and teaching through the church or support groups. For Danielle, this may be accomplished by training ministers how to help those who have lost a spouse or a child. She proposed one helpful way to assist those who were grieving is to offer grief support groups in Pentecostal churches, a ministry that is absent in her church. Kirsten specifically spoke of two levels of training to be offered in churches: one for leadership and one for those who are not in leadership. I recommend one way to provide formal or informal training is through the teaching of NVC to current and future leaders as well as laity. Such training would address the concern of the participants of how to improve the pastoral care offered by both Pentecostal clergy and laity to those who are suffering; thus, it would center on helping persons. Training on pastoral care would also attend to the view of many Pentecostals in regards to those persons who are suffering. For instance, Christy noticed that Pentecostals tend to equate an overcomer with one who does not cry and/ or one who has an absence of sorrow. In other words, those who are unable to be conquerors in this respect are somehow deficient in their faith and practice. Such an assessment, according to NVC, fails to see the humanity of others who are hurting and hinders the expression of empathy.

Besides addressing the negative view of persons who suffer, the participants also saw a need to educate Pentecostals on the concepts of suffering and grieving. As Christy asserted at the beginning of this chapter, "I think Pentecostals need to understand suffering a little bit better than they do. There needs to be more out there." She perceived that Pentecostals believe they are to avoid suffering or that as believers, they are not to suffer; thus, she saw the importance of Pentecostals learning "the benefits in suffering." Not only did the participants seek to address *how* Pentecostals ministered to sufferers as well as *what* Pentecostals' believed about suffering, but the participants also referred to a need to educate Pentecostals *where* God is in suffering. Kyle specifically stated, "I think the church could do a much better job . . . on teaching the people about the presence of God in suffering." This type of training would not only talk about where God is in suffering but also how to provide pastoral care with this central understanding in mind.

Finally, the chief way this project may be advanced for me is by each reader responding to sufferers through the expression of empathy, being present as God is present. When a connection is made through empathy, it nurtures a desire in others to act in a similar manner, spreading the influence of empathic responses. This invitation to be empathically present to sufferers (which I believe includes being present to myself as well) has been extended to me as I listen to these stories of Classical Pentecostals. Rather than fleeing, evading, or daydreaming away their hardships, I am invited to embrace the sufferers and their arduous actualities by sitting alongside for this is where the Spirit is. I extend this invitation to you, the reader, through Bob's words, "And I think that's my theology now is that we need to learn how to just let people live, be in the pain and join them in the pain instead of trying to fix the pain and make it go away."

Appendix A
Interview Protocol

NOTE: PRIOR TO THE interview, I will have collected the following two types of information for classification purposes: (1) general personal information, such as age, marital status, parental status, and education, and (2) personal Christian experience, such as the length of time the person has been a Christian, how long the person has been a part of the AG or PAOC, the person's church affiliation prior to being a part of the AG or PAOC, how frequently the person attends church, and in what ways the person is involved in the church.

1. What has been your experience as a Pentecostal?
    A. Describe for me what your church is like.
        i. How would you characterize your church?
        ii. It may be helpful to consider, "How would an outsider perceive your church?" As Pentecostal? Evangelical?
    B. How would you define a Pentecostal?
        i. Would you classify yourself as a Pentecostal?
        ii. Some define Pentecostals as those who have been baptized in the Holy Spirit with the initial physical evidence of speaking in tongues. Would you say that describes you?

2. As you know, I am interested in your story about your experience of suffering, particularly your experience with [I would name the way in which they suffered, e.g., the death of _____, your ongoing illness or permanent injury, or the multiple aspects of

Appendix A

suffering]. Before you tell me about that experience, describe for me your relationship with God and your relationships with people in your church prior to your experience of suffering.

    A. What were some of your most important beliefs or perceptions about God?

    B. What were some of your most important beliefs about suffering, such as sickness or an extended period of suffering?

        i. If a person suffered, what were the two or three significant factors that you believed contributed to that suffering?

        ii. If a person suffered, what were the main reasons that God did not intervene?

    C. What were some of your significant experiences with God?

        i. How would you define an experience with God?

    D. In what ways did you interact with people at your church?

        i. How authentic were you with the people at your church?

        ii. Describe an instance in your relationships at your church that illustrates for me the type of relationships you had?

3. Reflect upon your experience of suffering. Describe for me what transpired.

    A. Could you walk me through the events step by step?

    B. What was your initial reaction when you received the news?

        i. In whom did you first confide?

        ii. When did you confide with this person? In other words, how long did you wait before you told this person?

        iii. When did you inform people at the church?

    C. How would you describe some of the emotions you experienced during this period of suffering?

    D. What were your three main needs at this time?

    E. How were any of those needs met?

4. Describe for me how relationships with others were helpful and unhelpful during your suffering.

INTERVIEW PROTOCOL

A. What were some of the helpful/unhelpful responses during the beginning stages of the suffering? Please distinguish between Pentecostals, non-Pentecostals, and non-Christians.

B. What were the helpful/unhelpful responses during the later stages of the suffering?

C. In what ways were your relationships at the church affected?

D. How would you compare and contrast the responses of Pentecostals, non-Pentecostals, and non-Christians?

E. What was the most important thing that your relationships contributed to your journey through suffering?

5. Describe for me how your understanding of God may have changed in the mist of suffering.

A. What were your expectations of God?

B. In what ways were those expectations met or not met?

C. How did you feel or what did you think about God during this time and the fact God was not intervening?

D. In what ways was your prayer life affected?

6. Today as you look back on this experience of suffering, in what ways has your perception about God been affected?

A. How has your perception about how God interacts with the world been affected?

For example, what are the reasons God heals and/or keeps a person safe or the reasons God does not heal nor keep a person safe?

B. How have your expectations about God changed?

C. How has your perception about suffering been affected?

D. How do you reconcile your suffering with your belief that God intervenes?

[For instance, if the person is sick, I would ask, "How do you reconcile your illness with the belief that God heals?" If the person experienced several factors in his/her suffering over a period of a year, I would ask, "How do you reconcile your

Appendix A

    suffering with the belief that God delivers and keeps people safe?"].

7. Based on your experiences in the midst of suffering, how would you now respond to a friend who was suffering?

    A. In what ways would this response be different from what your responses would have been prior to your suffering?

8. What else have we not talked about that you want me to know?

Appendix B
Informed Consent Form

You are invited to be in a research study of Assemblies of God congregants who have experienced suffering. You were selected as a possible participant because you have self-identified as a person who expected an intervention from God in the midst of your suffering, which did not happen, and because you responded affirmatively to the letter. I ask that you read this form and ask any questions you may have before agreeing to be in the study.

This study is being conducted by me as part of my PhD dissertation in Pastoral Care and Counseling at Luther Seminary in St. Paul, MN. My adviser is Dr. Jessicah Krey Duckworth.

BACKGROUND INFORMATION

The purpose of this study is to gain insight into the experiences of Pentecostals who have suffered, particularly focusing upon their experiences with God and others in the midst of suffering. This insight will be used to help to improve pastoral care for Pentecostals.

PROCEDURES

If you agree to be in this study, I will ask you to participate in an interview that inquires about your experience of suffering. This interview, which will take approximately ninety minutes, will be digitally recorded and notes will be taken during the interview. I, then, will transcribe the interview. If you

Appendix B

choose to participate but decline to be recorded, please indicate that in the space below.

RISKS AND BENEFITS OF BEING IN THE STUDY

There are no direct risks involved in participating in the study. However, there may be indirect risks relating to the emotional health of the interviewees. In the event of such risks, consideration will be given to safeguarding your well-being and appropriate referral and follow-up will be done. If a need for referral arises, a phone number for a respective counseling center and/or counselor will be provided. However, payment for any such treatment must be provided by you or your third-party payer (such as health insurance, Medicare, etc.).

There are no direct benefits, such as money, credit, etc., for participating in this study. However, there are indirect benefits for you, the church at large, and academia. They include but are not limited to: increased self-awareness about suffering and the importance of relationships; increased congregational awareness on a more effective way to minister to those within our churches who are suffering; and additional contributions to the field of research and academia.

CONFIDENTIALITY

The records of this study will be kept confidential. Pseudonyms will be used (for persons and places) in all publications of this report. All data will be kept in a secured file in my personal computer; only my advisor, Dr. Jessicah Krey Duckworth, and I will have access to the data and, if applicable, any digital recordings. If the research is terminated for any reason, all data and recordings will be destroyed. While I will make every effort to ensure confidentiality, anonymity cannot be guaranteed due to the small number being studied.

All interviews will be digitally recorded, and only the researcher and her adviser will have access to these recordings, which will be used as part of the qualitative data analysis methodology. All raw data will be destroyed after three years of the project's completion, by 2020.

Informed Consent Form

VOLUNTARY NATURE OF THE STUDY

Your decision whether or not to participate will not affect your current or future relations with Luther Seminary, the congregation, and/or any other cooperating institutions. If you decide to participate, you are free to withdraw at any time without affecting those relationships.

CONTACTS AND QUESTIONS

I, Pam Walter Engelbert, am the one conducting this research. You may ask any questions and/or share any concerns by contacting me at XXX-XXX-XXXX or username@domain. My advisor can be reached at XXX-XXX-XXXX or username@domain.

You will be given a copy of this form to keep for your records.

STATEMENT OF CONSENT

I have read the above information or have had it read to me. I have received answers to questions asked. I consent to participate in the study.

Signature _____
Date _____

Signature of investigator _____
Date _____

I consent to be digitally recorded:

Signature _____
Date _____

I consent to allow use of my direct quotations in the published dissertation document.

Signature _____
Date _____

Appendix C
Coding Process

AFTER I TRANSCRIBED EACH recorded interview, I began the coding process. *Coding* is a way in which the researcher analyzes data in qualitative research by assigning symbols to the data, such as designating a word or a short phrase to a word, sentence, paragraph, or sections of the interviews. That is, I detected concepts, topics, and themes within the data and placed them into categories while reading the interviews repeatedly. My codes began with a gerund, e.g., *prayer* became "Petitioning God." Drawing from Kathy Charmaz's work, my coding process involved two phases: *initial and focused coding*.[1]

Initial coding is a four-step process in which I coded each interview by itself. I began with *word-by-word coding* in which I read through an interview more than once to identify words, phrases, or similar words/phrases frequently spoken by the participant and assigned them a code. The next step was *line-by-line coding*, which involved forming a code for each line (or two to three lines). Third was *incident-by-incident coding*, and it included reading the interview in conjunction with the previously created codes. Here I constructed a code for a larger section of the data, e.g., a specific incident in a story. The final step was *in vivo coding*. This refers to unique terms in the story or special words or phrases that are used by a specific people group, e.g., Spirit baptism, and these are coded verbatim. I also highlighted phrases or sentences that may be a relevant quote. Upon completing the coding process for each interview, I emailed to each participant the chief themes from his/her own interview (the word-by-word/incident-by-incident codes), inviting them to partner with me in this process. Seven

---

1. Charmaz, *Constructing Grounded Theory*.

of the eight participants responded, and each expressed their support of the themes.

I then turned to the second phase, which was *focused coding*. This began by comparing each coded interview to the other coded interviews. It included forming groups for the various codes (predominantly incident-by-incident codes) in accordance with the questions I had asked the participants. For example, a question that emphasized the participant's life prior to the stressful event(s) became a group. However, coding is not a linear process but is similar to a spiral. This was particularly evidenced when I compared data and codes within an interview as well as with other interviews, resulting in a revision of some incident-by-incident codes. Additionally, as I repeatedly read the interviews, I gained more insight into what the participants were communicating, which also resulted in a change of some initial codes. The next step was *axial coding*. In this step I carefully defined the parameters of the previously formed groups by drawing from my initial codes. In some cases, my groups and axial codes were identical, but in others, a different code emerged as I delineated the code's characteristics. An example of defining a code's characteristics is seen in the code "encountering God" in which there were: instances of intense presence and ongoing presence; encountering God alone and with others; and being shaped by human will and God's will.

The final step, which was *theoretical coding*, involved the forming of central categories from themes that repeatedly appeared in the interviews. Significant for this step was my writing spontaneously the ways in which these categories were related. This relates to another aspect of coding, which is *memo writing*. It was here I described the process and expressed thoughts, feelings, ideas, and reasons for changes in my codes.

Bibliography

Adams, Michael K. "'Hope in the Midst of Hurt': Towards a Pentecostal Theology of Suffering." Paper presented at the 25th Annual Meeting of the Society for Pentecostal Studies, Toronto, Ontario, Canada, March 7–9, 1996.

Adogame, Afe. "HIV/AIDS Support and African Pentecostalism: The Case of the Redeemed Christian Church of God." *Journal of Healthy Psychology* 12, no. 3 (2007) 475–84. doi: 10.1177/1359105307076234.

Albrecht, Daniel. *Rites in the Spirit: A Ritual Approach to Pentecostal/Charismatic Spirituality.* Journal of Pentecostal Theology Supplement Series 17. Sheffield, UK: Sheffield Academic, 1999.

Alexander, Kimberly Ervin. *Pentecostal Healing: Models in Theology and Practice.* Journal of Pentecostal Theology Supplement Series 29. Blanford Forum, UK: Deo, 2006.

Althouse, Peter. *Spirit of the Last Days: Pentecostal Eschatology in Conversation with Jürgen Moltmann.* Journal of Pentecostal Theology Supplement Series 25. London: T. & T. Clark, 2003.

Anderson, Allan. *An Introduction to Pentecostalism: Global Charismatic Christianity.* Cambridge: Cambridge University Press, 2004.

———. "Pentecostal Approaches to Faith and Healing." *International Review of Mission* 91, no. 363 (2002) 523–34. doi: 10.1111/j.1758-6631.2002.tb00365.x.

———. *To the Ends of the Earth: Pentecostalism and the Transformation of World Christianity.* New York: Oxford University Press, 2013.

———. "Varieties, Taxonomies, and Definitions." In *Studying Global Pentecostalism: Theories and Methods,* edited by Allan Anderson et al., 13–29. Berkeley: University of California Press, 2010. Kindle ed.

Anderson, Ray. "Christopraxis: The Ministry and the Humanity of Christ for the World." In *Christ in Our Place: The Humanity of God in Christ for the Reconciliation of the World; Essays Presented to Professor James Torrance,* edited by Trevor and Daniel Thimell Hart, 11–31. Exeter, UK: Paternoster, 1989.

———. *Ministry on the Fireline: A Practical Theology for an Empowered Church.* Eugene, OR: Wipf and Stock, 1993.

———. *The Shape of Practical Theology: Empowering Ministry with Theological Praxis.* Downers Grove, IL: InterVarsity, 2001.

———. *The Soul of Ministry: Forming Leaders for God's People.* Louisville: Westminster John Knox, 1997.

Anderson, Robert Mapes. *Vision of the Disinherited: The Making of American Pentecostalism.* New York: Oxford University Press, 1979.

Bibliography

Andrews, Courtney Jones. "Health and Salvation: The Social Construction of Illness and Healing in the Charismatic Christian Church." MA thesis, University of Alabama, 2012.

The Apostolic Faith. 312 Azusa Street. http://www.azusastreet.org/TheApostolicFaith.htm.

"The Apostolic Faith: 312 Azusa Street." *The Apostolic Faith*, November 1906. http://www.apostolicfaith.org/Library/Index/AzusaPapers.aspx.

Archer, Kenneth. *A Pentecostal Hermeneutic for the Twenty-First Century: Spirit, Scripture and Community.* New York: T. & T. Clark, 2004.

Archer, Melissa. "'Worship in Spirit and Truth': The Role of Worship in the Fourth Gospel in Concert with the Liturgy of the Apocalypse." Paper presented at the 45th Annual Meeting of the Society for Pentecostal Studies, San Dimas, CA, March 10–12, 2016.

Asamoah-Gyadu, J. Kwabena. *African Charismatics: Current Developments within Independent Indigenous Pentecostalism in Ghana.* Studies of Religion in Africa 27. Leiden: Brill, 2005.

———. *Contemporary Pentecostal Christianity: Interpretations from an African Context.* Eugene, OR: Wipf and Stock, 2013.

Attanasi, Katherine. "Pentecostal Theologies of Healing, HIV/AIDS, and Women's Agency in South Africa." *Pneuma: The Journal of the Society For Pentecostal Studies* 37 (2015) 7–20. doi: 10.1163/15700747–03701024.

Beasley-Murray, George. *John.* 2nd ed. Word Biblical Commentary 36. Nashville: Nelson, 1999. CD-ROM.

Beijer, Catharina J. "'Although 90% of the System Is against Us, We Are Able to Survive': An Exploratory Study of West-African Christian Migrants Living in the Netherlands on Healing Practices and Sources of Empowerment in Times of Social Distress." MA thesis, Universiteit van Amsterdam, 2006.

"Bible Pentecost: Gracious Pentecostal Showers Continue to Fall." *The Apostolic Faith*, November 1906. http://www.apostolicfaith.org/Library/Index/AzusaPapers.aspx.

Bjorck, Jeffrey, and Pamela Trice. "Pentecostal Perspectives on Causes and Cures of Depression." *Professional Psychology: Research and Practice* 37, no. 3 (2006) 283–94. doi: 10.1037/0735–7028.37.3.283.

Blumhofer, Edith. *"Pentecost in My Soul": Explorations in the Meaning of Pentecostal Experience in the Early Assemblies of God.* Springfield, MO: Gospel, 1989.

———. *Restoring the Faith: The Assemblies of God, Pentecostalism, and American Culture.* Urbana: University of Illinois Press, 1993.

Bosman, John-Eduard. "Some Are Not Healed: The Theory-Praxis Tension Regarding the Healing Ministry in a Pentecostal Church." PhD diss., University of South Africa, 1997.

Bosman, John-Eduard, and J. P. J. Theron. "Some Are Not Healed: Reflecting on the Experiences of Pentecostal Believers Who Have Not yet Been Healed through a Ministry of Healing to the Sick." *Practical Theology in South Africa* 21, no. 3 (2006) 1–16.

Brodin, Kari L. "Experience or Suffer?: Galatians 3:4 in Paul's Argument." Paper presented at the 36th Annual Meeting of the Society for Pentecostal Studies, Lee University, Cleveland, TX, March 8–10, 2007.

Brown, Brené. *Daring Greatly: How the Courage to Be Vulnerable Transforms the Way We Live, Love, Parent, and Lead.* New York: Avery, 2012.

———. *The Gifts of Imperfection: Let Go of Who You Think You're Supposed to Be and Embrace Who You Are.* Center City, MN: Hazelden, 2010.

———. *I Thought It Was Just Me: Women Reclaiming Power and Courage in a Culture of Shame*. New York: Gotham, 2007. Kindle ed.

———. *Rising Strong*. New York: Spiegel & Grau, 2015. Kindle ed.

Brown, Candy Gunther. *Testing Prayer: Science and Healing*. Cambridge, MA: Harvard University Press, 2012.

Browning, Don S. *A Fundamental Practical Theology: Descriptive and Strategic Proposals*. Minneapolis: Fortress, 1991. Kindle ed.

Bultmann, Rudolph, and Artur Weiser. "πιστεύω, πίστις, πιστός, πιστόω, ἄπιστος, ἀπιστέω, ἀπιστία, ὀλιγόπιστος, ὀλιγοπιστία." Translated by Geoffrey W. Bromiley. In *Theological Dictionary of the New Testament*, edited by Gerhard Friedrich and Geoffrey W. Bromiley, 6:174–228. Grand Rapids: Eerdmans, 1968.

Burge, Gary. *The NIV Application Commentary: John*. NIV Application Commentary. Grand Rapids: Zondervan, 2000.

Burgess, Stanley M., and Eduard M. van der Maas. "Introduction." In *The New International Dictionary of Pentecostal and Charismatic Movements*, edited by Stanley M. Burgess and Eduard M. van der Maas, xvii–xxiii. Grand Rapids: Zondervan, 2002.

Burns, Charlene. *Divine Becoming: Rethinking Jesus and the Incarnation*. Minneapolis: Augsburg Fortress, 2002.

Cartledge, Mark J. *Encountering the Spirit: The Charismatic Tradition*. Maryknoll, NY: Orbis, 2007.

———. "Pentecostal and Charismatic Theology Comes of Age." *Theology* 114 (2011) 363–70. doi: 10.1177/0040571X11411542.

———. *Speaking in Tongues: Multi-Disciplinary Perspectives*. Studies in Pentecostal and Charismatic Issues. Milton Keynes, UK: Paternoster, 2006.

———. *Testimony in the Spirit: Rescripting Ordinary Pentecostal Theology*. Surrey, UK: Ashgate, 2010.

Castelo, Daniel. "Patience as a Theological Virtue: A Challenge to Pentecostal Eschatology." In *Perspectives in Pentecostal Eschatologies*, edited by Peter Althouse and Robby Waddell, 232–46. Eugene, OR: Pickwick, 2010.

Chan, Simon. *Pentecostal Ecclesiology: An Essay on the Development of Doctrine*. Journal of Pentecostal Theology Supplement Series 38. Blanford Forum, UK: Deo, 2011.

Charmaz, Kathy. *Constructing Grounded Theory: A Practical Guide through Qualitative Analysis*. London: Sage, 2006.

Clifton, Shane. "The Dark Side of Prayer for Healing: Toward a Theology of Well- Being." *Pneuma: The Journal of the Society For Pentecostal Studies* 36 (2014) 204–25. doi: 10.1163/15700747-03602003.

———. "Theodicy, Disability, and Fragility: An Attempt to Find Meaning in the Aftermath of Quadriplegia." *Theological Studies* 76, no. 4 (2015) 765–84. doi: 10.1177/0040563915605263.

Courey, David. *What Has Wittenberg to Do with Azusa?: Luther's Theology of the Cross and Pentecostal Triumphalism*. London: Bloomsbury T. & T. Clark, 2015.

Crysdale, Cynthia. *Embracing Travail: Retrieving the Cross Today*. New York: Continuum, 1999.

Dau, Isaiah Majok. *Suffering and God: A Theological Reflection on the War in Sudan*. Nairobi, Kenya: Paulines, 2002.

Dayton, Donald W. *Theological Roots of Pentecostalism*. Grand Rapids: Baker Academic, 1987.

Bibliography

Decker, Edward E. "Pentecostalism and Suffering." In *Pentecostal Caregivers... Anointed to Heal*, edited by John Kie Vining, 51–65. East Rockaway, NY: Cummings and Hathaway, 1995.

DeYoung, Patricia. *Relational Psychotherapy: A Primer*. New York: Brunner-Routledge, 2003. Kindle ed.

Dilger, Hansjorg. "Healing the Wounds of Modernity: Salvation, Community and Care in a Neo-Pentecostal Church in Dar Es Salaam, Tanzania." *Journal of Religion in Africa* 37, no. 1 (2007) 59–83. http://www.jstor.org/stable/27594404.

Dunlap, Susan. *Caring Cultures: How Congregations Respond to the Sick*. Waco, TX: Baylor University Press, 2009.

Dusing, Michael L. "Toward a Pentecostal Theology of Physical Suffering." Paper presented at the 25th Annual Meeting of the Society for Pentecostal Studies, Toronto, Ontario, Canada, March 7–9, 1996.

Ellington, Scott A. "The Costly Loss of Testimony." *Journal of Pentecostal Theology* 8, no. 16 (2000) 48–59. doi: 10.1177/0966736907083264.

———. *Risking Truth: Reshaping the World through Prayers of Lament*. Eugene, OR: Pickwick, 2008.

Espinosa, Gastón. *William J. Seymour and the Origins of Global Pentecostalism: A Biography & Documentary History*. Durham, NC: Duke University Press, 2014.

Evans, G. W. "Fire Falling at Oakland." *The Apostolic Faith*, September 1906. http://www.apostolicfaith.org/Library/Index/AzusaPapers.aspx.

Eves, Richard. "'In God's Hands': Pentecostal Christianity, Morality, and Illness in a Melanesian Society." *Journal of the Royal Anthropological Institute* 16, no. 3 (2010) 496–514. http://search.ebscohost.com.naomi.fuller.edu:2048/login.aspx?direct=true&db=ap h&AN=52718329&site=ehost-live.

Fettke, Steven. *God's Empowered People: A Pentecostal Theology of the Laity*. Eugene, OR: Wipf and Stock, 2011.

———. "The Spirit of God Hovered over the Waters: Creation, the Local Church, and the Mentally and Physically Challenged, a Call to Spirit-Led Ministry." *Journal of Pentecostal Theology* 17 (2008) 170–82. doi: 10.1163/174552508X377475.

Fettke, Steven, and Michael L. Dusing. "A Practical Pentecostal Theodicy?: A Proposal." *Pneuma: The Journal of the Society For Pentecostal Studies* 38 (2016) 160–79. doi: 10.1163/15700747–03801002.

Friesen, Aaron T. *Norming the Abnormal: The Development and Function of the Doctrine of Initial Evidence in Classical Pentecostalism*. Eugene, OR: Pickwick, 2013.

Gabriel, Reuben Louis. "Response to Wonsuk Ma's 'Toward an Asian Pentecostal Theology.'" *Asian Journal of Pentecostal Studies* 2, no. 1 (1999) 77–85. http://www.apts.edu/index.cfm?menuid=94&parentid=54.

Gallagher, Robert L. "Hope in the Midst of Trial." Paper presented at the 33rd Annual Meeting of Society for Pentecostal Studies, Marquette University, Milwaukee, WI, March 11–13, 2004.

Gee, Donald. *Trophimus I Left Sick: Our Problems of Divine Healing*. London: Elim, 1952. http://www.dealpentecostal.co.uk/Trophimus I Left Sick—Gee, D.pdf.

Gill, Raj, Lucy Leu, and Judi Morin. *Nonviolent Communication (NVC) Toolkit for Facilitators*. Seattle: Freedom Project, 2009.

Goff, James R. *Fields White unto Harvest: Charles F. Parham and the Missionary Origins of Pentecostalism*. Fayetteville: University of Arkansas Press, 1988.

Bibliography

Gonzales, Robert. "Being Present with What's Alive and Juicy." Lecture, NVC Academy, Cornville, AZ, February 16—April 5, 2016. https://nvctraining.com/index.php.

———. "Living Compassion and Restoring Wholeness." Lecture, Compassionate Communication Center of Ohio, Columbus, OH, December 46, 2015.

Green, Chris E. "The Crucified God and the Groaning Spirit: Toward a Pentecostal *Theologia Crucis* in Conversation with Jürgen Moltmann." *Journal of Pentecostal Theology* 19, no. 1 (2010) 127–42. doi: 10.1163/174552510X489946.

Green, Joel B. "Death of Jesus." In *The Dictionary of Jesus and the Gospels*, edited by Joel B. Green et al., 146–63. Downers Grove, IL: InterVarsity, 1992.

Han, Sang-Ehil. "Weaving the Courage of God and Human Suffering: Issues and Challenges in the Doctrine of Atonement." In *Passover, Pentecost and Parousia*, edited by Steven J. Land et al., 171–90. Journal of Pentecostal Theology Supplement Series 35. Blanford Forum, UK: Deo, 2010.

Hardesty, Nancy. *Faith Cure: Divine Healing in the Holiness and Pentecostal Movements.* Peabody, MA: Hendrickson, 2003.

Harley, Justin L. "Pentecostal Christian View toward Causes and Treatment of Mental Health Disorders." PhD diss., Regent University, 2006. http://pqdtopen.proquest.com/pubnum/3248181.html?FMT=AI.

Harris III, W. Hall. "John." In *NET Bible®, First Edition Notes*, edited by W. Hall Harris III et al. Richardson, TX: Biblical Studies, 1996–2005. CD-ROM.

Hollenweger, Walter. *Pentecostalism: Origins and Developments Worldwide.* Peabody, MA: Hendrickson, 1997.

———. *The Pentecostals: The Charismatic Movement in the Churches.* Minneapolis: Augsburg, 1972.

Hollingsworth, Andrea. "Implications of Interpersonal Neurobiology for a Spirituality of Compassion." *Zygon* 43, no. 4 (2008) 837–60. http://onlinelibrary.wiley.com.luthersem.idm.oclc.org/journal/10.1111/(ISSN)1467-9744.

Holm, Randall. "Healing in Search of Atonement: With a Little Help from James K. A. Smith." *Journal of Pentecostal Theology* 23 (2014) 50–67. doi: 10.1163/17455251-02301007.

Hooyman, Nancy R., and Betty J. Kramer. *Living through Loss: Interventions across the Life Span.* Edited by Frederic G. Reamer. New York: Columbia University Press, 2006. Kindle ed.

Hunsinger, Deborah van Deusen, and Theresa Latini. *Transforming Church Conflict: Compassionate Leadership in Action.* Louisville: Westminster John Knox, 2013. Kindle ed.

Ingalls, Monique M. "Introduction: Interconnection, Interface, and Identification in Pentecostal-Charismatic Music and Worship." In *The Spirit of Praise: Music and Worship in Global Pentecostal-Charismatic Christianity*, edited by Monique M. Ingalls and Amos Yong, 1–25. University Park, PA: Pennsylvania State University Press, 2015.

Jang, Kwang-Jin. "The Role of the Holy Spirit in Christian Suffering with Reference to Paul's Experience of Suffering and to Korean Church Suffering 1910–1953." DLitt et Phil diss., Rand Afrikaans University, 2003.

Jaye, Chrystal. "Embodied Integrity: Suffering and Healing among Pentecostals, Christian Scientists, and Medical Professionals." PhD diss., University of Otago, 1998.

Jordan, Judith V. *Relational-Cultural Therapy.* Washington, DC: American Psychological Association, 2010. Kindle ed.

Bibliography

Karen, Robert. *Becoming Attached: First Relationships and How They Shape Our Capacity to Love*. New York: Oxford University Press, 1994.

Kärkkäinen, Veli-Matti. "Pentecostal Hermeneutics in the Making: On the Way from Fundamentalism to Postmodernism." *The Journal of the European Pentecostal Theological Association* 18 (1998) 76–115. http://www.eptaonline.com/journal-articles/.

———. "The Pentecostal Understanding of Mission." In *Pentecostal Mission and Global Christianity*, edited by Wonsuk Ma et al., 26–44. Eugene, OR: Wipf and Stock, 2014.

———. "Pneumatologies in Systematic Theology." In *Studying Global Pentecostalism: Theories and Methods*, edited by Allan Anderson et al., 223–44. Berkeley: University of California Press, 2010.

———. *Pneumatology: The Holy Spirit in Ecumenical, International, and Contextual Perspective*. Grand Rapids: Baker-Academic, 2002.

———. "Theology of the Cross: A Stumbling Block to Pentecostal/Charismatic Spirituality?" In *The Spirit and Spirituality: Essays in Honor of Russell P. Spittler*, edited by Wonsuk Ma and Robert P. Menzies, 150–63. London: T. & T. Clark, 2004.

———. *Toward a Pneumatological Theology: Pentecostal and Ecumenical Perspectives on Ecclesiology, Soteriology, and Theology of Mission*. Edited by Amos Yong. Lanham, MD: University Press of America, 2002.

Kay, William. *Pentecostalism*. London: SCM, 2009.

Keener, Craig. *The Gospel of John: A Commentary*. 2 vols. Grand Rapids: Baker Academic, 2003.

Kitamori, Kazoh. *Theology of the Pain of God*. Eugene, OR: Wipf and Stock, 1958.

"A Know-So Salvation." *The Apostolic Faith*, October 1906. http://www.apostolicfaith.org/Library/Index/AzusaPapers.aspx.

Kydd, Ronald A. N. *Healing through the Centuries: Models for Understanding*. Peabody, MA: Hendrickson, 1998.

Lakika, Dostin, et al. "Violence, Suffering and Support: Congolese Forced Migrants' Experiences of Psychological Services in Johannesburg." In *Healing and Change in the City of Gold: Case Studies of Coping and Support in Johannesburg*, edited by Ingrid Palmary et al., 101–19. Cham, Switzerland: Springer, 2015. doi: 10.1007/978-3-319-08768-9.

Land, Steven J. *Pentecostal Spirituality: Passion for the Kingdom*. Cleveland: CPT, 2010. Kindle ed.

Latham, Steve. "'God Came from Teman': Revival and Contemporary Revivalism." In *On Revival: A Critical Examination*, edited by Andrew Walker and Kristin Aune, 171–86. Carlisle, UK: Paternoster, 2003.

Leavey, Gerard. "The Appreciation of the Spiritual in Mental Illness: A Qualitative Study of Beliefs among Clergy in the UK." *Transcultural Psychiatry* 47, no. 4 (2010) 571–90. doi: 10.1177/1363461510383200.

———. "U.K. Clergy and People in Mental Distress: Community and Patterns of Pastoral Care." *Transcultural Psychiatry* 45, no. 1 (2008) 79–104. doi: 10.1177/1363461507087999.

Lerner, Melvin J. *The Belief in a Just World: A Fundamental Delusion*. New York: Plenum, 1980.

Levinas, Emmanuel. *On Thinking-of-the-Other*. Translated by Michael B. Smith and Barbara Harshav. European Perspectives: A Series on Social Thought and Cultural Criticism. New York: Columbia University Press, 1998.

Bibliography

Lugo, Luis, et. al. *Spirit and Power: A 10-Country Survey of Pentecostals*. Washington, DC: The Pew Research Center, 2006. http://www.pewforum.org/2006/10/05/spirit-and-power/.

Luhrmann, T. M. *When God Talks Back: Understanding the American Evangelical Relationship with God*. New York: Knopf Doubleday, 2012. Kindle ed.

Ma, Wonsuk. "Asian (Classical) Pentecostal Theology in Context." In *Asian and Pentecostal: The Charismatic Face of Christianity in Asia*, edited by Allan Anderson and Edmond Tong, 46–72. Eugene, OR: Wipf and Stock, 2011.

Ma, Wonsuk, et al. "Introduction: Pentecostalism and World Mission." In *Pentecostal Mission and Global Christianity*, edited by Wonsuk Ma et al., 1–9. Eugene, OR: Wipf and Stock, 2014.

Mabitsela, Lethabo. "Exploratory Study of Psychological Distress as Understood by Pentecostal Pastors." MA thesis, University of Pretoria, 2003.

Macchia, Frank. "Theology, Pentecostal." In *The New International Dictionary of Pentecostal and Charismatic Movements*, edited by Stanley M. Burgess and Eduard M. van der Maas, 1120–41. Grand Rapids: Zondervan, 2002.

Maré, Leonard P. "A Pentecostal Perspective on the Use of Psalms of Lament in Worship." *Verbum et Ecclesia* 29, no. 1 (2008) 91–109. http://www.ve.org.za/index.php/VE/article/view/7/7.

Maringira, Godfrey, et. al. "Between Remorse and Nostalgia: Haunting Memories of War and the Search for Healing among Former Zimbabwean Soldiers in Exile in South Africa." In *Healing and Change in the City of Gold: Case Studies of Coping and Support in Johannesburg*, edited by Ingrid Palmary et al., 79–100. Cham, Switzerland: Springer, 2015. doi: 10.1007/978-3-319-08768-9.

Marti, Gerardo. "The Adaptability of Pentecostalism: The Fit between Prosperity Theology and Globalized Individualization in a Los Angeles Church." *Pneuma: The Journal of the Society for Pentecostal Studies* 34, no. 1 (2012) 5–25. doi: 10.1163/157007412X621662.

McAffee, Jeff. "The Theology of Co-Suffering as a Model of Spiritual Help and Companionship." Paper presented at the 34th Annual Meeting of the Society for Pentecostal Studies, Regent University, Virginia Beach, VA, March 10–12, 2005.

McClendon, Gwyneth, and Rachel Beatty Riedl. "Individualism and Empowerment in Pentecostal Sermons: New Evidence from Nairobi, Kenya." *African Affairs* 115, no. 458 (2016) 119–44. doi: 10.1093/afraf/adv056.

McCoy, Andrew M. "Salvation (Not Yet?) Materialized: Healing as Possibility and Possible Complication for Expressing Suffering in Pentecostal Music and Worship." In *The Spirit of Praise: Music and Worship in Global Pentecostal- Charismatic Christianity*, edited by Monique M. Ingalls and Amos Yong, 45–59. University Park, PA: Pennsylvania State University Press, 2015.

McGhee, Faith. "Holiness and the Path of Suffering: Lessons for Pentecostals from the Book of Hebrews." In *A Future for Holiness: Pentecostal Explorations*, edited by Lee Roy Martin, 57–85. Cleveland, TN: CPT, 2013.

McMahan, Oliver. "Grief Observed: Surprised by the Suffering Spirit." In *Passover, Pentecost & Parousia: Studies in Celebration of the Life and Ministry of R. Hollis Gaus*, edited by Steven J. Land et al., 296–314. Journal of Pentecostal Theology Supplement Series 35. Blanford Forum, UK: Deo, 2010.

Mead, Samuel. "New-Tongued Missionaries for Africa." *The Apostolic Faith*, November 1906. http://www.apostolicfaith.org/Library/Index/AzusaPapers.aspx.

Bibliography

Menzies, William. "Reflections on Suffering: A Pentecostal Perspective." In *The Spirit and Spirituality: Essays in Honor of Russel P. Spittler*, edited by Wonsuk Ma and Robert Menzies, 141–49. Journal of Pentecostal Theology Supplement Series 24. London: T. & T. Clark, 2004.

Menzies, William, and Robert Menzies. *Spirit and Power: Foundations of Pentecostal Experience*. Grand Rapids: Zondervan, 2000. Kindle ed.

Mercer, Jean. "Deliverance, Demonic Possession, and Mental Illness: Some Considerations for Mental Health Professionals." *Mental Health, Religion & Culture* 16, no. 6 (2013) 595–611. http://dx.doi.org/10.1080/13674676.2012.706272.

Mikulincer, Mario, and Phillip R. Shaver. *Attachment in Adulthood: Structure, Dynamics, and Change*. New York: Guilford, 2007. Kindle ed.

Miller, Jean Baker, and Irene Pierce Stiver. *The Healing Connection: How Women Form Relationships in Therapy and Life*. Boston: Beacon, 1997.

Miller-McLemore, Bonnie J. "Introduction: The Contributions of Practical Theology." In *The Wiley Blackwell Companion to Practical Theology*, edited by Bonnie J Miller-McLemore, 1–20. Chichester, West Sussex, UK: Wiley-Blackwell, 2012. Kindle ed.

Milton, Grace. *Shalom, the Spirit and Pentecostal Conversion: A Practical-Theological Study*. Global Pentecostal and Charismatic Studies 18. Leiden: Brill, 2015.

Mittelstadt, Martin. *Reading Luke-Acts in the Pentecostal Tradition*. Cleveland, TN: CPT, 2010. Kindle ed.

———. "Spirit and Suffering in Contemporary Pentecostalism: The Lukan Epic Continues." In *Defining Issues in Pentecostalism: Classical and Emergent*, edited by Steven M. Studebaker, 144–73. Eugene, OR: Pickwick, 2008.

———. *The Spirit and Suffering in Luke-Acts: Implications for a Pentecostal Pneumatology*. London: T. & T. Clark, 2004.

Moloney, Francis J. *Love in the Gospel of John: An Exegetical, Theological, and Literary Study*. Grand Rapids: Baker Academic, 2013.

Morris, Leon. *The Gospel of John*. New International Commentary on the New Testament. Grand Rapids: Eerdmans, 1995. CD-ROM.

Murray, Iain. *Revival and Revivalism: The Making and Marring of American Evangelicalism, 1750–1858*. Edinburgh: Banner of Truth Trust, 1994.

Neumann, Peter. *Pentecostal Experience: An Ecumenical Encounter*. Eugene, OR: Pickwick, 2012. Kindle ed.

"No Bottom." *The Apostolic Faith*, September 1906. http://www.apostolicfaith.org/Library/Index/AzusaPapers.aspx.

Noll, Mark A. *A History of Christianity in the United States and Canada*. Grand Rapids: Eerdmans, 1992.

North, Wendy E. S. "'Lord, If You Had Been Here . . .' (John 11.21): The Absence of Jesus and Strategies of Consolation in the Fourth Gospel." *Journal for the Study of the New Testament* 36, no. 1 (2013) 39–52. doi: 10.1177/0142064X13495135.

Núñez, Lorena. "Faith Healing, Migration and Gendered Conversions in Pentecostal Churches in Johannesburg." In *Healing and Change in the City of Gold: Case Studies of Coping and Support in Johannesburg*, edited by Ingrid Palmary et al., 149–68. Cham, Switzerland: Springer, 2015. doi: 10.1007/978-3-319-08768-9.

"The Old Time Pentecost." *The Apostolic Faith*, September 1906. http://www.apostolicfaith.org/Library/Index/AzusaPapers.aspx.

Onyinah, Opoku. "God's Grace, Healing and Suffering." *International Review of Mission* 95, nos. 376–77 (2006) 117–27. doi: 10.1111/j.1758-6631.2006.tb00546.x.

———. "Suffering and Dr. Yonggi Cho's Theology of the Cross." *Journal of Youngsan Theology* 22 (2011) 9–46.

Osmer, Richard Robert. *Practical Theology: An Introduction*. Grand Rapids: Eerdmans, 2008. Kindle ed.

Parker, Stephen. "Working with Pentecostal-Charismatic Beliefs in Therapy." Paper presented at the 40th Annual Meeting of the Society for Pentecostal Studies, Memphis, TN, March 10–12, 2011.

Payne, Jennifer Shepherd. "'Saints Don't Cry': Exploring Messages Surrounding Depression and Mental Health Treatment as Expressed by African-American Pentecostal Preachers." *Journal of African American Studies* 12, no. 3 (2008) 215–28. doi: 10.1007/s12111-008-9044-7.

———. "Variations in Pastors' Perceptions of the Etiology of Depression by Race and Religious Affiliation." *Community Mental Health Journal* 45, no. 5 (2009) 355–65. doi: 10.1007/s10597-009-9210-y.

Peltomaki, Denise A. "An Afflicted Waiting." *International Journal of Children's Spirituality* 13, no. 3 (2008) 223–33. doi: 10.1080/13644360802236649.

"The Pentecostal Baptism Restored." *The Apostolic Faith*, October 1906. http://www.apostolicfaith.org/Library/Index/AzusaPapers.aspx.

Poloma, Margaret M. "An Empirical Study of Perceptions of Healing among Assemblies of God Members." *Pneuma: The Journal of the Society For Pentecostal Studies* 7, no. 1 (1985) 61–82. doi: 10.1163/157007485X00058.

———. "Pentecostal Prayer within the Assemblies of God: An Empirical Study." *Pneuma: The Journal of the Society for Pentecostal Studies* 31, no. 1 (2009) 47–65. doi: 10.1163/157007409X418149.

Quayesi-Amakye, Joseph. "Coping with Evil in Ghanaian Pentecostalism." *Exchange* 43, no. 3 (2014) 254–72. doi: 10.1163/1572543X-12341327.

Rance, Valerie. "Biblical Personalities and Trauma: Towards a Theology of Well-Being." Paper presented at the 43rd Annual Meeting of the Society for Pentecostal Studies, Evangel University, Springfield, MO, March 6–8, 2014.

———. "Trauma and Coping Mechanisms among Assemblies of God World Missionaries: Towards a Biblical Theory of Missionary Well-Being." PhD diss., Assemblies of God Theological Seminary, 2017.

Rasmussen, Steven Dale Horsager. "Illness and Death Experiences in Northwestern Tanzania: An Investigation of Discourses, Practices, Beliefs, and Social Outcomes, Especially Related to Witchcraft, Used in a Critical Contextualization and Education Process with Pentecostal Ministers." PhD diss., Trinity International University, 2008. http://www.whrin.org/wp-content/uploads/2012/11/ILLNESS-AND-DEATH-EXPERIENCES-IN- NORTHWESTERN-TANZANIA.pdf.

Robbins, Joel. "Anthropology of Religion." In *Studying Global Pentecostalism: Theories and Methods*, edited by Allan Anderson et al., 156–77. Berkeley: University of California Press, 2010. Kindle ed.

Robeck, Cecil M., Jr. *The Azusa Street Mission and Revival: The Birth of the Global Pentecostal Movement*. Nashville: Nelson Reference and Electronic, 2006.

Robeck, Cecil M., Jr., and Amos Yong. "Global Pentecostalism: An Introduction to an Introduction." In *The Cambridge Companion to Pentecostalism*, edited by Cecil M. Robeck Jr. and Amos Yong, 1–10. New York: Cambridge University Press, 2014.

Root, Andrew. *Christopraxis: A Practical Theology of the Cross*. Minneapolis: Fortress, 2014. Kindle ed.

Bibliography

———. "Evangelical Practical Theology." In *Opening the Field of Practical Theology: An Introduction,* edited by Kathleen Cahalan and Gordon S. Mikoski, 2097–2664. Lanham, MD: Rowman & Littlefield, 2014. Kindle ed.

Rubin, Herbert J., and Irene S. Rubin. *Qualitative Interviewing: The Art of Hearing Data.* 3rd ed. Los Angeles: Sage, 2012.

Seymour, William J. "William J. Seymour's Doctrine and Discipline." *312 Azusa Street,* edited by River of Revival Ministries. Accessed December 8, 2017. http://www.azusastreet.org/WilliamJSeymourDiscipline.htm.

Simmons, Daniel J. "They Shall Recover: Towards a Pneumatological and Eschatological Understanding of the Atonement in Pentecostal Healing." Selected Honors Thesis, Southeastern University, 2015. http://firescholars.seu.edu/cgi/viewcontent.cgi?article=1019&context=honors.

Skaggs, Rebecca. *The Pentecostal Commentary on 1 Peter, 2 Peter, Jude.* Pentecostal Commentary Series 17. New York: T. & T. Clark, 2004.

———. "The Problem of Suffering: A Response from 1 Peter." Paper presented at the 37th Annual Meeting of Society for Pentecostal Studies, Duke Divinity School, Durham, NC, March 13–15, 2008.

Sloan, Robert. "The Absence of Jesus in John." In *Perspectives on John: Method and Interpretation in the Fourth Gospel,* edited by Robert B. Sloan and Mikeal C. Parsons, 207–28. NABPR Special Studies Series 11. Lewiston, NY: Mellen, 1993.

Smith, James K. A. *Thinking in Tongues: Pentecostal Contributions to Christian Philosophy.* Grand Rapids: Eerdmans, 2010. Kindle ed.

Solivan, Samuel. *The Spirit, Pathos and Liberation: Toward an Hispanic Pentecostal Theology.* Journal of Pentecostal Theology Supplement Series 14. Sheffield, UK: Sheffield Academic, 1998.

Stewart, Adam. *The New Canadian Pentecostals.* Waterloo, ON: Wilfrid Laurier University Press, 2015.

Swinton, John, and Harriet Mowat. *Practical Theology and Qualitative Research.* London: SCM, 2006. Kindle ed.

Synan, Vinson. *The Holiness-Pentecostal Tradition: Charismatic Movements in the Twentieth Century.* 2nd ed. Grand Rapids: Eerdmans, 1997.

Synan, Vinson, and Charles R. Fox. *William J. Seymour: Pioneer of the Azusa Street Revival.* Alachua, FL: Bridge-Logos, 2012.

Tankink, Marian. "'The Moment I Became Born-Again the Pain Disappeared': The Healing of Devastating War Memories in Born-Again Churches in Mbarara District Southwest Uganda." *Transcultural Psychiatry* 44, no. 203 (2007) 203–31. doi: 10.1177/1363461507077723.

Thomas, Andrew James. "Pathways to Healing: An Empirical-Theological Study of the Healing Praxis of 'the Group' Assemblies of God in Kwazulu-Natal, South Africa." ThD diss., University of South Africa, 2010.

Thomas, John Christopher. *The Devil, Disease and Deliverance: Origins of Illness in New Testament Thought.* Journal of Pentecostal Theology Supplement Series 13. Sheffield, UK: Sheffield Academic, 1998.

———. *Footwashing in John 13 and the Johannine Community.* 2nd ed. Cleveland, TN: CPT, 2014.

Thompson, Luke. "Rising above a Crippling Hermeneutic." MA thesis, University of South Florida, 2014. http://scholarcommons.usf.edu/etd/5140.

Thompson, Marianne Meye. "'God's Voice You Have Never Heard, God's Form You Have Never Seen': The Characterization of God in the Gospel of John." *Semeia* 63 (1993) 177–204. https://luthersem.idm.oclc.org/login?url=http://search.ebscohost.com/login.aspx?d irect=true&db=rfh&AN=ATLA000.

———. "John, Gospel of." In *Dictionary of Jesus and Gospels,* edited by Joel B. Green and Scot McKnight. 368–83. Downers Grove, IL: InterVarsity, 1992. CD-ROM.

———. *John: A Commentary.* Louisville: Westminster John Knox, 2015.

———. "The Living Father." *Semeia* 85 (1999) 19–31. https://luthersem.idm.oclc.org/login?url=http://search.ebscohost.com/login.aspx?d irect=true&db=keh&AN=6539638&site=ehost-live&scope=site.

Thomson, Mathew K. "Minister between Miracles: A Pentecostal Model of Pastoral Care." In *Soul Care: A Pentecostal Charismatic Perspective,* edited by John Kie Vining and Edward D. Decker, 129–39. East Rockaway, NY: Cummings and Hathaway, 1996.

"To Our Correspondents." *The Apostolic Faith,* October 1906. http://www.apostolicfaith.org/Library/Index/AzusaPapers.aspx.

Tomberlin, Daniel. *Pentecostal Sacraments: Encountering God at the Altar.* Cleveland, TN: Center for Pentecostal Leadership & Care, 2010. Kindle ed.

"Tongues as a Sign." *The Apostolic Faith,* September 1906. http://www.apostolicfaith.org/Library/Index/AzusaPapers.aspx.

Torr, Stephen C. *Dramatic Pentecostal/Charismatic Anti-Theodicy: Improvising on a Divine Performance of Lament.* Eugene, OR: Pickwick, 2013.

Torrance, James B. "The Vicarious Humanity of Christ." In *The Incarnation: Ecumenical Studies in the Nicene-Constantinopolitan Creed A.D. 381,* edited by Thomas F. Torrance, 127–47. Edinburgh: Handsel, 1981.

Tramel, Terry. *The Beauty of the Balance: Toward an Evangelical-Pentecostal Theology.* Franklin Springs, GA: LifeSprings Resources, 2009. Kindle ed.

Twenge, Jean M. *Generation Me: Why Today's Young Americans Are More Confident, Entitled—and More Miserable Than Ever Before.* New York: Free, 2006.

"Two Works of Grace and the Gift of the Holy Ghost." *The Apostolic Faith,* September 1906. http://www.apostolicfaith.org/Library/Index/AzusaPapers.aspx.

Villafañe, Eldin. *The Liberating Spirit: Toward an Hispanic American Pentecostal Social Ethic.* Lanham, MD: University Press of America, 1992.

Vining, John Kie. "Soul Care in the Pentecostal Tradition." In *Soul Care: A Pentecostal-Charismatic Perspective,* edited by John Kie Vining and Edward E. Decker, 15–33. East Rockaway, NY: Cummings and Hathaway, 1996.

Viorst, Judith. *Necessary Losses: The Loves, Illusions, Dependencies, and Impossible Expectations That All of Us Have to Give Up in Order to Grow.* New York: Free, 1986.

Wacker, Grant. "Searching for Eden with a Satellite Dish: Primitivism, Pragmatism, and the Pentecostal Character." In *The Primitive Church in the Modern World,* edited by Richard T. Hughes, 139–66. Urbana: University of Illinois Press, 1995.

Walker, Rebecca, and Glynis Clacherty. "Shaping New Spaces: An Alternative Approach to Healing in Current Shelter Interventions for Vulnerable Women in Johannesburg." In *Healing and Change in the City of Gold: Case Studies of Coping and Support in Johannesburg,* edited by Ingrid Palmary et al., 31–58. Cham, Switzerland: Springer, 2015. doi: 10.1007/978-3-319-08768-9.

Wanje, George Horace. "'It Is Not a Sin Going for the Test': A Qualitative Study of Attitudes Towards HIV Testing in Pentecostal Churches in Mombasa, Kenya." MPH thesis,

University of Washington, 2012. https://digital.lib.washington.edu/researchworks/handle/1773/20691.

Warren, E. Janet. *Cleansing the Cosmos: A Biblical Model for Conceptualizing and Counteracting Evil*. Eugene, OR: Pickwick, 2012.

———. *Holy Housekeeping: Understanding Evil and Living Godly Lives*. Bellville, ON: Essence, 2017.

Warrington, Keith. "Acts and the Healing Narratives: Why?" *Journal of Pentecostal Theology* 14, no. 2 (2006) 189–217. doi: 10.1177/0966736906062132.

———. "Healing and Kenneth Hagin." *Asian Journal of Pentecostal Studies* 3, no. 1 (2000) 119–38. http://www.apts.edu/index.cfm?menuid=94&parentid=54.

———. "Healing and Suffering in the Bible." *International Review of Mission* 95, no. 37677 (2006) 154–64. doi: 10.1111/j.1758-6631.2006.tb00551.x.

———. *Healing and Suffering: Biblical and Pastoral Reflections*. Milton Keynes, UK: Paternoster, 2005.

———. "James 5:14–18: Healing Then and Now." *International Review of Mission* 93, nos. 370–71 (2004) 346–67. doi: 10.1111/j.1758-6631.2004.tb00464.x.

———. *Jesus the Healer: Paradigm or Unique Phenomenon?* Carlisle, UK: Paternoster, 2000.

———. "The Path to Wholeness: Beliefs and Practices Relating to Healing in Pentecostalism." *Evangel* 21, no. 2 (2003) 45–49. http://www.luthersem.edu/library/auth_resource.aspx?resource_link=http://search.ebscohost.com/login.aspx?direct=true&db=rfh&AN=A TLA0001577009&site=eh ost-live&scope=site.

———. *Pentecostal Theology: A Theology of Encounter*. London: T. & T. Clark, 2008.

———. "A Response to James Shelton Concerning Jesus and Healing: Yesterday and Today." *Journal of Pentecostal Theology* 15, no. 2 (2007) 185–93. doi: 10.1177/0966736907076337.

———. "The Role of Jesus as Presented in the Healing Praxis and Teaching of British Pentecostalism: A Re-Examination." *Pneuma: The Journal of the Society for Pentecostal Studies* 25, no. 1 (2003) 66–92. doi: 10.1163/157007403765694420.

———. "A Spirit Theology of Suffering." In *The Suffering Body: Responding to the Persecution of Christians*, edited by Harold D. Hunter and Cecil M. Robeck Jr., 24–36. Milton Keynes, UK: Paternoster, 2006.

———. "Suffering." In *Handbook of Pentecostal Christianity*, edited by Adam Stewart, 201–4. DeKalb: Northern Illinois University Press, 2012.

———. "The Use of the Name (of Jesus) in Healing and Exorcism with Partial Reference to the Teachings of Kenneth Hagin." *Journal of the European Pentecostal Theological Association* 17, no. 1 (2015) 16–36. http://www.eptaonline.com/wp-content/uploads/2013/07/JEPTA-1997-17.pdf.

Wenk, Matthias. "An Incarnational Pneumatology Based on Romans 8.18–30: The Spirit as God's Solidarity with a Suffering Creation." Paper presented at the 43rd Annual Meeting of the Society for Pentecostal Studies, Evangel University, Springfield, MO, March 6–8, 2014.

———. "*Missio Spiritu* —Why Pentecostals Have an Ecumenical Responsibility." *Journal of the European Pentecostal Theological Association* 35, no. 1 (2015) 26–33. doi: 10.1179/1812446114Z.0000000005.

Wilkinson, Michael, "Pentecostalism in Canada: An Introduction." In *Canadian Pentecostalism: Transition and Transformation*, edited by Michael Wilkinson, 3–12. Montreal: McGill-Queen's University Press, 2009.

———. *The Spirit Said Go: Pentecostal Immigrants in Canada.* American University Studies 7, Theology and Religion 247. New York: Lang, 2006.

"William J. Seymour's Doctrine and Discipline." 312 Azusa Street. http://www.azusastreet.org/WilliamJSeymourDiscipline.htm.

Wolfelt, Alan. *Death and Grief: A Guide for Clergy.* Bristol, PA: Accelerated Development, 1988.

———. *Understanding Your Grief: Ten Essential Touchstones for Finding Hope and Healing Your Heart.* Fort Collins, CO: Companion, 2003.

Yong, Amos. *The Bible, Disability, and the Church: A New Vision of the People of God.* Grand Rapids: Eerdmans, 2011. Kindle ed.

———. "Many Tongues, Many Senses: Pentecost, the Body Politic, and the Redemption of Dis/Ability." *Pneuma: The Journal of the Society for Pentecostal Studies* 31 (2009) 167–88. doi: 10.1163/027209609X12470371387688.

———. *Renewing Christian Theology: Systematics for a Global Christianity.* Waco, TX: Baylor University Press, 2014. Kindle ed.

———. *Theology and Down Syndrome: Reimagining Disability in Late Modernity.* Waco, TX: Baylor University Press, 2007.

www.ingramcontent.com/pod-product-compliance
Lightning Source LLC
Chambersburg PA
CBHW070257230426
43664CB00014B/2562